Pondering Pearls of Wisdom

Patricia Lee Appelt

PublishAmerica
Baltimore

First printing

PublishAmerica has allowed this work to remain exactly as the author intended, verbatim, without editorial input.

Hardcover 978-1-4560-6920-9
Softcover 978-1-4560-6921-6
PUBLISHED BY PUBLISHAMERICA, LLLP
www.publishamerica.com
Baltimore

Printed in the United States of America

Pondering Pearls
of Wisdom

January 1 Resolutions

Scripture Text: Genesis 1:1

"In the beginning God created the heaven and earth."

God's Resolution: Genesis 1: 2-5

In the beginning God created the heaven with all His angels, and with His light. In the beginning God resolved to create light on the darkness of His earth. May I resolve to allow God's plan for me to include being a light to shine for His world!

Man's Resolution: Genesis 2:26

In the beginning God created man with all His creatures, and with His gardens. In the beginning God resolved to create man to tend His garden. May I resolve to allow God's plan for me to include being His gardener for His world!

New Year's Resolution: John 1:1

In the beginning God created man with all His words, and with His Word (The Holy Bible). In the beginning God resolved to create man to share His Word. May I resolve to allow God's plan for me to include being his writer for His world!

Prayer: Thank you Lord, for a new year, new beginnings, new Resolutions that you create in your new creatures. I resolve to let you lead in this new year!

January 2 Resolutions

Scripture Text: Genesis 3: 6

"And when the woman saw that the tree was good for food, and that it was pleasant to the eyes, and a tree to be desired to make one wise, she took of the fruit thereof, and did eat, and gave also unto her husband with her; and he did eat."

God's Resolution: Genesis 2: 15-17

God created man to tend to His garden which included the tree of the knowledge of good and evil. God's resolution included a consequence: if fruit from this particular tree was eaten; death would follow! I believe that our God in His wisdom was speaking of spiritual death.

Man's Resolution: Genesis 3:8

God created man to choose between good and evil. God's resolution included a consequence: if man knows good and evil; eviction would follow. I believe that our God in His wisdom was speaking of spiritual eviction.

New Year's Resolution: John 1:6

God sent a man to bear witness of the Light. God's resolution for Saint John included a gospel message: that all men through Him might believe. I believe that our God in His wisdom speaks of spiritual witnessing.

Prayer: Thank you Lord, for new mornings to be sent by you to be your witness through your wisdom!

January 3 Resolutions

Scripture Text: Genesis 4: 2

"And she (Eve) again bare His (Cain's) brother Abel. And Abel was a keeper of sheep, but Cain was a tiller of the ground."

God's Resolution: Genesis 4: 3,4

God created man to tend to His fruit (Cain's job!) and His cattle (Abel's job!). God's resolution included keepers and tillers. I believe that God has chosen us to be His keepers, tillers of His earth!

Man's Resolution: Genesis 4: 8

God created siblings to take on different jobs. God's resolution included respect and repentance. I believe that God has chosen us to respect His earth and repent when we abuse His humans!

New Year's Resolution: John 1:14

God sent His Son Jesus to be the Word. God's resolution for Saint John included the Word living on earth and being full of grace and truth. I believe that God in His wisdom speaks of redeeming grace and everlasting truth.

Prayer: Thank you Lord, for allowing us to be your Family; keepers and tillers for your Earth of grace and truth.

January 4 Resolutions

Scripture Text: Genesis 4: 25

"And Adam knew his wife again; and she bare a son, and called his name Seth: for God, said she, hath appointed me another seed instead of Abel, whom Cain slew."

God's Resolution: Genesis 5:8

God created man to record their genealogy. Moses' first book: Genesis contains ages of Adam (nine hundred and thirty), and Seth (nine hundred and twelve. We also read of Moses' recording of children born. God in His wisdom resolved to have His children to multiply! I believe that the Lord; the Way showed the path of His salvation!

Man's Resolution: Genesis 6:3

God created man to live on earth for an hundred and twenty years. Moses includes in his genealogy the population of giants and how God in His wisdom resolved to destroy His wicked man from the earth! I believe that the Lord; the Way prepared the path of His salvation!

New Year's Resolution: John 1:23

God sent His Son to be the Way. God's resolution for Saint John included the Way announced by a voice crying in the wilderness; making straight the path of the Lord. I believe that the Lord; the Way invites us to make straight the path of His salvation!

Prayer: Thank you Lord for being the Way and that we can help make the way straight for Your salvation!

January 5 Resolutions

Scripture Text: Genesis 7:1

"And the Lord said unto Noah, ' Come thou and all thy house into the ark; for thee have I seen righteousness before me in this generation'."

God's Resolution: Genesis 6:19

God created an ark to survive the flood of waters on the earth. Moses included in his record of Noahs ark and how God in His wisdom resolved to begin a generations of His people that will follow righteousness. I believe that our Lord Righteous wished us to survive the earth's wickedness.

Man's Resolution: Genesis 8:13

God created a wind to pass over and dry the earth. Moses included in his record of Noah's ark landing on dry land and how God in His wisdom resolved to allow Noah to build an altar for offerings to Him! I believe that our Lord Righteous wished us to thank Him for leading us to safety!

New Year's Resolution: John 1:32

God sent His Son to be baptized on earth. God sent His Spirit to desend on His Son. God's resolution for Saint John included His people to be baptized with the Holy Ghost. I believe in the baptism by the Trinity; God the Father, Jesus His Son, and the Holy Spirit!

Prayer: Thank you Lord for sending your Son and Spirit to baptize us with Your holiness!

January 6 Resolutions

Scripture Text: Genesis 12: 2

"And I (the Lord) will make of thee (Abram) a great nation, and I will bless thee, and make thy name great; and thou shalt be a blessing."

God's Resolution: Genesis 12:1

God created a new land for Abram. Moses included in his record of Abram and his family leaving their country and how God resolved to begin a new nation that will be blessed. I believe that our Lord Blessed began new, and great lands of people!

Man's Resolution: Genesis 12: 5

God created family and substance for Abram. Moses included in his record of Abram and his family entering the land of Canaan and how God resolved to begin a new nation that will reside. I believe that our Lord Blessed began new and great nations of people!

New Year's Resolution: John 1:38

God sent His Son to live on Earth. God sent His Spirit to follow His Son. God's resolution for Saint John included his record of His Son living on Earth and how God resolved to have His Disciples seek and ask of where He lived. I believe that our Lord Blessed began new and great nations of disciples!

Prayer: Thank you Lord, for sending your Son and Spirit to bless us with the ability to seek and ask as disciples!

January 7 Resolutions

Scripture Text: Habakkuk 2: 2

"And the Lord answered me (Habakkuk) and said, Write the vision, and make it plain upon tables, that he May run that readeth it."

God's Resolution: Habakkuk 1: 1,2

God inspired prophets to write the truth. Habakkuk shared his burden. He wrote about God's judgment on the violent Chaldeans. He wrote to God to ask for salvation from the iniquity. Habakkuk included in his vision God's majesty, power, and creation working in His people. I believe our Majestic God's daily resolution includes salvation for His people.

Man's Resolution: Habakkuk 2:1

God inspired prophets to write the truth. Habakkuk shared his promise. He wrote about God's salvation for those who watched for Him. He wrote to God to promise to watch from the tower. Habakkuk included in his vision God's protection, power and creation working for His people. I believe our Protective God's daily resolution includes watching by His people.

New Year's Resolution: II Timothy 4: 2

God inspired His Apostle Paul to write to Timothy (his son in the faith). Timothy was to prepare himself to be reproved by God. Paul shared his vision. He wrote about God's rebuking and exhorting. His letter to Timothy included a vision of God's guidance for a new young leader. I believe our Protective God's daily resolution includes guiding His leaders.

Prayer: Thank you Lord, for sending your apostles, preachers to write the vision through God's reproving, rebuking and exhorting!

January 8 Resolutions

Scripture Text: Habakkuk 2:2

"And the Lord answered me, and said, Write the vision, and make it plain upon tables, that he May run that readeth it."

God's Resolution: Habakkuk 1:5

God inspired His Prophet Habakkuk to write the plain truth. Habakkuk wrote of the wonder of God's work; even among the heathen. The prophet included in his vision God's wonderful work among the heathen. I believe that our Wonderful God's daily resolution includes the sharing of His Plain Truth.

Man's Resolution: II Timothy 2: 15

God inspired the Apostle Paul to encourage Timothy to write the plain truth. He encouraged the study and sharing of God's plain word for all people. He included in his epistle God's wonderful wisdom among his people. I believe that our Wonderful God's daily resolution includes studying His Plain Truth found in His scriptures.

New Year's Resolution: Habakkuk 2:2

God inspired me; Patricia Appelt to encourge my readers to read the plain truth. I encourage the study and sharing of God's plain word for all readers of PEARLS OF WISDOM. I include in my book God's wonderful wisdom among my readers. I believe that our Wonderful God's daily resolution includes studying His Plain Truth found in His Holy Bible.

Prayer: Thank you Lord, for inspiring us to study and share Your Plain Truth, Your Word, Your Holy Bible!

January 9 Resolutions

Scripture Text: Matthew 1: 1

"The book of the generation of Jesus Christ, the son of David, the son of Abraham."

God's Resolution: 1:17

God inspired His Saint Matthew to continue Habakkuk's resolution: Write the plain vision (truth). Matthew wrote in his gospel about the fourteen generations from Abraham to David, fourteen more from David to those of Babylon, and fourteen final generations from Babylon to Christ. The saint included in his gospel the birth, life, death, and the resurrection of His Son; Christ. I believe that our Father God's daily resolution includes us continuing the recording of His generations!

Man's Resolution: Matthew 28: 19

God inspired Saint Matthew to encourage future generations to write His Truth. Matthew wrote a quote from God's Son; Jesus Christ : "Go, ye therefore, and teach all nations, baptizing them in the name of the Father, and of the Son, and of the Holy Ghost..." The saint included in his gospel the baptism by the Trinity. I believe that our Father God's daily resolution includes us continuing the teaching of His generations!

New Year's Resolution: Matthew 28: 20

God inspired me to encourage my readers to teach His Truth. I read the last verse of Matthew; Jesus Christ's last words here on earth according to Saint Matthew: "...Teaching them to observe all things whatsoever I have commanded you: and lo I am with you alway, even unto the end of the world." Saint Matthew included in his gospel the teaching by the Trinity. The saint concluded with: "Amen" ! I believe that our our Father God's daily resolution includes us continuing the teaching of His Word until the end of His World!

Prayer: Thank you Lord, for inspiring us to study past generations and share your teachings to Your World! Amen!

January 10 Resolutions

Scripture Text: Mark 1: 1,2

"The beginning of the gospel of Jesus Christ, the Son of God; As it is written in the prophets, Behold I send my messenger before thy face, which shall prepare thy way before thee."

God's Resolution: Mark 1: 45

God inspired Saint Mark to continue the Prophet Habakkuk's resolution: "Write the plain vision (truth)". Mark wrote in his gospel about the ministry of John the Baptist; the preparation for Jesus' ministry on earth. The saint included in his gospel the 'publishing', the 'blazing' by John The Baptist of the ministry of Jesus (against His wishes!) I believe that our Father God's daily resolution includes us spreading His Word, even against our own human wishes!

Man's Resolution: Mark 16: 19

God inspired Saint Mark to encourage future followers of Christ to record His Truth. The saint included in his gospel the 'receiving up into heaven' and the 'sitting on the right hand of God' by Jesus (against His wishes!) I believe that our Father God's daily resolution includes us joining His Word, even against our own human wishes!

New Year's Resolution: Mark 16: 20

God inspired me to encourage my readers to prepare His Truth. I read the last verse of Mark: The last event that took place as Jesus was received by His Heavenly Father: "And they went forth, and preached everywhere, The Lord working with them, and confirming the Word with signs following." Saint Mark included in his resolution the working of the Truth. The saint concluded with "Amen" ! I believe that our Father God's daily resolution includes us working with His Word, even against our own human desires!

Prayer: Thank you Lord, for inspiring us to study about Your past messengers and share Your Works with Your World! Amen!

January 11 Resolutions

Scripture Text: Luke 1: 3

"It seemed good to me also, having had perfect understanding of all things from the very first, to write unto thee in order, most excellent Theophilus."

God's Resolution: Luke 1:2

God inspired Saint Luke to continue the Prophet Habakkuk's resolution: to write the plain truth. Luke wrote specifically to Theophilus and included what 'eyewitnesses' and 'ministers of the word' had delivered. I believe that our God of Wisdom's daily resolution includes us reporting and ministering His Word!

Man's Resolution: Luke 24: 52

God inspired Saint Luke to read the plain truth. Luke wrote as an eyewitness to Jesus; and included that Jesus was the Minister of the Word. I believe that our God of Wisdom's daily resolution includes us being reporter and followers in sharing His Word!

New Year's Resolution: Luke 24:53

God inspired me to encourage my readers to praise His Word. I read the last verse of Luke: the last event that took place when Jesus was carried up into heaven: "They worshipped Him...and were continually in the temple praising and blessing God." Saint Luke included in his resolution the ministering of the Word. The saint concluded with "Amen"! I believe that our God of Wisdom's daily resolution includes us being worshippers and praising followers of His Word!

Prayer: Thank you Lord, for inspiring us to read your writer's messages and share the Word with the World! Amen!

January 12 Resolutions

Scripture Text: John 1: 1,2

"In the beginning was the Word, and the Word was with God, and the Word was God. The same was in the beginning with God."

God's Resolution: John 1: 29

God inspired Saint John to continue the Prophet Habakkuk's resolution: to commune with the Word. John wrote specifically about the Lamb of God, and includes that He takes away the sin of the world. I believe that our Heavenly Father's daily resolution includes us being recipients of His Word!

Man's Resolution: John 21:24

God inspired Saint John to testify to what is true; the Word. John wrote as a testimony to God's Word, and included that he was a disiple of Jesus. I believe that our Heavenly Father's daily resolution includes us being Disciples of His Word!.

New Year's Resolution: John 21:35

God inspired me to encourge my readers to testify to His Word. I read the last verse of John: "many other things Jesus did; should be recorded. Saint John included in his resolution the world not being able to contain the books; the Word that should be written. He concluded with; "Amen"! I believe that our Heavenly Father's daily resolution includes us being Writers of the Word!

Prayer: Thank you Lord, for inspiring us to write with your writers, and to share in the writing of your Word along with the World. Amen!

January 13 Resolutions

Scripture Text: Revelation 1: 1,2

"The Revelation of Jesus Christ, which God gave unto him, to shew unto his servants things which must shortly come to pass; and he sent and signified it by his angel unto his servant John: Who bare record oof the word of God, and of the testimony of Jesus Christ, and all things that he saw."

God's Resolution: Revelation 1: 3

God inspired Saint John The Divine to continue the resolution of the Prophet Habakkuk: to keep the Word (the plain truth). John the Divine wrote specifically about the testimony of Jesus Christ, and includes what will come to pass. I believe our Giving God's daily resolution includes us reading, hearing and keeping His Word until the end of the World!

Man's Resolution: Revelation 22: 20

God inspired Saint John The Divine to testify to what is to come. John wrote specifically about Jesus coming quickly, and includes how the saint asks Him to come. I believe our Giving God's daily resolution includes us saying to Jesus: "Even so, come", to your world, Lord Jesus!

New Year's Resolution: Revelation 22: 21

God inspired me to testify to what is to come. I read the last verse of Revelation: "Our Lord Jesus Christ be with you all". Saint John The Divine wrote specifically a blessing to His readers and includes grace from Jesus. He concluded with: "Amen"! I believe our Giving God's daily resolution includes us receptive to grace for God's world!

Prayer: Thank you Lord, for inspiring us to testify to your grace and to wait for Your coming. Amen!

January 14 Resolutions

Scripture Text: Proverbs 1: 1,2

"The proverbs of Solomon the son of David, king of Israel ; to know wisdom and instruction; to perceive the words of understanding."

God inspired King Solomon to write proverbs. God's resolution for His world included wisdom; instruction. I believe our Ruler God's daily resolution for us includes understanding His Wisdom!

New Year's Resolution :

Proverbs 1:7

"The fear of the Lord is the beginning of knowledge..." Fear can be either a negative or positive reaction to our Lords wisdom. Fear of the Lord is a prerequisite for daily receiving or sharing of knowledge.

God inspired me to present this pearl of wisdom:

Fear can affect our faith.

Emotions can alter our faith.

Awe can cause us to have positive faith.

Respect is a prerequisit for faith in our Lord.

Our hearts can be either healthy or unhealthy recipients of the Lord's wisdom. A receptive heart is a prerequisite for daily receiving and sharing pleasant aspects of knowledge.

Daily we receive, adore, revere, trust in our God of wisdom.

Prayer: Let us fear and trust you with our healthy hearts, Oh, God Only then May we receive Your pleasant wisdom!

January 15 Resolutions

Scripture Text: Proverbs 3: 5,6

"Trust in the Lord with all thine heart; and lean not unto thy own understanding, In all thy ways acknowledge him, and he shall direct thy paths. "

We can trust in the Lord or we can trust in man. A trusting heart is

16

a prerequisite for daily direction from God. God inspired my friend and special sister; Barbara Torbitt to present her pearl of wisdom (her New Year's resolution):

"Do my best, and let God do the rest."

Barbara submitted this resolution in the local newspaper where she was Executive Director of the Housing Authority and resident of Rockville Centre, Long Island. She trusts the truth with all her heart. She relies on her Lord for wisdom and understanding. Daily, she seeks God for direction and prays with thankfulness and gratitude.

New Year's resolution:

Do your best, and let God do the rest! What is your best?

What do you allow God to do for you?

Prayer: Dear God, I trust in you; with my whole heart! I lean not on my own understanding. I acknowledge all Thy ways! PS: Dear God: Bless my friend and co-worker; Sheri! Today is her birthday! I have witnessed her trust in You. Sheri acknowledges all Your ways! You direct her paths daily!

January 16 Resolutions

Scripture Text: Proverbs 15: 23

"A man hath joy by the answer of his mouth; and a word spoken in due season, how good is it!"

We can express words of joy or words of sorrow. A joyful word is a prerequisite for God's daily wisdom and direction. My friend and special sister, Phyllis Culkin wrote this New Year's Resolution Poem:

Follow Your Dreams "Follow your dreams wherever you go. Dreams are something that you never let go. If you have no dreams, you have no hope. Hold on to your dreams with all your heart. Wherever you go, your dreams go too!"

Phyllis moved from Long Island to Canandaigua, N.Y. in the late 1990's. She had already joined the Care-giver Team for Retired Salvation Army Officer; Mrs. Orpha Spellman. Daily, Phyllis delights in dreaming with God, reaching out to Him, enters in prayer and in the presence of an awesome, majestic God and worthy to be adored.

Prayer: Dear God, I follow the dreams that you allow me to keep, to share and to cherish!

January 17 Resolutions

Scripture Text: Proverbs 16: 8

"Better is a little with righteousness than great revenues without right."

We can offer a little amount of words or offer a lot! We can do little acts as a prerequisite for God's wisdom and righteousness.

Love is such a little thing that means alot. Interesting acts are prerequisites for God's wisdom, and the timing of these acts is precious.

Talents are meant to be shared, while laughter and love go hand in hand. Exceptance of God's righteousness and immersion of yourself in His wisdom prepares you to go and tell others.

Daily we can help others find righteousness and tell how God inspires you.

New Year's Resolution:

Resolve to do right with God's righteousness.

Prayer: Dear Righteous God, I resolve to hold, cherish and follow in Your righteousness.

January 18 Resolutions

Scripture Text: Proverbs 19: 1

"Better is the poor that walketh in his integrity..."

We can walk in poorness or richness. We can walk with integrity as we follow God's wisdom and righteousness.

Walk in God's wisdom. Adore and love Him appropriately and in luxury! Know of God's knowledge while involving yourself in His interesting plan of new and nice goals.

Think thoughtfully of God's righteousness; even to the end of the day. Gracefully and with a glad heart walk with God for right reactions can make you rich.

Imagine what good you can do with God as you trust His timing.

Yesterday is gone so yield today.

New Year's Resolution: Resolve to walk in integrity whether poor or rich.

Recognize our richness in God's wisdom and rightousness.

Prayer: Dear God, I walk in Your integrity; little by little yielding to You!

January 19 Resolutions

Scripture Text: Proverbs 22: 6

"Train up a child in the way he should go; and when he is old, He will not depart from it. "

A child can be trained or neglected on life's path. Daily we can be a youthful child of God our King in training. Children can be curious so we need to help them to hear about God. Show them individual interest in them and God's plan for them. Let love for self and others go hand in hand,

Dare to dream for God's plan for everyone; training and teaching God's truths. Reach out to the children with proper reasons; motives. Act with an appropriate attitude, involving others with God given intellect. Simple, but noble and nice acts will do for God.

New Year's Resolution: Dare to daily delve in God's word.

Prayer: Dear God, thank you for training us; your children; in your reasonable wisdom!

January 20 Resolutions

Scripture Text: Proverbs 24: 5

"A wise man is strong; yea, a man of strong knowledge increaseth strength."

A man is either wise or foolish in knowledge. A man is either strong or weak in knowledge. Whether you are wise or weak in wisdom, God sees us as individuals where sincerity and sensitivity need to go hand in hand.

Endurance is for the wise followers of God. Strength from God can spread through tough times as we reach out to God for rigorous strength. Only by God's strength can enthusiasm enter our weak bodies.

Now we become nimble and quick, going forth with our Great God. We are taught and trained by God's teachers to go forth with our Awesome God who instills healthy habits with His infinite wisdom.

New Year's Resolution: Go forth with God's strength as wise followers.

Prayer: Dear God, thank you for training us for with your infinite wisdom and for Your Kingdom!

January 21 Resolutions

Scripture Text: Proverbs: 25: 11

"A word fitly spoken, is like apples of gold in pictures of silver."

The spoken word can be fit or unfit to be heard. The spoken word can be colorful and rich to the ear. How receptive we are when we hear fit and rich words.

Apples are often associated with the spoken word and often associated with temptation. Think of the golden and glossy fruit taken by Adam and Eve! Upon eating of the golden fruit there was the opening of their eyes and the failing to obey God.

There was the learning about lurking evil, and the disobedience due to the delving into the delicious but forbidden fruit. pictures of goodness were severely clouded by evil.

There is evil lurking yet today while shiny, smooth apples are eaten. There is the interruption of the eating of this fruit by the appearance of a blemish. The recipient of that golden apple recognizes the bad and the good and tries to form vivid pictures of better looking apples. It is as if evil has entered and is trying to destroy and ruin God's power over goodness.

New Year's Resolution:

Speak God's word with caution from destruction.

Prayer: Thank you God, for giving us wisdom in our prepartion to speak Your Word; Your Wisdom."

January 22 Resolutions

Scripture Text: Proverbs 27: 1

"Boast not thyself of tomorrow; for thou knowest not what a day may bring forth."

We can pray or boast about tomorrow. We do not know what God has planned for tomorrow. Plan to pray to God daily and plead for His performance. Listen to His loving wisdom and lean on His love. Acquire God's advice and adopt His plan while noticing how noteworthy and newsworthy today can be for each of us.

Take time to think about today; only one minute counts at a time. Maybe months will pass by quickly. Prayer may take place over the course of one hour.

Round the clock the hands do run, reaching a revolution of time. One can only allow God to plan with His infinite wisdom in our ifinite weakness.

New Year's Resolution: Live each day without boasting of thyself but of God!

Prayer: Dear God, Thank you for giving untimely wisdom to share with others!

is the expanding of their exquisite webs as the wise spider is resolved to reach a wide span of God's world. They are the best teachers of how to dwell and expand while being immersed in God's world!

These four small creatures are God's exceeding wise creations. Each one in their God given wisdom is resolved to find their "place" on God's earth.

New Year's Resolution:

May we be resolved to find our place on God's earth.

Prayer: Thank you God, for the wise examples of these four, small, yet wise reatures.

January 26 Resolutions

Scripture Text: Proverbs 31: 10

"Who can find a virtuous woman? For her price is far above rubies."

Our creator God's resolution for a virtuous woman includes the use of her whole being. You could say she wears her pearls with dignity and pride.

A virtuous woman uses her healthy hands to hug her children from God. They are her precious pearls who need attention.

A virtuous woman depends on God's actions, never noticing the callouses from attending to her precious pearls.as she diligently delves in her duties.

A virtuous woman becomes a servant of family and to her God. Each evening she examines each child as she secretly is yearning for their youthfulness. She finds herself explaining God's plan for each child through speaking, singing, or sometimes scolding.

One such viruous woman became the Mother of our Saviour Jesus Christ. Mary continues to be our example of obedience. Her sincere understanding and knowledge is unhindered by the world.

A virtuous woman is daily teaching others and being taught by her children and husband. Oh how happy she is to wear her perls of wisdom as she hears her God speaking! She can daily be acting in honesty and truth which are priceless.

New Year's Resolution: Women of God must be virtuous servants for family.

Prayer: Thank you God, for virtuous women who use their gifts of your power and gace!

January 27 Resolutions

Scripture Text: Ecclesiastes 1: 3

"What profit hath a man of all his labour which he taketh under the son?"

The remaining devotionals for January will expound on Ecclesiastes or The Preacher's proclamation that "all is vanity". His resolution includes the statement that all things are full of labour and he gave his heart to seek and search out by wisdom all things. (see 1: 13).

Wisdom excelleth folly:

2:13

As far as light excelleth darkness, wisdom extendeth beyond the excelling folly. Labour and love go hand in hand. So you must involve yourself with interest internally. You must be giving God the glory for His grace. You must be helping in His harvesting of healthy habits. You must be thinking trusting thoughts today!

Wisdom is offered with works and labour: 2:11

That which is good in God's kingdom.comes from hard works and steady labour. Working wonders is God's way of displaying his omnipotence and observation of our needs. Daily He is reaching out His working hands and already knowing how to keep us in His Earthly Kingdom.

Wisdom is offered with knowledge and joy: 2:26

That which is good in God's sight has to include the joining of Jesus in joy and justice first. Then the joiner finds others opening themselves to the same joy in Jesus. Only then will you be able to yield yourselves just as you did yesterday.

New Year's Resolution: We resolve to labour for God's profits and wisdom.

Prayer: Thank You God, for wisdom; knowlege, joy, works, and labour amidst folly!

January 28 Resolutions

Scripture Text: Ecclesiastes 3: 1

"To everything there is a purpose, and a time to every purpose under the heavens: "

The Preacher of the book of Ecclesiastes shares his wisdom about time. He preaches of God's infinite wisdom in creating time on His created earth! I believe that God's preachers should keep Resolutions (promises) made aboutGod's creation of time and purpose: (3: 12).

We rejoice for a new-born and do good for God's child from life to death. We rejoice for a new plant and do good for God's plant by tending and plucking. We witness killing and resolve to do good for God's family by spiritual healing.

We resolve to break down barriers and to do good for God's house by building up. We witness weeping and resolve to do good to witness rejoicing and laughing! We mourn for God's family and resolve to do good to witness dancing through life!

We resolve to cast away stones and to gather stones for building God's House. We resolve by God's given wisdom to recognize when to embrace or to refrain. We rejoice in getting God's gifts and resolve to do good even when losing them.

We resolve to keep God's purpose and resolve to cast away man's faulty purposes. We rejoice in rending God given material and do good to mend man's torn lives. We rejoice in silence and do good to speak up for God's will for His children.

We rejoice by loving one another and do good by hating that which is evil. We witness war on God's earth and resolve to do good...to keep peace among us.

Prayer: Thank You God, for allowing us to rejoice and to do good at all times!

January 29 Resolutions

Scripture Text: Eccclesiastes 9: 11

"I returned, and saw under the sun, that the race is not to the swift, nor the battle to the strong, neither yet bread to the wise, nor yet riches to men of understanding; nor yet favour to men of skill; but time and chance happeneth to them all."

Resolutions made often depend on time and chance.

God's Resolution: Ecclesiastes 9: 2

There is one "event" for the "righteous" and for the "wicked"! We are all in the same race! May we each resolve to go for the same goal...Heaven !

Man's Resolution: Ecclesiastes 9: 18

It only takes one man...one child of God to destroy "much good" ! We are all sinners seeking to fight the same battle! My we resolve to go forth in the same battle...fighting for God's Kingdom !

New Year's Resolution: Ecclesiastes 12: 13

It only takes one day...to wander away and stray from God ! We all are prone to wander from His Will for His Kingdom! May we resolve to go forth in this new year...following God's Will !

Prayer: Thank You, God for Your Heaven, Your Kingdom, and Your Will !

January 30 Resolutions

Scripture Text: Song of Solomon 8: 7

"Many waters cannot quench love, neither can the floods drown it;

if a man would give all the substance of his house for love, it would utterly be contemned. "

Resolutions made are often dependent on the giving of substance and love.

God's Resolution: Song of Solomon 2 :4

There is only invititation made by God for His Children. He resolves to invite us to His banquet table with His Trinity Team! The banner over that table is: "L O V E '' !

Man's Resolution: Song of Solomon 3: 9, 10

It only took one king chosen by God...King Solomon, to build a chariot. His resolution involves making a chariot from the wealth of God's earth. He protects his kingdom of Israel with threescore "valiant" men!

May we resolve to protect God's Kingdom (His World) by being His valiant army!

New Year's Resolution: Song of Solomon 8: 11

It only takes one day...to neglect and to forget to tend God's Garden! We are all prone to neglect the fruits of His valleys and the flowers of His gardens. May we resolve to begin this new year tending to God's World!

Prayer: Thank You, God, for your love and guiding us to love your KIngdom!

January 31 Resolutions

Scripture Text: Colossians 3: 23

"And whatsoever ye do , do it heartily as to the Lord, and not unto men..."

The Apostle Paul's advise to the church of Colosse is my new year's resolution. I I I promise to God to do whatever....whenever, however, for Him and do so heartily!

Resolutions are met to be promises that are reachable! Resolutions are met to be shared with others at times. Resolutions are helpful to keep us reaching for goals.

My sister Sue has graciously agreed to illustrate this devotional book and support each monthly theme. Her illustrations will be displayed starting in February. Sue will have the last day of the months of February through November to support each theme with her drawings.

May this final day of January serve as the presentation of each monthly theme:

January:

Resolutions February:

Love Chapter March:

Foundations April:

Music May:

Bouquets June:

Precious Stones July:

Wise Creatures August:

Wise Words September:

ABC's of Wisdom October:

Wit and Wisdom November:

Thanks Be To God December:

The Road Taken

Each monthly title reveals to the reader a resolution for the new year!

Prayer: Thank You God, for helping me keep my resolution all year!

February 1 Love Chapter

Welcome to a new month which will feature devotionals with the main theme being love. I would like to give February the title; Love Chapter. Each entry or daily devotional will introduce the loves of our lives.

My first love is being a recipient of God's love and have known since childhood the scripture verse studied and memorized from the Holy Bible; John 3:16: "For God so loved the world, that He gave His only begotten Son, that whosoever believeth in Him should not perish, but have everlasting life."

My first love therefore includes thanksgiving for God sending His Son, the salvation received from Jesus Christ and the everlasting life breathed in from the Holy Spirit.

My first love also includes teaching. I thank God for sending me down the path of teaching, preaching, and sharing His love with others. I remember most vividly an important step on the path of teaching, preaching, and sharing God's love with others: being a substitute, stand-in, baby sitter, relief, assistant, or aide.

I introduce to the reader the poem entitled "Substitutes" found on page 25 of my first poetry book; HORIZONS. I ask you to read again the scripture quoted at the beginning of this devotional; John 3:16. Now I present:

Substitutes

Substitute teachers follow a plan... to help other teachers.

Substitute sugars provide a purpose... to help us stay healthy.

Substitute runners give relief... to help us rest and gain strength.

Substitute....Jesus...gave salvation... to fulfill God's plan for each person!

Prayer: Dear God, as we start a new month of devotionals, pearls of wisdom, May we pause to thank you for our most precious substitute; your Son, Jesus!

February 2 Love Chapter

Today I quote John 3:17 before I introduce the poem; C.P.R. which is found on page 26 of HORIZONS:

"For God sent not His Son into the world to condemn the world; but that the world through him might be saved."

C. P. R.

Cardiovascular...Christian receive a healthy heart from the salvation of Jesus Christ

Confession by Christians should come from a healthy heart.

Dear God, I confess with all my heart that I am a sinner saved by your Son.

Pulmonary...Christians receive a pair of healthy lungs from the Holy Spirit.

Professsion by Christians should from a pure tongue.

I profess with all my lungs that I am a sinner saved by your Son

Resuscitation...Christians receive a healthy body from the creation of Almighty God

Revival by Christians should be a daily experience.

I am revived with each breath that I take as a sinner saved by your Son.

Prayer: Dear God, Thank you God, and your Trinity Team as I accept C.P.R.

February 3 Love Chapter

I love to drive! Now, it took me until after college years to be comfortable behind the wheel of any vehicle! Then I bought my first car; Chevy Vega Hatchback! I even sat behind the wheel of The Salvation Army Emergency Canteen as I drove through the Hoboken, New Jersey Tunnel ! Many cars and jobs later....I drive a Toyota Corolla to work and as Activities Assistant, often drive a fifteen passenger handicapped accesible bus. I still love to drive!

We have been taught, reminded to check our mirrors when driving. We do have to look out for the other drivers! But, more important than that, we have to drive safely and use every precaution behind the wheel. I believe that in our daily ride with God we have to be safe and use every precaution. I quote from one of Saint Paul's letters to the Church of Ephesians:

"Blessed be the God and Father of our Lord Jesus Christ, who hath blessed us with all spiritual blessings in heavenly places in Christ: according as He hath chosen us in Him before the foundation of the world, that we should be holy and without blame before Him in love: having predestinated us unto the adoption of children by Jesus Christ to Himself, according to the good pleasure of His will." Ephesians 1: 3-5

The following poem is found on page 27 of HORIZONS:

Rearview Mirror

Driving down life's highway... Looking in my rear-view mirror... Other people pass me by. but, I'm keeping a watchful eye! Policemen May give tickets that cost! God is giving a message to the lost!

Driving down life's highway... Looking in my rear-view mirror... Others have traveled far away. but, I'm keeping a watchful eye! The road May be curved or straight! Following God's highway is never too late!

Prayer: Thank you God for keeping a watchful eye as I travel your King's highway.

February 4 Love Chapter

There is a chapter in the Holy Bible known as the Love Chapter and that is I Corinthians 13: 1-13. This passage is read at wedding ceremonies and I would like to quote verse 13:

"And now abideth faith, hope, charity, these three, but the greatest of these is charity."

Often we hear the word "love" substituted for the word "charity".... the greatest is love. I have written a poem that is found on page 28 of HORIZONS:

Two Lives (A Wedding Prayer)

Two lives have been joined together. God continues to unite!

May your love for each other be: delicate as a butterfly's wings... colorful as the storm's rainbow... gentle as the springtime rains... flexible as a tender sapling...

May your lives with each other be: flexible under pressure... bending towards God... towards His refreshing love!

Prayer: Thank you God for weddings! Thank you for uniting two lives.

February 5 Love Chapter

My Mother, Virginia Appelt loved to take home movies! But, she hid behind the camera leaving her out of family pictures! My Oma, Maria Appelt loved to take pictures with her camera. And, she was captured on camera taking a picture of her daughter, my Aunt Elsbeth Smail, who was being captured by her daughter, my cousin Cindy Smail, who was being captured by my sister Sue Appelt, who ended up hiding behind her camera!

I remember my first camera; I fondly called my lovely brownie box Kodak! And, I captured some interesting pictures; unique pictures; because I always forgot to advance the film to the next frame! My double exposure pictures became a "hit" in our family albums! My favorite was the kittens all lined up on the sliding barn door as if they were hanging on for a ride!

Another important feature on my first camera was the refocus button and I have to admit that zooming in and out was fun! It became fun for me to focus in on small flowers, creatures, people's faces, and tried hard to capture my love for nature and family!

God has given each of us an inner camera where the refocus button is used to capture His will for us daily. We read in the Holy Bible another letter from Paul to the Thessalonian Church; I Thessalonians 2:12:

"...called you unto His kingdom and glory. "

God inspired me to write the following poem that can be found on page 29 of HORIZONS.

Refocus God, help me to refocus daily... Re-enter holiness daily! Enjoy your fellowship! Freely give of myself! Open your word daily! Come into your presence! Understand your love! Seek your will daily!

Prayer: Our Father, who art in Heaven....(recite the rest of the Lord's prayer)

February 6 Love Chapter

Motel 66 has a motto...."We'll leave the light on" ! How welcoming to come home from a long day which stretched into the night hours and find a light on! We follow that light until we are safely home!

God said (in Genesis 1:3) while his creation was "coming forth" : "Let there be light. ". We are grateful for God loving us so much to send light into this world!

The Psalmist David said (in Psalm 27:1) while he was a shepherd: "The Lord is my light and my salvation.".

We are grateful for God's servant professing love for His Lord!

The Apostle Paul writes to the Church of Ephesus (in Ephesians 5:8): "...walk as children of light...". We are grateful for God's churches sharing love for their Lord! I express my gratitude in the following poem:

"Light the Way, Lord "

Lord, you are my light. Illumine my path. Guide me daily. Help me to follow you. Take me with you always!

We are grateful for God's messengers sharing love for their Lord!

Prayer: Thank you Lord, for being my light, shining, guiding, helping me daily.

February 7 Love Chapter

My Dad, Herbert Appelt was a magician on our small dairy farm five miles outside of Prattsburg, New York! He would entertain his wife and children with acts of magic to keep our small dairy farm running smoothly! One lesson he taught us within his magic tricks was the "slip-knot". I loved learning from Dad what he was taught in his Navy days!

I love the memories that came from learning how to create the slip knot!

The magic of the slip-knot became helpful in our farm chores; especially to help tie the calves safely in their pens and away from their mother's huge bodies that could crush them!

The magic of the slip-knot went beyond the tending of the calves; especially when the imagination of five children learning the secret together! We became cow-hands as we would swing our created magical ropes around the necks of those precious calves! Well, at least most of the time...when we were not chasing and roping each other (around our waists of course)!

The magic of the slip-knot went beyond the dairy farm for me. I shared the magic of slip-knots as a camp counselor, associate pastor, teacher, and activities associate. The rope is colorful like multi-colored yarn. I share my love for my Lord and how He knows all my problems (as I create small slip-knots on this multi-colored rope). Then I seek help from my audience to pull each end of the rope. We literally watch all the problems slip away!

The Psalmist David in Psalm 109: 26 & 27 wrote: "Help me Lord my God: Oh save me according to thy mercy: that they May know that this is thy hand: that thou, Lord, hast done it."

I wrote on page 31 of HORIZONS:

Slip Knots

Lord, my soul is like a rope with slip knots... hurt feelings, anxiety, inability to pray.

Holy Spirit, tug gently at those slip knots... they disappear.. I'm free to do your will again!

Prayer: Dear Trinity, thank you for freeing me from my problems (slip knots).

February 8 Love Chapter

Here in New York State during the month of February if I mentioned the word breeze, one would not think of cool but cold! I love the cold breeze on my face and I love to think of the summer breeze to keep me warm!

In Portal, Arizona during the month of February, my parents didn't have to think of the warm breeze; they felt it! I learned that while visiting them several times in the house they built; stone by stone! I also found out how important a breeze can be!

During one of my visits in Portal, I was fascinated by the butterflies gliding in the breeze! I was inspired by the birds as they flew in the breeze. Oh, the beauty I saw in the spider webs swaying in the breeze; until I noticed a butterfly lying still in the web...no more to fly. I reacted by writing this poem, which is found on page 32 of HORIZONS:

Let the Breeze Take Hold!

Butterfly, caught in a web... unable to fly... wish you could hold on to the breeze that sways the flower!

Friends, caught in a web... unable to move... wish you could hold on to the breeze that of the Holy Spirit!

The breeze of the Holy Spirit is precious to hold on to daily. We read in Acts 1:8 the importance of receiving the power of the Holy Ghost: (I love holding on to the power!

"But ye shall receive power, after that the Holy Ghost is come upon you: and ye shall be witnesses unto me both in Jerusalem, and in all Judea, and in Samaria, and unto the uttermost part of the earth."

Prayer: Dear God, I am so grateful for the power that comes from Your Holy Ghost.

February 9 Love Chapter

I love the Bible story about Noah's ark. All the animals that saved from the flood! Noah's family was saved and God made a covenant with him. To help Noah remember the covenant, God made sure he had a visible sign; the rainbow!

I love rainbows! I was inspired to write the following poem from reading the story of Noah's ark (which can be found in Genesis; Chapters 7-9:

God's Rainbow

God's world is like a rainbow, filled with many colors; red sunsets and apples green grass and trees blue skies and seas indigo blossoms and mountains All nature is happy together!

God's word is like a rainbow, filled with many colors; red blood of salvation green growth of grace blue purity of holiness indigo majesty of power All the world love and honor together!

Prayer: God, your rainbow is so brillantly shown in the sky and the colors symbolize your love for each one of us and our lives!

February 10 Love Chapter

Today, I continue to share my love for nature. I love to experience the watching of the different weather patterns. I thank God for giving us such beauty in the changes we notice in weather. I would invite you to read over the creation story found in Genesis Chapter 1: 1-20 the passage that inspired me to write this poem found on page 34 of HORIZONS:

When... When it rains, we see the washing away of natural stains!

When it snows, we see the cleansing of natural foes!

When the sun shines, we take in the healing of deep, corrupted mines!

When the wind blows, we catch the clearing of sorrow and woes!

Prayer: God, of our daily weather patterns, thank you for sending us the rain, snow, sun and wind to catch, take in and feel for daily cleansing, healing and clearing!

February 11 Love Chapter

Do you remember the lyrics to the song entitled "Pass It On?" I remember "...a wondrous time is Spring "and how this season is compared to God's love and how we would want to pass His love on to others! I thought of my favorite season: Autumn and wrote lyrics to create another verse for Pass It On! This poem can be found on page 35 of HORIZONS, and I quote from the Bible: Matthew 28: 19-20.

"Go ye therefore, and teach all nations, baptizing them in the name of the Father, and of the Son, and of the Holy Ghost: teaching them to observe all things whatsoever I have commanded you: and lo, I am with you alway, even unto the end of the world. Amen."

Pass it On

A wondrous time is Autumn when all the leaves are changing! The colors are so bright they need no re-arranging!

That's how it with God's love, once you experience it. It's bright as fall and nothing small. You'll want to pass it on!

Prayer: Dear Lord of the seasons we witness changing four times a year and the reminder of the beauty and power within them. Thank you for guiding us to pass on our love for you and your creation!

February 12 Love Chapter

The month of February contains holidays when we can express our love and recognize our loved ones. No wonder we recognize our 16th President of the United States of America today on his birthday. Abraham Lincoln is remembered for his ability to share his "pearls of wisdom" that he wrote for our country; the most famous being the Gettysburg Address.

The month of February in 2004 will be a memorable one for me; when I was teaching a college course at Finger Lakes Community College's Newark Site, in Canandaigua, New York. As an adjunct instructor within the Social Sciences Depart- ment, I was assigned to teach "Foundations of Childcare". Meanwhile, I was still substituting within the Canandaigua Elementary and Manchester/Shortsville Elementary Schools. I vividly remember starting the writing of a poem about foundations.

On page 36 of HORIZONS and pages 29-37 of PONDERING OUR HORIZONS the creation and expansion of this poem can be read.

Foundations of Life Mortar by mortar stone by stone we build our home on a firm foundation wherever we May roam!

Muscle by muscle bone by bone we build our skeleton on a firm foundation whatever we are given!

Step by step moment by moment we build our precious time on a firm foundation whenever we find reason or rhyme !

Scripture reference: Apostle Paul's letter to the Philippian Church; Philippians 4:8

"Finally, brethren, whatsoever things are true, whatsoever things are honest, whatsoever things are just, whatsoever things are pure, whatsoever things are lovely, whatsoever things are of good report; if there be any virtue, and if there be any praise, think on these things."

Prayer: Thank you God our Father, that you are living still! May we recognize, review, and refresh our memories this day on the foundations laid before us by our "fore-fathers".

February 13 Love Chapter

At the end of each devotional I have closed with a prayer. For today's devotional I would like to begin with a prayer! Let us begin today by praying the Lord's prayer. What pearls of wisdom are contained in the prayer our Lord taught us to pray! For those readers who wish to recite and any who wish to read the prayer let us have our bibles open to Matthew 6:9-13.

There are five pearls written in the following poem that was originally published on page 37 of HORIZONS:

Purity of Prayer

Prayer is ... Understanding Respect Intercession Trusting Yielding

Prayer is: Understanding...Look at Matthew 6:9.

We pray with understanding that God is our Father, He is in heaven, and his name is understood.

Prayer is : Respect...Look at Matthew 6:10

We pray with respect that God's kingdom will come, God's will will be done, and His heaven is respected.

Prayer is: Intercession...Look at Matthew 6:11

We pray with intercession that God will give us our daily bread by interceeding.

Prayer is: Trusting...Look at Matthew 6:12

We pray, trusting God to forgive our sins as we forgive others who trespassed against us; losing our trust in them.

Prayer is: Yielding...Look at Matthew 6:13

We pray, yielding to God who leads us, delivers us, and allows us to yield to His kingdom, power and glory forever! Amen!

Prayer: Thank you God for the purity of prayer so beautifully expressed by our reciting or reading the prayer you taught us to pray.

February 14 Love Chapter

"Be Mine", "True Love" , "Hugs and Kisses", and "Always Yours" are phrases found on candy and cards for Valentine's Day! I would like to add another phrase: "Let Go". Why? We have been given words of wisdom that love is letting go. Look at the Apostle Peter's letter (I Peter 5:6,7):

"Humble yourselves therefore under the mighty hand of God, that He May exalt you in due time: Casting all your care upon Him; For He careth for you."

God allows us daily to cast our care upon Him (letting go) because He cares for us and our lives to let go. I express this thought in a poem found on page 38 of HORIZONS:

Let Go Let go of grief! Grab on to peace!

Let go of grudges! Grasp the good!

On this Valentine's Day give a heart...let go all that hinders!

Prayer: Dear God of love, thank you for the short messages we can keep close to our hearts. You ask us to be yours, trust you and to let go!

February 15 Love Chapter

Did you ever have someone make you a comforter; beautifully made with meaningful patterns, patches of love? I think of how that material is so cozy and how we would miss the comforter if it became lost.

Did you ever lose someone who gets along beautifully with you, matched with love? I think of how that person you cuddle up to and we could miss this comforter if he or she became lost.

Did you ever wander away from God's love; missing His comforting ways? I think of how God sent His Son, Jesus Christ to save us and how we hear His comforting words:

"And I will pray the Father, and He shall give you another

Comforter, that He May abide with you for ever;..." John 14:16

The following poem first written for HORIZONS; pg. 39 was inspired by God's comforting words found in John 14:16 and by my dear sister Sue's gift; a patched comforter.

Comforting Ways

Your loved one is missed today in each though and heart.

What words of comfort can we say? consoling can we impart?

Your loved one leaves comfort if we would gently hold.

Your loved one's smile lingers...gently easing pain and sorrow.

Your loved one's touching fingers firmly grasping comfort for today and for tomorrow.

Prayer: Dear God and your Trinity Team, thank you for sending comfort our way! Help us to accept you and your team's comforting ways!

February 16 Love Chapter

There is a conversation recorded in the book of Luke; chapter 18: 18-25. The dialogue is between a rich ruler and Jesus (he called Jesus the Good Master). There is the main question by the rich ruler: "What must I do to inherit eternal life?"

Jesus answers by reminding the rich ruler of the commandments and the rich ruler professes to have kept these commandments from his youth. Then Jesus goes for the rich ruler's first love; his treasures, his riches. and commands him to sell all and distribute to the poor. Unfortunately the rich ruler is sorrowful; Jesus picks up on this and commands the situation by stating: "...It is easier for a camel to go through a needle's eye, than for a rich man to enter into the kingdom of God..."

A rich man according to Jesus will have to sacrifice in order to move towards the kingdom of God and all His riches! I challenge the reader to look at the life God has allowed for you; some riches, while others poverty. Either way we have to approach each day by moving on. You can find the following poem on page 40 of HORIZONS:

Move On When your way become rough and life is tough, Move on with the power of God!

When your day becomes lost and you're paying the cost, your task seems long and there's no song. You can smile at every trial, and Move on with the power of God!

Prayer: God you sent your Son to guide us on our way and we know that no matter what treasures we have on earth, we know to move on with your power.

February 17 Love Chapter

In your days of youth, do you remember receiving advise from your pastor? Well, Timothy received exhortations from the Apostle of Paul who wrote to many church groups such as the Philippians, Colossians, and Corinthians. In Second Timothy 4: 2 we read:

"Preach the word; be instant in season, out of season; reprove, rebuke, exhort with all longsuffering and doctine."

As a member of The Salvation Army Church, I have received some advise such as Paul gave to Timothy and I have reacted by writing the following poem that can be found on page 41 of HORIZONS:

Tis' the Season

Tis' the season to be ready for the coming of the Lord!

Tis' the season to be steady for the preaching of God's word!

For convincing May be unwelcome 'out of season' by those who fear!

But, the season will still be coming! Some will not want to be near!

Tis' the season to be ready! Be steady, though the way be long! Be steady, through word or song!

Prayer: We thank you, God for sending the youthful Timothy to listen under the Apostle Paul's ministry. May we be ready ... any season!

February 18 Love Chapter

I love being happy. I love making others around me happy. I love what we read in the Holy Bible about being happy. Take a look at the Apostle Paul's letter to the Church of Phillipi in Philippians 4:4:

"Rejoice in the Lord alway: and again I say, rejoice."

I love creating acrostics. I love coming up with phrases for each letter of a given topic; word of interest. For today's devotional I share my love for the word "happiness" with this poem found on page 43 of HORIZONS:

Happiness

Happiness is a healthy habit Acquired and appreciated Partaken by parents Passed on by siblings Introduced to others Nipping the negative Endeavoring to edify Simply smiling Specializing in sharing!

Prayer: Happiness is knowing your healthy habit, dear God! We thank you for you and your "Trinity Team's "examples in sharing happiness!

February 19 Love Chapter

I love the name given to our class at The Salvation Army School For Officers' Training, in Suffern, New York. Our session was given this name in 1976 to carry while in school for two years and then keep with us upon graduation in 1978. In our class, we started out with twelve single men (and May I add designated as out twelve disciples!). We knew the command Jesus gave his eleven disciples as He spoke to them about the power they would receive upon their appointments: (found in Matthew 28:19-20), would be the same for the 60+Disciples of Jesus being given their appointments in June of 1978:

"God ye therefore, and teach all nations, baptizing them in the name of the Father, and of the Son, and of the Holy Ghost: teaching them to observe all things whatsoever I have commanded you: and lo, I am with you alway, even unto the end of the world."

I wrote another poem using part of our session name: Disciples of

Jesus (found on page 44 of HORIZONS):

Disciple of Jesus

Daring to be a disciple of Jesus Interested in serving others Singing in God's Salvation Army Continuing to study God's Word Insisting on following Jesus Praying for family and others Lifting up the banner 'Blood and Fire' Ever, always, doing God's Will!

Prayer: God, we claim to be your disciples of your Son. May we be guided daily to live up to the name we were given.

February 20 Love Chapter

I loved hearing and reading about how my parents met: Virginia Jeanne Seabury and Herbert Ewald Appelt attended Syracuse University School of Forrestry in New York State at the same time! I also loved finding out about their wedding day and how their lives united throughout fifty plus years!

For their 50th (Golden) Anniversary the family sent special greetings by creating a collage made up of each of our pictures and I personally wrote a poem (found on page 45 of HORIZONS) that was inspired by what we call the Golden Rule (recorded in the Gospel of Matthew 7:12). May I quote the scripture reference first:

"Therefore all things whatsoever ye would that men should do to you, do ye even so to them: for this is the law.."

Golden Anniversary May 31, 1947

Beginnings for you, my dear parents Virginia and Herbert Appelt Special anniversaries with special gifts:

5th anniversary the gift of wood family dairy farm surrounded by woods!

10th anniversary the gift of aluminum/tin your children carrying lunch boxes of tin!

25th anniversary the gift of silver graduations brought a few hairs of silver!

30th anniversary the gift of pearl weddings..two sons and your middle girl!

40th anniversary the gift of ruby Arizona sunrises and sunsets of beauty!

50th anniversary the gift of gold gold medal for weavings presented and sold!

HAPPY GOLDEN ANNIVERSARY, MOTHER AND DAD

God's blessings and lots of love, Patricia

PS.....75th anniversary the gift of diamond continue to let your life glimmer and shine!

Prayer: Thank you God for the union of our parents, the celebrations, and the gifts you presented through the years of anniversaries.

February 21 Love Chapter

Many of you readers love to try out new recipes! Some of you will follow step by step, while others will be more comfortable just baking with ease! Do you remember making gingerbread men? I must confess I remember eating those cookies without much thought about the recipe!

Let's pause to think about the recipe and what three main ingredients we would include: cookie dough, icing or frosting, and decorations. We would need measuring spoons and cups, mixing bowl and utensils to prepare for the baking of the gingerbread men! Unfortunately the life of the gingerbread man is short-lived, but not the taste!

One of God's writers of wisdom; David wrote in Psalms 34:8 about tasting: "O taste and see that the Lord is good: blessed is the man that trusteth in him."

I share a poem that encourages us to greet each day: (the original title of this poem was "The New Year" found on page 46 of HORIZONS" :

A New Day

A new day is approaching near! Will we face this new day with hope? Will we turn and run with fear?

Come, our new day! We greet you with open arms around a huge bowl of stirred mix: Cups of Love Spoonfuls of Joy Pounds of Peace!

Come, our new day! We greet you with open arms around a huge gingerbread boy: Chocolate chip eyes of Love Red Licorice smile of Joy White frosting clothes of Peace!

Come, our new day! We greet you with open arms around a huge world to stay: Long-Lasting Love Everlasting Joy Endless Peace!

Prayer: Thank you Lord, that we can greet each new day you created with open arms!

February 22 Love Chapter

Today we recognize the birthday of our first president of the United States and the father of our country; George Washington. In American History classes, we learned about him as General and President. We recognize deep love for his country of America and how he began a tradition of seeking God's guidance as the leader of our nation. I would compare President Washington with a leader we read about the Holy Bible: Abraham. For a brief review let us look at the Apostle Paul's letter to the Hebrews in which he recognize Abraham as the Father of many nations (Hebrews 6:13-15):

"For when God made promise to Abraham, because he could swear by no greater, he sware by himself, saying, 'Surely blessing I will bless thee, and multiplying I will multiply thee."

Today I recognize the deep love my father; Herbert E. Appelt had for our U.S.A. (born in Indianapolis, Indiana, raised in Rochester, New York, and tended to his family and farm five miles outside of Prattsburg, in the Pultney area). I introduce you to the following poem which can be found on page 47 of HORIZONS:

We Will Remember, Dad

December 21, 1924-May 26, 2001

We will remember, Dad the lessons of life you taught us love for nature: from cultured sunflowers to names of trees beauty of life: raising a family as a faithful companion to Mother love for people: Prattsburg, N.Y. farm community Portal, A.Z. friendly, quaint place commitment to country serving in the Navy and whistling patriotic tunes! We will remember, Dad You will never be forgotten!

Prayer: Dear Heavenly Father, thank you for the promises you made to Abraham, President Washinton, and my Dad. May the oath never be forgotten.

February 23 Love Chapter

One of the favorite places our family loved on the farm was the apple orchard. We would spend hours playing around what we fondly called "Our Family Tree". The branches of this particular tree were low and thick enough for climbing, swinging and hiding our treasures. We would scramble up the tree when a game of tag or hide-go seek would be in session! We would swing from a branch that eventually had our hands imprinted as a result of the wearing off of the bark! We would hide our treasures of stone, wood, and even a precious marble or yo-yo! We even made a club house protected by the shade of the tall, stately apple tree! Even in the winter months we would find ourselves gathering near the club house! And I wrote my first poem there:

Appelt' Famous Club (created in the 1960's)

Five children: Linda, John, Sue, Pat and Bill Appelt family with parents: Virginia and Herbert Make a club house in the apple orchard Outside with nature on our dairy farm Under the shade of our family tree Sharing a poem written by Patricia Lee:

Mr. Amos was so famous He planted a flower that grew like a tower. When he looked down at his feet They were as red as a beet!

Oath: We promise to protect our farm by planting floweres, raising animals, and learning about the birds,bees and trees!

Scripture Reference: Yesterday's bible passage from Hebrews 6: 13-15

Prayer: God, Lord, and Holy Spirit, guide us to daily receive your promises and to daily keep our oath to you!

February 24 Love Chapter

It was Labor Day of 1975 that I was introduced to my new boss; Captain Barbara Torbitt, Corps Officer (Pastor) of The Wellsville Salvation Army Citadel (Church). That same day, I was introduced to her Mother, Dorothy and their poodle, Pierre. I would be starting a new job; Associate with Captain Barbara Torbitt. Her family from Oleo Acres, Oswego, New York would become my extended, "Special Family".

Paul writes in Ist Corinthians (13:4) "Charity suffereth long, and is kind..."

Special Family of Oleo Acres

Trustworthy, "Special" Torbitt family from Oswego, New York Thanks, Mom (Dorothy) and Dad (Raymond) for welcoming another Patricia!

Open-door and open-arms for family and friends Thanks, "Special" Sister (Barbara) for introducing me to your Mom and Dad!

Ready to travel to Long Island and Canandaigua, New York Thanks, "Special" Sister (Barbara) for inviting me to meet the Spellmans from Canandaigua, the Chosen Spot!

Bringing family together with re-unions and holidays Thanks "Special" siblings: Bob, Toby, Ray, Jack, Bill, Barbara, Doreen, & Larry for those delicious chicken barbeques!

Inviting others to join the family Thanks "Special" siblings: Helen, Caroline, Mimi, Lorainne, Alice, Pat, Lynn, Nancy, and Esther or sharing your children and pets!

Thoughtful, tactful, and true to friends Thanks "Special" family: Torbitts for business transactions and auto sales!

Tender-Loving Care Team (T.L.C.!) Thanks "Special" Mom, Dad, Bob, and Jack, for you have gone to your rest!

Prayer: Thank you Lord for extended families, extended loved ones who have been given the name: "Special Family" . Guide me daily to show that same love (charity) that suffereth long and is kind.

February 25 Love Chapter

Today's devotional will begin with the same scripture reference as yesterday. Apostle Paul's definition of charity (love) inspired me to write about my "spiritual" family that I met through my "special" sister; Barbara Torbitt. The following poem is found on page 51 of HORIZONS:

Spiritual Family of The Chosen Spot

Spiritual Spellman family of Canandaigua, New York Thanks Mom (Orpha) & Dad (Francis) for introducing me to your Salvation Army!

People-oriented and community conscious Thanks for your Music and leadership within worship and club meetings.

Enthusiasts for the Lord and His people Thanks for your sermons and programs at church and community centers.

Listening to God's call and service Thanks for your visitation and meetings with the motto; "Saved to Serve".

Leaning on God's strength and power Thanks for your example of faith on a daily basis!

Making room for three "spiritual" daughters: Phyllis Culkin, Barbara Torbitt, Patricia Appelt; in your Mayflower Dr. Home!

Always aware of others and their needs Thanks for reaching above and beyond!

Never giving up on others Thanks for being spiritual care-givers!

Prayer: Thank you Lord for extended families, extended loved one who have been given the name: "Spiritual Family". Guide me daily to show that same love (charity) that suffereth long and is kind.

February 26 Love Chapter

Often, we say "Three is a charm" and that is why we will refer to Paul's pearl of wisdom for the third time! Refer back to the devotionals and scripture reference on February 24th and 25th. I preface another poem of HORIZONS found on pages 52 with the same introduction.

Blended Families

Biological families have the same genes, traits and looks keeping our precious memories in albums and scrapbooks. I am proud to be a part of the Appelt family!

Special families have similar hobbies, loves and interests sharing so there never exists an empty nest. I am proud to be a part of the Torbitt family!

Spiritual families have similar beliefs and values in life living so others see see how we best handle stress or strife. I am proud to be a part of the Spellman family!

Prayer: Thank you Father, Son, and Holy Spirit for blended families. Guide me daily to show the same love (charity) that "suffereth long" and is "kind".

February 27 Love Chapter

We are coming to the end of February and the Love Chapter. I have loved sharing my poems from HORIZONS and expounding on them for the month of February's devotionals. There is one last poem in my first poetry book and I refer to the prophet Habakkuk's pearl of wisdom before I share it: Habakkuk 2:2

"And the Lord answered me, and said, 'Write the vision, and make it plain upon tablets, that he May run that readeth it'..."

Epilogue

Clouds will continue to float across our skies Lives will continued to be inspired by these billowy white objects to write poems for others to read.

Lives will continue to grow across the centuries Humans will continue to be inspired by these unique individuals to write poems for future readers.

Poetry will continue to flow across pages of books Readers will continue to be inspired by a variety of works by poets of the future.

Prayer: Dear God, thank you for the 'clouds' of life we encounter because you first loved us, formed us in your loving hands, and inspired us to share your love through your Son, Jesus and your Holy Spirit, the Comforter.

February 28 Love Chapter

Every four years on our calendar we are reminded that this date; February 28th is not the last day of February. Leap year is recognized on February 29th. I will share a devotional today and allow my sister Sue to share her pearls of wisdom through her illustration tomorrow.

In today's devotional let's leap! Do you remember the childhood game: Leap Frog? Have you ever leaped for joy? Have you ever made a leap of faith? Well, I have to say my second poetry book: PONDERING OUR HORIZONS was a leap! It followed HORIZONS after a few years of leaping into prayer and guidance from God! Each poem is preceded or followed by an exposition. Often the exposition contains scriptural reference to The Holy Bible. I even invited two co-writers to take the leap of faith with me!

I would like to quote from the introduction of PONDERING OUR HORIZONS for today's devotional: "... a collection of my poetry, a path others can follow to receive inspiration and insight. "

I would like to give scriptural reference from the Psalmist David: Psalm 108:4 "For Thy mercy (O Lord) is great above the heavens, and Thy truth reacheth the clouds..."

Prayer: Dear Lord, Thy mercy (love) is great above the heavens! Thank you for making a leap of love for each one of us...by sending your Son, the Saviour of the world!

February 29 Love Chapter

Scripture Text: I John 4: 19

"We love him, because he first loved us. "

Saint John the Divine wrote about His God of love...and how we love Him too! This month we have been promised His everlasting love. May we love heartily unto the Lord! This will help us keep our Resolutions to God!

Thank you for leaping to this page and not waiting for a leap year to see the first of my sister Sue's monthly illustrations.

Today we give God thanks for the wisdom learned through talented illustrators.

Prayer: Thank You, Lord for allowing my sister Sue to take her first leap into making a contribution through her drawing for February's Love Chapter.

March 1 Foundations

May 2004 was when I began a new job within the Activities Team at Clifton Springs Hospital and Clinic. I continued substitute teaching within the Manchester- Shortsville and Canandaigua School Districts and continued to teach as an adjunct instructor at the Newark, NY. site for Finger Lakes Community College. The course within the Social Sciences department was "Foundations of Childcare".

When Scott, one of the co-workers at Clifton Springs shared interest in the course I was teaching, he expressed how we needed to have a more important course: Foundations of Life. His suggestion became the catalyst for a survival manual that I had been compiling for at least ten years. For the month of March I wish to share sections of this survival manual and will start today with a brief introduction:

I quote first from the Apostle Paul's letter to the church of Corinth; I Corinthians 3:10:

"According to the grace of God which is given unto me, as a wise masterbuilder, I have laid the foundation and another buildeth thereon. But let every man take heed how he buildeth thereupon."

I dedicate the sections of this survival manual to my parents; Virginia and Herbert Appelt. They will always be remembered as social workers and masterbuilders! From the foundations on the dairy farm just outside the town of Prattsburg, NY to the foundations of their new home in Portal, AZ, my parents inspired me to write a poem that expresses my theory of life. The poem has seven stanzas that expound on what I believe are the seven basic foundations of life.

Ponder your horizon: What do you believe are some basic foundations of life?

Prayer: Dear God, masterbuilder of the foundations of the earth, thank you for inspiring us to ponder our horizons and the foundations of life!

March 2 Foundations

Once again we will refer to Paul's letter to the Church of Corinth and his reminder to the people that God is the "masterbuilder" (Corinthians 3:10)

I believe that God is the builder of our home. I introduce my first basic foundation of life and expound my theory in the first stanza of "Foundations of Life":

MORTAR

Mixture of cement; often lime with sand and water. Much time must be spent as taught by my mother and father.

Mixture of our enviroment; family, friends, and nature. Much time has been spent as shown by a home so secure.

Stone by stone mortar by mortar we continue building foundations of life.

Ponder your horizons:

What was your home address as a child?

Mine was: RD#1 Prattsburg, NY

What kind of building did you have as a home?

Ours was: a farm house that I found out was built in the late 1800's

How was your home furnished?

I remember the closets underneath my bunk bed, and kitchen benches used for storage and for us children to sit around a huge, sturdy table.

How secure was your home?

We were taught rules to keep the foundation of our home secure.

Prayer: Dear God, the masterbuilder of our homes, thank you for laying the foundation of a secure, safe home that helps us in building the same strong foundation of home with families of our own!

March 3 Foundations

Let us continue our study of the first foundation of life: Home. Many of us will remember the scene in the story; "The Wizard of Oz" when Dorothy clicks her red shoes together and repeats: "There's no place like home". She dreamt that her home was literally torn away from its foundations! No one likes to see their home destroyed by natural causes such as fire, wind, or floods. No one likes to see their home torn away from its foundations.

Let us look up in the Holy Bible; Matthew 7:24. This scripture supports our first foundation of life; "home". It contains a lesson (parable) taught by Jesus.

"Therefore whosoever heareth these sayings of mine, and doeth them, I will liken him unto a wise man, which built his house upon a rock."

What sayings of Jesus needed to be heard?

If we look back at Matthew 4: 25 and 5:1 we read how Jesus saw the people, multitudes from Galilee, Decapolis, Jerusalem, Judea, and from beyond Jordan. They were eager to listen to this "teacher", "Rabbi". They would listen to lessons He taught that we know today as: "The Beatitudes", "Parables" (ie. lessons on salt and light), "Commandments", "The Lord's Prayer" and our lesson found in Matthew 7:24.

How would these sayings of Jesus be done?

If we look back at our own childhood we will remember lessons taught by parents, guardians, teachers, siblings, and pastors. I remember being told these lessons and also witnessed how they were not only said but done by my mentors. I know now as an adult that lessons in life taught in our homes are meant to be "done", shared, and most of all, passed on down.

Do we build our homes upon a rock?

When I look back at one of my childhood past-times, I remember the climbing of rocks...trying to be the "King of the Mountain"! My strategy was simple....I would choose a rock that I could climb upon without hurting myself! I believe we choose our homes that protect us from harm. We know about the natural disasters that can ruin our homes; ie floods. We also have learned how to build firm foundations for our homes to help us deal with natural disasters. We recognize rock as a firmer foundation than sand!

Prayer: Let us pray the prayer that Jesus taught us to pray: "The Lord's Prayer".

March 4 Foundations

Today's scripture is within another letter from the Apostle Paul: Romans. He writes in chapter 12: 1:

"I beseech you therefore, brethren, by the mercies of God, that you present your bodies a living sacrifice, holy, acceptable unto God, which is your reasonable service."

I believe God is the masterbuilder of our bodies. I introduce the second basic foundation of life, and expound my theory in the second stanza of "Foundations of Life":

Muscle

Mixture of tissue Often contracting and relaxing An important health issue as shown by my parents' nurturing.

Mixture of our environment Family and physical nature Much time has been spent creating a healthy stature.

Bone by bone muscle by muscle we continue building foundations of life.

Ponder your horizons:

How would you best describe your childhood physical body? Mine was short, skinny, bony, sunburned easily, and leaning (lazy legs!)

What physical challenge did you have growing up? I remember having to wear glasses (not pretty ones!) starting in Kindergarten to correct a lazy eye. The lazy legs corrected themselves by then!

What lesson have you learned about the differences in body

development? Mine would be the reading of the poem by John G. Saxen as a student and then as a substitute teacher: "The Blindmen and the Elephant". It is all about what we observe (and not just by sight)!

Prayer: Dear God, the masterbuilder of our bodies, thank you for laying the foundation of a strong, healthy body that helps us build strong, healthy bodies in our homes.

March 5 Foundations

Scripture review: Romans 12:1 (see yesterday's devotional)

Let us continue our study of the second foundation of life: body. I would like to compare the Apostle Paul' advise found in Romans 12:1 with the Psychologist Maslow's "Hierarchy of Needs" I learned in Social Science classes. Apostle Paul' advise on how to present our healthy bodies to God can be compared to Maslow's theroy of our main need being "physical". and this being the foundation (or base) of the hierarchy of needs.

The Apostle Paul directs us to present our body...By the mercies of God... Count your blessings! Maslow's theory was also called "Self-Actualization psychologist. He believed in focusing on productivity and happiness instead of problems.

The Apostle Paul directs us to sacrifice our body...As a sacrifice to God...not burnt offerings...but living, reasonable service! Maslow's theory refers to development. He stated that our body has to be daily developed...satisfied!

The Apostle Paul directs us to prepare our body...Holy unto God...daily holiness ...spiritually and physically prepared! Maslow's theory refers to being in tune. He states that our body has to be daily developed...tuned!

Prayer: As we pray the Lord's prayer, May we thank you God, for our physical bodies.

March 6 Foundations

Today's scripture was written by David. Remember the shepherd boy David and how he defeated the giant Goliath? This same youth would become a king and be recognized as a song writer. Let us look at Psalm 37: 30 & 31:

"The mouth of the righteous speaketh wisdom, and his tongue talketh of judgment. The law of his God is in his heart; none of his steps shall slide."

I believe God is the masterbuilder of our steps. I introduce today the third foundation of life and expound my theory in the third stanza of "Foundations of Life":

Step

Mixture of skips and leaps Often twists and turns in our walks Many flips and flops But, how we enjoyed the talks!

Mixture of our environment Family and friends who teach Much time has been spent helping us our goals to reach!

Path by path step by step we continue building foundations of life!

Ponder your horizons:

How old were you when you took your first step? I took longer than my siblings, and only know this because Mother included our "firsts" in our individual and personalized scrapbooks.

What family talents would you share? Sketching, drawing, painting, making collages, and playing the piano.

What important step did your family take together? We were together for Sue; the middle girl. She walked down the aisle with Dad to marry Ben LaSpagnoletta! We each possess this memory of September 6, 1975!

Prayer: Dear God, the masterbuilder of our steps, thank you for laying the foundation of important steps that help us build, or take significant steps in our lives.

March 7 Foundations

Scripture review: Psalm 37: 30,31 (see yesterday's devotional)

Let us continue our study of the third foundation of life: step. I would like to compare King David's advise in Psalm 37: 30,31 with research found in this decade of an increase of children, youth, and adults diagnosed with ADHD; Attention Deficit Hyperactive Disorder (ADHD). It is a medical disorder and has symptoms that affect the daily steps in life.

King David directs the righteous to speak wisdom. Talk to God first, seek His wisdom, and only then share wisdom. The medical field includes doctors, parents talking to God firstabout ADHD, seeking professional help and only then share the helpful steps to create a healthier physical environment.

King David directs the righteous to have the law of God in their hearts. Learn God's laws, obey His laws, and teach His laws. The medical and educational field include instructors, teachers that have learned God's laws, research professional advances for ADHD, and only then share the helpful steps to create a healthier physical environment.

King David encourages that none of the righteous "steps" shall slide. Seek God's guidance if one of your loved one needs treatment for ADHD. Learn from God and "experts" He sends your way the medical advances for ADHD, and only then share the helpful lessons you have learned to create a healthier physical environment.

Prayer: Dear God, you sent us the "Great Physician" (your Son, Jesus) to save us in our often physically upset world. We seek His daily guidance to prevent those with physical disorders from being untreated.

March 8 Foundations

Today's scripture is the Apostle Paul's letter to Timothy (who he calls his "son of faith"). Let us look at II Timothy 4:2:

"Preach the word; be instant in season, out of season; reprove, rebuke, exhort with all longsuffering and doctrine."

I believe God is the masterbuilder of our time. I introduce today the fourth foundation of life and expound my theory in the fourth stanza of "Foundations of Life".

Time

Mixture of intervals multidirectional time spent birth and school work and retirement always movement!

Mixture of our environment family of each special season much time has been spent making of life rhyme or reason!

Day by day moment by moment we continue building foundations of life!

Ponder your horizons:

When did you learn to tell time? Some of us learned first by following the sun in the sky way before we read a clock, or a wristwatch!

What is the best time of day for you and why? Some of us are early risers when we read, write, and pray, being ready for bed before the night owls find their best time to read, write, and pray!

What is your favorite way to spend your free time? Some of us love to be outdoors with nature, searching the clouds and star gazing while others enjoy love to be inside with the comforts of home.

Prayer: Dear God thank you for helping us to live daily in your presence.

March 9 Foundations

Scripture review: II Timothy 4:2 (see yesterday's devotional)

Let us continue our study of the fourth foundation of life: time. I would like to compare the Apostle Paul's advise for Timothy's preaching to be instant in season, with God's instant omnipotent power in season.

The Apostle Paul advises Timothy to reprove in season; to find fault with the sinful world. Timothy needs to preach repentance, salvation, holiness instantly! God reproves in each season; finds fault with the sinful world and has given us a saviour to offer us instant salvation if we instantly admit our faults.

The Apostle Paul advises Timothy to rebuke in season; to criticize sharply about our sinful world. Timothy needs to instantly convict, scold, plead! God rebukes in each season; convicts us to repent for our sins.

The Apostle Paul advises Timothy to exhort in season; to teach instantly! God exhorts in each season; with all long suffering (He sent His Son, Jesus to be the Saviour for our sinful world. God exhorts with doctrine (He sends each of us sinners to share His doctrine of salvation through Jesus Christ.

Prayer: Dear God, thank you for preparing us to preach the word; the truth.

March 10 Foundations

Today's scripture is Saint Luke's gospel 23:42:

"And he (one of the malefactors which were hanged on a cross) said unto Jesus, Lord, remember me when thou comest into Thy kingdom."

I believe God is the masterbuilder of our memory. I introduce the fifth foundation of life and expound my theory in the fifth stanza of "Foundations of Life".

Memory

Mixture of retaining and recalling often explicit and gradual much time in gathering experiences: sensitive or logical

Mixture of our environment social, emotional, physical walls much time has been spent traveling down life's halls

Experience by experience memory by memory we continue building foundations of life

What do you recall as a painful, childhood memory? I remember witnessing my sister falling out of a tree and had a concussion.

What do you recall as a pleasant, childhood memory? I remember family visits to grandparents, cousins, and rides in the car.

How do you keep your "memories" alive? I am continuing the scrapbook that Mother gave each of us five children around when we graduated from High School.

Prayer: Thank you Lord for remembering us daily and helping us to recall memories.

March 11 Foundations

Let us continue our study of the fifth foundation of life: memory. I would like to refer to the Mind & Body Special Issue of Time; January 29, 2007. Recent research has supported within neuroscience that one of the brain's functions; remembering, can be changed; altered by the support of transmission received by our senses.

When we re-read the scripture from yesterday's devotional: Luke 23:42, we read how the malefactor (hanging one one of the crosses alongside Jesus) pleads to Jesus to remember him when Christ "comes into His kingdom". Even the malefactor recognizes that Christ is all knowing! When His kingdom comes:

Christ will remember my pleas of forgiveness, even when I do not remember how many times we have asked! The malefactor who wished Jesus to remember him did rebuke the other malefactor by asking him; "Dost not thou fear God...?" (Luke 23:40). We are reminded how emotions affect our memories!

Christ will remember my seeking for salvation even if I do not remember the actual date myself! The malefactor continues his conversation and reminds the other malefactor that; "...we receive the due reward of our deeds." (Luke 23:41). We are reminded how circumstances affect our memories!

Christ will remember who has their name written in the book of life, even if we do not remember all the experiences we have had as a sinner! The malefactor turns from the other malefactor and directs his plead to Christ: "...remember me...(Luke 23:42). Jesus replies: "...to day shalt thou be with me in paradise" (Luke 23:43). We are reminded how our whole being affects our memories!

Prayer: Dear God we pray the words of the Lord's prayer by memory!

March 12 Foundations

Today's scripture is the Gospel of John 1:1:

"In the beginning was the Word, and the Word was with God, and the Word was God."

I believe God is the masterbuilder of our words. I introduce the sixth foundation of life and expound my theory in the sixth stanza of "Foundations of Life".

Syllable

Mixture of instruction and cognition often phonetics or language much room for expression experiences taught and understood!

Mixture of our environment social, emotional, physical impressions much time has been spent our words being reflections!

Word by word syllable by syllable we continue building foundations of life!

What memories do you have about learning to talk?

I have the memories in a scrapbook made by my parents which includes my firsts! It was recorded that my first word was: "cat"....or was I trying to say my name; Pat?

What was the first book you remember reading as a child?

I remember reading POKEY LITTLE PUPPY by Janette S. Lowrey!

What memories do you have about learning about God, the Word, the Bible?

I remember family conversation around the supper table, attending services in church (one specifically where we memorized the entire book of John!), and listening to the radio stations (one I continue to listen to; Family Radio).

Prayer: Thank God for being the Word, sharing the Word, and guiding us through daily reading of Thy Word!

March 13 Foundations

Let us continue our study of the sixth foundations of life: word. I would like to compare the creation of this devotional book with God, the creator of the Word, remaining with and being the Word.

In the beginning of each daily entry of this devotional book, I quote from God's Word. We live in a world where there are so many translations of God's Word!

In this third month of this devotional book, I continue to recognize that I am inspired with God's Word to share by communicating through writing. We live in a world where there are numerous forms of technology to share God's Word!

As each month of this devotional book unfolds, I will continue to share God, communicate with the readers pearls of wisdom that I have attained. We live in a world where readers have freedom of religion; being with God, being with the Word!

Prayer: Dear God, you inspired the writing of the Holy Bible; the Word because you began the Word, you are with the Word and always will be the Word!

March 14 Foundations

Today's scripture is the Apostle Paul's letter of II Timothy 3:16:

"All scripture is given by inspiration of God, and is profitable for doctrine, for reproof, for correction, for instruction in righteousness..."

I believe God is the masterbuilder of our beliefs. I introduce the seventh; and final foundation of life and expound my theory in the seventh (last) stanza of "Foundations of Life":

Belief

Mixture of theory and regulations often learned and created many opinions or convictions experiences modeled!

Mixture of our environment social, emotional, physical, spiritual theory much time has been spent creating a life with less worry!

Value by value, belief by belief, we continue building foundations of life!

What religion does your family practice?

I hope each reader recognizes the freedom of religion and worship!

What values do you try to reinforce daily?

I hope each reader recognizes and lives by the "Golden Rule" (Luke 6:31).

What family philosophy do you still carry with you?

I remember ours being: "Does the choice you make bring happiness?

Prayer: Thank you God for the freedom of religion, values and philosphy passed down from your family. May we continue sharing this freedom!

March 15 Foundations

Let us continue our study of the seventh (last) foundation of life: belief. I would like to summarize the seven theories of "Foundations of Life"; my belief! Each foundations of life is mentioned and supported in a very well-known passage in the Holy Bible: Psalms 23: 1-6. The reading of this passage also reminds us that all scripture is given by inspiration of God and is profitable. (II Timothy 3:15). Let us review:

We read in verse 1 of Psalms 23: "The Lord is my shepherd...". We are his flock, his family, given a place to live, a home.

We are promised a heavenly home!

We continue to read verse 1 of Psalms 23: "...I shall not want." We are His recipients, His family, our needs supplied. We are promised a perfect body!

We read in verse 2 of Psalms 23: "He maketh me to lie down in green pastures: He leadeth me beside the still waters." We are His consumers, His family, our supplies provided.

We are promised healthy steps!

We read in verse 3 of Psalms 23: "He restoreth my soul: He leadeth me in the paths of righteousness for His name's sake." We are His followers, His family, our moments planned. We are promised precious time!

We read in verse 4 of Psalms 23: "Yea, though I walk through the shadow of death, I will fear no evil: for Thou art with me; Thy rod and Thy staff comfort me." We are His sheep, His family, our memories refreshed. We are promised precious memories!

We read in verse 5 of Psalms 23: "Thou preparest a table before me in the presence of mine enemies: Thou annointest my head with oil; my cup runneth over. We are His guests, His family, our communication is with Him daily. We are promised inspiration from God, the Word!

We read in verse 6 of Psalms 23: "Surely goodness and mercy shall follow me all the days of my life: and I will dwell in the house of the Lord for ever." We are His, His goodness and mercy believed, valued, daily. We are promised guidance from God, in Whom we believe!

Prayer: God of our lives; our foundations of life, we give you thanks for inspiring us to receive, give, and share life with You!

March 16 Foundations

Today's Scripture- Acts of the Apostles 1:7,8

"And He (Jesus) said unto them (apostles) , It is not for you to know the times or the seasons, which the Father has put in His own power. But, ye shall receive power, after that the Holy Ghost is come upon you: and ye shall be witnesses unto me both in Jerusalem, and in all Judea, and in Samaria, and unto the uttermost ends of the earth."

God inspired Luke, the writer of this book to record the acts of the apostles, the disciples, the followers of Jesus Christ. But before he recorded these acts, Luke mentions the power of God, the salvation of Jesus Christ, and the baptism by the Holy Ghost. The Trinity lays the foundations for allowing future missions possible. The Trinity is a team of masterbuilders! What better team can we have in our homes!

We witness the power of God...Creator... Masterbuilder of the Garden of Eden God created the first healthy home! The home for Adam and Eve is described in Genesis 2:8. Unfortunately, unhealthy choices make foundations weaken. May we strive to make healthy choices with God's power!

We witness the salvation of Christ...Carpenter...Masterbuilder within Nazareth Jesus built healthy homes! He was called the carpenter's son in Matthew 13:54-58 Unfortunately unhealthy attitudes make foundations weaken. May we strive to have healthy attitudes by Christ's salvation!

We witness the power of The Holy Spirit...Comforter... Masterbuilder at Jerusalem The Holy Spirit restored homes! He would abide (live) with the Apostles in Acts 1:6-8 Unfortunately unhealthy practices make foundations weaken. May we strive to have healthy practices by The Holy Spirit's power!

Prayer: Dear Trinity Team, thank you for your power of creation, salvation, and restoration. May we daily seek you God, Christ, and The Holy Spirit as we strive to live healthy lives.

March 17 Foundations

Today's scripture: I Corinthians 3:16

"Know ye not that ye are the temple of God, and that the Spirit of God dwelleth in you?"

God inspired the Apostle Paul to write to the Church of Corinth some advice they needed to follow as Christians. He mentions God's work, Christ's grace, and The Holy Spirit's presence. Once again, the Trinity is a team of masterbuilders of our bodies!

We witness God's work...Father (Abba)...Masterbuilder of Adam and Eve God created the first healthy, couple...Genesis 3:21-24. Unfortunately, unhealthy choices were made. Let's strive to make healthy choices for our temples (bodies) by God's work!

We witness Christ's ordination of twelve individuals...Mark 3: 13-19 God created the opportunity for twelve strong (in different ways!) to follow Christ. Unfortunately, unhealthy mistakes were made. Let's strive to have healthy, perfect temples (bodies) by Christ's grace!

We witness the Holy Spirit's filling of the saints...Romans 1: 1-7 God created the vessel (our bodies) to receive the power to follow Christ. Unfortunately, unhealthy reactions to saints were made. Let's strive today to honor one saint especially...Spirit filled...St. Patrick!

Prayer: Dear God, as we remember St. Patrick's Day by wearing the green, May we also carry on the mission to help others join the Christian family; temples of God.

March 18 Foundations

Today's Scripture: Romans 4:12

"....walk in the steps of that faith of our father Abraham...."

God inspired the Apostle Paul to write to the church in Rome reminding them of our forefathers such as Abraham.

He mentions God's direction, Jesus' example and the Holy Spirit's guidance. The Trinity Team works together to be the masterbuilders of our steps!

God created the Garden of Eden as a place to walk...Genesis 2:8-9 & 3:1-3 God's direction for Adam and Eve was clear as they were allowed to walk in the Garden of Eden, but step away from eating from a certain fruit tree! Unfortunately, unhealthy choices were made. We are all sinners and must step up daily to God and His direction.!

Jesus walked His earthly home, preaching salvation...Matthew 5: 1-11 Jesus presented the Beatitudes as clear steps for His followers to hear on the mountain, and to assist them in taking steps toward His

Kingdom! Unfortunately, unhealthy mistakes were made. We are all sinners and must step with our Saviour, following His example!

The Holy Spirit guides His churches to walk with Him...Galations 5: 13-17 The Spirit led the churches in their walks but to fulfil the lust of the flesh! Unfortunately, unhealthy reactions were made. We are all sinners and must step daily in the Spirit, following His liberty!

Prayer: Dear God, as we step, walk, run, or ride around our earthly home May we seek your direction, your Son's example and your Spirit's guidance!

March 19 Foundations

Today's Scripture: Ecclesiastes 3: 1

"To every thing there is a season, and a time to every purpose under the heaven: "

King David's son Solomon; preacher of the words of Ecclesiastes; wrote about time (Ecclesiastes 3: 2-8). He mentions the Trinity (Father, Son, & Holy Ghost) and the purpose of this team to be masterbuilders of our time.

The Trinity works together in times of birth, death, planting, and harvesting. We thank the Trinity for each life brought into this pattern of life!

The Trinity works together when there is killing, healing, breaking down and building up. We thank the Trinity for each life guided during the patterns of life!

The Trinity works together during weeping, laughing, mourning and dancing. We thank the Trinity for allows for expression during patterns of life!

The Trinity works together when stones are cast away or gathered, and whether there is embracing or refraining from embracing. We thank the Trinity for showing us the way through patterns of life!

The Trinity works together in times of getting, losing, keeping, and casting away. We thank the Trinity for preparations for the patterns of life!

The Trinity works together during love, hate, war and peace. We thank the Trinity for walking with us in experiencing life!

Prayer: Our Father, Our Saviour, Our Spirit...thank you for being our trinity team that works together at all times; in all seasons.

March 20 Foundations

Today's Scripture: I Corinthians 15, 1 & 2

"Moreover, brethren, I declare unto you the gospel which I preached unto you and wherein ye stand; by which also ye are saved if ye keep in memory what I preached unto you, unless ye have believed in vain."

The Apostle Paul wrote to the Church of Corinth reminding them of the master building of their memories by the Trinity.

God built up Paul's courage to preach what he once believed in vain. We thank God for building up our courage to share the gospel!

Christ built up Paul's witness to preach what others believed in vain. We thank Christ for building up our courage to live the gospel!

The Holy Spirit built up Paul's memory of promises he now believed. We thank the Holy Spirit who builds up our memories of the gospel!

Prayer: We remember, God, for awesome creation of memories! We remember, Christ, for vivid life-saving memories! We remember, Holy Ghost, for deep breath- taking memories!

March 21 Foundations

Today's scripture: I John 5:7

"For there are three that bear record in heaven, the Father, the Word, and the Holy Ghost: and these three are one."

The Apostle John wrote to Christians, followers of the masterbuilders of exhortations to brotherly and christian love; the Trinity Team!

God, our Father bears record in heaven; all-knowing of christian love. (I John 5:11) "And this is the record that God hath given us eternal life..." God keeps His Word...we each read or hear His promises!

Christ, the Word bears record in heaven; teaching of christian love. (I John 5:12) "He that hath the Son hath life; ..." Christ is the Word... we each read or hear His testimony!

The Holy Ghost, the Spirit bears record in heaven; living in christians. (I John 5:10) "He that believeth on the Son of God hath the witness in himself..."

The Spirit bears the Word.. we each read or hear about Him daily !

Prayer: Dear Trinity Team, I invite you to go with me daily as I study from Thy Word, carry Thy Word closely, and live and breathe Thy Word eagerly!

March 22 Foundations

Today's Scripture: II Thessalonians 2: 13

"But we are bound to give thanks always to God for you, brethren beloved of the Lord, because God hath from the beginning chosen you to salvation through anctification of the Spirit and belief of the truth..."

The Apostle Paul wrote with Silvanus and Timotheus to the church of the Thessalonians a second epistle (letter); an exhoration to steadfastness as a christian church with the grace of God, Jesus and The Holy Ghost; the Trinity. The masterbuilders from generation to generation knowing that the day of Christ is at hand. (II Thessalonians 2: 2)

God's steadfastness is evident as He from the beginning chose each of us to salvation. Have you chosen to believe in God's preparing a place for you? "...hold the traditions which ye have been taught..." II Thessalonians 2:15

Christ's steadfastness is evident from the beginning of His birth was chosen to salvation. Have you chosen to believe in Christ's saving you from sin? "...He hath given us everlasting consolation and good hope through grace." II Thessalonians 2:16

The Holy Ghost's steadfastness is evident from His presence at the Garden of Eden. Have you chosen to believe in the Spirit's daily sanctification? "...Comfort your hearts, and stablish you in every good word and work." II Thessalonians 2:17

Prayer: We thank you God for your servants who have shared their belief of your Son Jesus Christ who believes in saving us and for their belief in a life of holiness through your Spirit!

March 23 Foundations

For the remainder of the month of March I would like to share with the reader advise from family, friends and "acquaintances" about how to build!

Today's Advise:

"Whatever you want to do in life, make sure you're happy!"

Today's Advisors: My parents: Virginia and Herbert Appelt

Today's Scripture: Psalm 128: 1 & 2

"Blessed is every one that feareth the Lord; that walketh in His ways. For thou shalt eat the labour of thine hands: happy shalt thou be and it shall be well with thee."

David, a shepherd boy, played the harp and sang, defeated the Giant; Goliath, ruled as King and shared his songs (prayers) to God (author of the book of Psalms). David feared the Lord, walked in His ways and happiness was evident.

My parents used concrete, stone, bricks to build foundations at their first home together in Prattsburg, New York. The address was even; "Stone Road" ! They eventually taught us children the techniques of building when we had the milk house added on to the barn. We were allowed hands on experience as we joined our parents in what made them happy; building a farm family together!

My parents used books, radio, talks to build foundations for their five children. We were brought up with plenty of nature books, WHAM radio quiz show, and the sharing of knowlege for all the Science Fair Projects! We were allowed hands on experience as we joined our parents in what made them happy; respecting the plants, trees, and animals that come with farm life!

My parents used discipline, fairness, advise to build foundations for the future of each of their five children. We were brought up with neighbors, their families, 4-H Club, baseball, games, car pools for Sunday School and Church, parties, and even sharing the raising of different farm animals. We were allowed to choose what made us happy; respecting the siblings, neighbors, religions, and how God became a masterbuilder for each of us individually.

Prayer: Thank you God for being the masterbuilder my parents happiness!

March 24 Foundations

Today's Advise:

"Know Thyself"

Today's Advisors: Principal Farley from Prattsburg Central School

Today's Scripture: II Timothy 2:15

"Study to show thyself approved unto God, a workman that needeth not to be ashamed, rightly dividing the word of truth."

The Apostle Paul's second letter to Timothy was full of instruction for a youth, a new young leader, teacher, and a soldier of Jesus Christ.

Principal Farley of Franklin Academy of Prattsburg, New York was the leader of the only school I attended from Kindergarten to a Senior in High School. He made himself visible to faculty and students and families. His daily walk in the hallways and into the classrooms showed him as a gentle, but firm leader. He had an office which the students did not want to frequent too often!

There was a tradition each year called "Career Day" for the Seniors of Franklin Academy. I remember vividly how one of my classmates became Principal for the day and how Principal Farley made himself visible; taking on the role of that classmate! His walk that day in the classrooms showed him as a fun, but alert student!

His teaching team had one teacher for each grade level and the class sizes when I attended (1957-1970) averaged around 30-35 students. When my class graduated and their was the signing of yearbooks and autograph books, Principal Farley wrote down his advise to many of us graduates: "Know Thyself". He made himself visible; showing himself as a gentle, firm, fun, alert advisor!

Prayer: Thank you God, for educators who helped us know ourselves.

March 25 Foundations

Today's Advise:

Hide the Holy Scriptures in your heart!

Today's Advisor:

Religious Instructors from Prattsburg, NY churches

Today's Scripture: Psalm 119:11

"Thy word have I hid in my heart that I May not sin against Thee."

The words of the Psalmist David are often quoted the most, memorized the most, and hidden in our hearts the most!

Several religious instructors from the Prattsburg churches taught us to quote, memorize and hide scriptures in our hearts. There were Bible lessons, Bible drills, and Bible Choruses in Sunday School, Church Service, and Released Religious Instruction(early dismissal from school).

I began hiding verses from the Bible in my heart when I accepted a unique challenge: Memorize the entire Gospel of John. I joined a group of youth in this endeavor which also drew me closer to learning about salvation. Our "reward" was receiving a picture illustrated Bible (which I still own!)

It was not until I was a college student and working my summer job that I was taught (by a child camper) about salvation from sin. It was at The Salvation Army's Long Point Camp on Seneca Lake near Penn Yan, N.Y. All those memorized verses became my answers to many soul searching questions!

Not only did I hide God's word in my heart but also poetry He inspired me to write while I was continuing as a college student. It was not until 2003 when I accepted another challenge: Share your poetry. I joined another poet pal in submitting my inspirations from God's word, God's world, and God's will to encourage others to follow the plan of salvation!

Prayer: Thank you God, for the Bible (your word) and as you taught us to pray: "Our Father...." (recite the Lord's Prayer!)

March 26 Foundations

Today's devotional is written by my special sister who is celebrating her birthday! Happy Birthday, Barbara Torbitt! Thank you for sharing your advise:

Scripture Text: Matthew 14: 31

"And immediately Jesus stretched forth his hand, and caught him, and said unto him, 'O ye of little faith, wherefore didst thou doubt?' "

Jesus had just performed the miracle known as the Feeding of the Five Thousand. The disciples had been with Him during the healing of the sick, the blind, the lame, and the dumb. No wonder Jesus directed His disciples to get in a boat; to get some well deserved rest! Meanwhile Jesus would send the multitudes home and He would go up to the mountains to rest and spend time in prayer with His Heavenly Father.

Jesus was just about to perform another miracle, and this one we recognize as the Calming of the Waters. The peaceful waters surrounding the disciples on their boat were changing; visible to Jesus up on that mountain top. As any fisherman knows, the winds can rise; causing turmoil on the water. Panic sets in and even more fear when the troubled disciples watch helplessly this 'spirit' approaching them.

Jesus speaks up 'straightway' (14: 27): "Be of good cheer, it is I , be not afraid."

Jesus allows Peter to come to Him, allows him to panic, flounder and finally ask for help (14: 30)..." Lord, save me. "

Jesus immediately stretches forth His hand; catches him and sighs these words: "O thou of little faith, wherefore didst thou doubt "

Jesus was recognized and worshipped by the disciples on the boat that day. He has reminded His disiples of words He has preached; commanded to them so many times before: "All You Have To Do Is Ask! "

Jesus speaks to us 'straightway' amidst the turmoils of life. We need not be afraid! Jesus allows us to panic, flounder. We call out for help! Jesus immediately stretches forth His hand; catches us. He reminds us of our doubt!

Jesus identifies Himself to us. We finally (often as a last resource) ask for help!

Prayer: Dear Jesus, thank You for your words of comfort. All I have to do is ask!

March 27 Foundations

Scripture Text: Job 38:4

"Where wast thou (Job) when I (God) laid the foundations of the earth? declare, if thou hast understanding."

God laid His hand! He allows Job to go through affliction, be reproved by Eliphaz, shown God's, justice by Bildad, shown man's wickedness by Zophar, and hear Elihu's words of wrath against Job who justified himself rather than God. Only then does God answer Job out of the whirlwind!

God allows us to go through affliction, be reproved, shown His justice, shown man's wickness, and hear a "messenger" words of wrath against us who justify ourselves rather than God. God continues to lay His Hand on His earth!

God prepared the world! God allows Job to fear Him, eschew evil, bare seven sons and three daughters, be recognized as the greatest of all the men of the east. and allows Satan to afflict Job but save His life! Only then does God answer Job out of the whirlwind!

God allows us to fear Him, eschew evil, live with family, justice and wickedness. He allows Satan to tempt us to move away from God. God continues to prepare with His hand in His world!

God laid foundations! God allows Job to show patience, acknowledge His confidence in God, and repent his ways. Only then does God answer Job out of the whirlwind!

God allows us to show patience, be confident in God and repent. God continues to lay foundations as He has prepared heaven!

Prayer: Thank you God for laying the foundations for your earth, world and heaven!

March 28 Foundations

Scripture Text: Luke 14: 28,29,30

"For which of you, intending to build a tower, sitteth not down first and counteth the cost, whether he have sufficient to finish it? Lest haply, after he hath laid the foundation, and is not able to finish it, all that behold it begin to mock him, saying, 'This man began to build and was not able to finish'."

Man laid his hand! Man has shown good intentions, planned, counted the cost of laying a foundation, only to find out they are unable to finish. God sent a man; His son, Jesus with good intentions, planning and counting the cost of laying down His life, and able to say "It is finished"!

Man has been mocked! Man has lost respect, confidence in himself, and only wants to hide. Jesus, the Son of Man lost respect, confided in God; only wanting to Save!

Man has been Saved! Man has often mocked, refused, and had

lame excuses. Jesus the man of God, was mocked, refused by many, only wanting to excuse the sinful world!

Prayer: Thank you God for allowing your Son to become a human and show us He has to lay the foundation of salvation!

March 29 Foundations

Scripture Text: Nehemiah 2:5

"And I (Nehemiah) said unto the king (Ar-ta-xerx-es), ' If it please the king, and if thy servant have found favour in thy sight, that thou wouldest send me unto Judah, unto the city of my fathers' sepulchres, that I May build it.' "

Nehemiah was pleasing the king. Nehemiah was the king's cup-bearer (Nehemiah 1:11). He was to go up to the king and present him with wine. This time, when he goes before the king, he is noticed because of his sad countenance (2:2,3). The king questions Nehemiah; whether he is sick!

We are cup-bearers for our King; Jesus Christ. We are to go up to Him and present Him with our lives. There will be times when we go before our Lord, He will notice our sad countenances. Jesus questions us; whether we trust Him!

Nehemiah has oncerns for the kingdom. Nehemiah then shares his concern for the sad condition of Judah, and the crumbled down walls of Jerusalem. Only then does the king seek his request (Nehemiah 2:4).

We share our concerns for the sad condition of earth, and the crumbled down walls of our lives. Only then does our King; Christ Jesus, seek our requests.

Nehemiah had walls to build. Nehemiah presents his request to build the walls of Jerusalem (2:5). He already presented this request to God. God led His servant to a leader who would help build the destroyed walls and gates of the kingdom of Judah.

We present our request to build the walls of our lives. We must present this request to God. God leads his servants to His leaders (His Son and His Holy Ghost) who would help build the destroyed walls and gates of His Kingdom here on earth.

Prayer: Our Father, who art in heaven, hallowed be Thy name. Thy kingdom come...

March 30 Foundations

Scripture Text: Revelation 22:14

"And the wall of the city (Jerusalem) had twelve foundations, and in them the names of the twelve apostles of the Lamb."

Saint John asks: What have you seen? John shares in chapters 1-3 what he has witnessed: the works of the seven churches of Asia (Ephesus, Smyrna, Pergamos, Thyatira, Sardis, Philadelphia, and Laodicea).

We are witnesses: the works of churches in seven continents (Africa, Antarctica, Asia, Australia, Europe. North America, South America).

Saint John asks: How are things? John shares in chapters 4-18 what he has heard: the vision of God's throne containing a book with seven seals, seven trumpet sounding, seven angels pouring out seven vials of wrath upon the earth.

We have heard the sounding of seven trumpets: the call to war, the call to peace, the call to life, the call to death, the call to marriage, the call to service, and the call to team work.

Saint John asks: What is yet to come? John shares in chapters 19-22 what one of the seven angels showed him: Jerusalem had a wall with twelve foundations and in them the names of the twelve apostles(disciples) of the Lamb: Simon Peter, Andrew, James, John Philip, Bartholomew, Matthew, Thomas, James (son of Alphaeus), Simon (called Zelotes), Judas (brother of James), and Matthias. (See Luke 6:13-16 and Acts 1: 16-26).

We have read about the holy Jerusalem and are familiar with

the names of the twelve foundations "garnished with all manner of Precious Stones": jasper, sapphire, chalcedony, emerald, sardonyx, sardius, chrysolite, beryl, topaz, chrysoprasus, jacinth, and amesthyst. What is coming as we prepare to enter gates of twelve pearls and walk the streets of gold of heaven (Revelation 21: 19-21)?

Prayer: Behold, Lord you come quickly and blessed am I that keepeth the sayings of the prophecy of Revelation (See 22:7)!

March 31 Foundations

Scripture Text: II Corinthians 5: 1

"For we know that if our earthly house of this tabernacle were dissolved, we have a building of God, an house not made with hands, eternal in the heavens."

The Apostle Paul writes in his second letter to the Church of Corinth how earthly houses; not matter how sturdy the foundation will not last, but that made of God will!

My sister Sue and I know from experience, observation, and example of how important a strong foundation is to making a sturdy building! All we have to do is remember our own feeble attempts to build tree forts! We also received our parents guidance in pouring concrete for the foundaton of the milkhouse. We witnesse in person our parents' new, hand-made (stone by stone) home in Portal Arizona!

It is time to have Sue's illustration for March's theme:

Foundations.

Prayer: Thank You God for an eternal home built by You and Your Trinity Team.

April 1 Music

Scripture Text: Genesis 1:1-3

"In the beginning God created the heaven and the earth. And the earth was without form and void; and darkness was upon the face of the deep, And the Spirit of the Lord moved upon the face of the waters."

The Prophet Moses' first book; Genesis, records the well known Creation Story. I believe as God created the heaven and the earth, He used His power to include the creation of Music.

We read of God's Music in Genesis 1-3. Our Omnipotent God created Music to His ears; the calling of the wind, the rushing of the waves, the rolling thunder, the sounds of creatures, and the voices of man. He created man; in His own image to listen to His Music! Unfortunately, man failed to listen to His commands and would no longer be able to listen to the Music in the Garden of Eden!

We read of man's Music - Genesis 4. Our Omnipotent God created Music for Adam and Eve beyond Eden. Their son Cain's family lived in tents and raised cattle. His family included Musicians such as"Jabal; the father of all such as handle the harp and organ, and Tu-balcain, an instructor of every artificer in brass and iron." (4:21,22) God created Musicians and instruments!

We read of man's first singer - Exodus 15: 1,2. Our Omnipotent God created a safe way for the Israelites to cross the sea! Israel's leader and God's servant, Moses in his second book; Exodus sang:

"I will sing unto the Lord, for He hath triumphed gloriously: the horse and the rider hath He thrown into the sea. The Lord is my strength and song, and He is become my salvation: He is my God, and I will prepare Him an habitation: my father's God, and I will exalt Him."

These same words were echoed by children of the Israelites as they walked safely on dry ground, and with the help of Musicians:

"Miriam the prophetess took a timbrel in her hand; and all the women went after her with timbels and with dances. (Exodus 15: 20,21)

Prayer: Oh, Lord you are my strength, song, salvation, my God! I will exalt you!

April 2 Music

Scripture Text: I Chronicles 15:16

"And David spake to the chief of the Levites to appoint their brethren to be the singers with instruments of Musick, psalteries and harps and cymbals, sounding, by lifting up the voice with joy."

God's Musician: I Samuel 16:23 and I Chronicles 15:1-14

God inspired David as a shepherd boy to play a harp not only for the sheep under his care but also for the troubled Saul. He becomes a ruler of his own city; in the city of David, Levites are chosen to minister unto God forever!

Man's Musicians: I Chronicles 15: 17-24

God would be ministered unto by the assigned Musicians: Singers: He-man, A-saph, and E-than would sound with cymbals and brass. Zech-ari-ah, A-zi-el, She-mi-ra-hmoth, Je-hi-el, Un-ni, E-li-ah, Ma-a-sei-ah, and Be-nai-ah were assigned psalteries (strings are drawn over a box resonator and struck with a rod).Mat-ti-thi-ah, E-liph-e-leh, Mik-nei-ah, O-bed-e-dom, Je-i-el, and Az-a-zi-ah were assigned harps. Chen-a-ni-ah (Chief of the Levites), instructed about the song for the ark. Ber-e-chi-ah, El-ka-nah, O-bed-e-dom,and Je-hi-ah were doorkeepers. Sheb-a-ni-ah, Je-hosh-a-phat, Neth-a-neel, A-ma-sau, Zech-a-ri-ah, Be-nai-ah, and El-i-e-zer, the priests did blow with the trumpets.

Man's first orchestra: I Chronicles 15: 26-28

The Levites' orchestra offered to God seven bullocks and seven rams. David presented himself in white linen and an ephod (priestly garment), as did Chen-a-ni-ah (Chief of Levites and song instructor).

There was shouting and sounds of the cornet, trumpets, cymbals, and noise with the psalteries and harps.

Man's Audience: I Chronicles 15:29

Michal, (the daughter of troubled Saul), is seen watching from a window!

Prayer: Oh, Lord, you are the conductor of my daily orchestrated life!

April 3 Music

Scripture Text: Daniel 3: 4,5

"Then an herald cried aloud, To you it is commanded, O people, nations, and languages, That at what time ye hear the sound of the cornet, flute, harp, sackbut, psaltery, dulcimer, and all kinds of Musick, ye fall down and worship the golden image that Neb-u-chad-nez-zar the king hath set up..."

God's Audience: Daniel 1:8

During the reign of King Nebuchadnezzar, Daniel "purposed in his heart" that as God's Music was performed before the king, he would not defile himself with the portion of the king's meat and wine for ten days.

Man's Audience: Daniel 2: 28 & 44

During the reign of King Nebuchadnezzar, Daniel interpreted a dream that only his God could reveal and make known! God's kingdom with its Music shall never be destroyed.

Man's Worship: Daniel 3:14 & 29

During the reign of King Nebuchadnezzar, Bel-te-shaz-ar (Daniel), Shadrach, Mechach, and Abednego continued to worship God rather than the king when they heard the sound of all kinds of Music. Their lives were spared in the fiery furnace. The king's decree included that there is no other God that can deliver after this sort!

Prayer: O, Lord, you deliver us from the fiery furnaces of life and allow us to hear the sounds of all kinds of your created Music!

April 4 Music

Scripture Text: Psalm 33: 1-3

"Rejoice in the Lord, O ye righteous: for praise is comely for the upright. Praise the Lord with harp; sing unto Him with the psaltery and an instrument of ten strings. Sing unto HIm a new song; play skilfully with a loud noise."

God's Performance: Psalm 32: 7

God, with His omnipotent power "preserves from trouble" and "shalt compass me about with songs of deliverance". We rejoice, praise, and sing to God; "my hiding place". God performs for us just as He created us...individually! Do we allow God to deliver us daily?

Man's Performance: Psalm 33:1,2

God, with His omnipotent power, is worth to be praised by the upright, righteous, and skilfully. We perform in front of our God with what He helped us create! God performs through us just as He created us...individually! Do we allow God to perform through us daily?

Man's Instrument: Psalm 33:2

God, with His omnipotent power created instruments played by man. We perform with harp, psaltery (an instrument of ten strings), and with another instrument of ten. God prepared our hands (an instrument of ten fingers). Do we praise God; clap for Him daily?

Prayer: O, Lord, you created our bodies to include hands to lift you up, to pray to you, to clap for you, and praise you for your ominipotent power!

April 5 Music

Scripture Text: Luke 2: 7

"And she (Mary) brought forth her firstborn son, and wrapped him in swaddling clothes, and laid him in a manger; because there was no room for them in the inn."

God's Lullaby: Luke 1:35

God with His omnipotent power sends an angel to prepare Mary to give birth to Jesus. "The power of the Highest shall overshadow thee"...God's lullaby is holy and comforting to the concerned Mary and her unborn baby. Do you hear God's soothing, comforting lullaby to His children?

Man's Lullaby: Luke 1:44

God with His omnipotent power sends Mary to barren Elisabeth; who proclaims to Mary that "as soon as the voice of thy salutation sounded in my ears, the babe leaped in my womb for joy" ! God's lullaby is a promise of joy for us to pass to our families. Do you hear God's voice blend with man's lullaby to babies?

Man's Cradle: Luke 2:7

God with His omnipotent power sends Mary to a manger in Bethlehem; the first cradle surrounded by shepherds and the animals that resided there. God's lullaby was heard in a "lowly manger"; a crude cradle by a new born king; Jesus! Do you hear God's voice blend with man's lullaby to baby Jesus?

Prayer: Thank you Lord, for your love and lullaby of comfort!

April 6 Music

Scripture Text: Luke 2: 40

"And the child (Jesus) grew, and waxed strong in spirit, filled with wisdom: and the grace of the God was upon Him."

God's Wisdom: Luke 2:38

God with His omnipotent power sent the Prophetess; Anna, to the child Jesus. She chanted thanks before speaking to all of them that "looked for redemption in Jerusalem". God's wisdom is with rhyme and reason for those who are nursed in HIs love. Do you allow God to chant and nurse you to be strong in the spirit?

Man's Wisdom: Luke 2: 39

God with His omnipotent power allowed for the chanting of Mother Goose's Nursery Rhymes by His children! Two of these rhymes contain the name of Jesus' mother; Mary:

"Mary had a little lamb...it followed her to school one day"! Mother Mary had a child (her little lamb!)...He followed her to the temple one day! He (the lamb) made the children "laugh" and "play" !

"Mary, Mary...how does your garden grow...?" Mother Mary's son (Jesus) was led to the Garden of Gethsemane to pray! Jesus (the lamb) made it so all of God's children could come to Him! Do you as God's child daily chant prayers and praise to His lamb, Jesus?

Man's Rhymes: Luke 2:40

God with His omnipotent power allowed His child Jesus to "grow, wax strong in spirit, be filled with wisdom and His grace". Jesus spent time in God's temple. Jesus prepared the way with rhyme and reason! Do we spend time in God's temple being filled with Jesus' wisdom and reason?

Prayer: Thank you Lord, for filling us with wisdom; with rhyme for daily living!

April 7 Music

Scripture Text: Exodus 23: 20,21

"Behold, I send an Angel before thee (Moses), to keep thee in the way, and to bring thee into the place which I have prepared. Beware of him (the Angel), and obey his voice..."

God's Angel: Exodus 23: 14, 17

God's children from their youth were to keep a feast for Him three times a year; Feast of Unleavened Bread, Feast of Harvest, and the

Feast of Ingathering. The Voice of God's Angel would be obeyed as His children would go to the place prepared for the feasts. The voice of an angel chants us to come to feast with our God!

Man's Angel: Luke 2:41,42

God's Son, at age twelve, joined His parents in Jerusalem for the yearly Feast of the Passover. The yearly custom would include the voice of God's Angel to be obeyed by His Children following God's ways! The voice of an angel chants to all of God's children to follow His ways!

Man's Voice of an Angel: Luke 2:49

God's Son, remained at the Feast of the Passover, and was eventually found by His worried parents! Naturally their voices spoke of concern and sorrow towards Jesus. He responded with the voice of an angel: "How is it that ye sought me? Wist ye not that I must be about my Father's business? "

Prayer: Thank you, Lord for the angels here on earth that lift their voices of comfort, praise, and songs for your omnipotent power!

April 8 Music

Scripture Text: Luke 4:18,19

"The Spirit of the Lord is upon me, because He hath appointed me to preach the gospel to the poor; He hath sent me to heal the broken-hearted, to preach deliverance to the captives, and recovering of sight to the blind, to set at liberty them that are bruised, to preach the acceptable year of the Lord."

God's Parables: Luke 4:17

Jesus taught in the synagogues, such as in Nazareth. He stood up and read from the book of the prophet "E-sai-as" the words found in today's scripture text. God allows us to sing the words of the Prophet Isaiah 40: 31: "They that wait upon the Lord shall renew their strength; they shall mount up with wings as eagles; they shall run, and not be weary; and they shall walk, and not faint."

Jesus' Parables: Luke 4: 21

Jesus' introduction after reading from the scriptures was: "This day is the scripture fulfilled in your ears". He spoke in parables that are recorded in the four Gospels of Matthew, Mark, Luke, and John. God allows us to sing a chorus from a parable found in Luke 6: 48.49: "The foolish man built his house upon the sand...The wise man built his house upon the rock..." Do we build our houses on the Lord Jesus Christ?

Man's Parables: Mark 1:16,17

Mark writes about a scene at the sea of Galilee where Jesus calls two brothers as they cast their fishing nets. God allows us to sing a chorus from Mark's parable of fishers of men: "I will make you fishers of men, fishers of men, fishers of men. I will make you fishers of men if you follow me...!" Are we fishers of men for our Lord Jesus Christ?

Prayer: Thank you Lord, for the builders, the fishers of men, as they live following your daily plan for us!

April 9 Music

Scripture Text: Leviticus 25: 10

"And ye shall hallow the fiftieth year, and proclaim liberty throughout all the land unto all the inhabitants thereof; it shall be a jubile unto you; and ye shall return every man unto his possession, and every man unto his family."

God's Celebrations: Leviticus 23: 1,2

The Prophet Moses writes down in his third book laws given by God: "There will be the presentation to God of offerings, possessions and family" Every fifty years this presentation could be called a jubile! God allows us to celebrate fifty years of service; gathering up His harvest!

Jesus' Celebrations: Luke 12: 36

The Lord Jesus Christ teaches His disciples the laws given by God.

There will be the presentation to God of offerings, possessions and family. Every fifty years this presentation could be called a "golden" anniversary! God allows us to celebrate fifty years of marriage; gathering up His people!

Man's Celebrations: Acts 1: 12-14

The Holy Spirit gathers the disiples of Jesus, Mary, the mother of Jesus, and His brethren into an upper room. There will be the presentation to God of offerings, possessions and family. Every fifty years this presentation could be called a reunion! God allows us to celebrate fifty years of family; gathering up His plans!

Prayer: Thank you Lord, for years of planning for family and service!

April 10 Music

Scripture Text: Romans 6: 13

"Neither yield ye your members as instruments of unrighteousness unto sin: but yield yourselves unto God, as those that are alive from the dead, and your members as instruments of righteousness unto God."

The Apostle Paul reminds the Church of Rome that they are instruments of righteousness unto God through the death and resurrection of Christ. When we sing Charles Wesley's hymn: "Christ The Lord Is Risen Today", May we sing praises to God for sending His Risen Son of Righteousness!

Man's Righteousness: Romans 6:23

The Apostle Paul preaches to the Romans that they are dead in sin; but alive in God through the death and resurrection of the Lord Jesus Christ. When we sing James Rowe's hymn: "Love Lifted Me", May we testify of God's Saving Son of Righteousness!

God's Performers: Romans: 8: 28,29

The Apostle Paul preaches to the Romans that they cannot become "separated from the love of God which is in Christ Jesus our Lord".

When we sing Anna B. Warner's hymn: "Jesus Loves Me", May we tell others of God's Loving Son of Righteousness!

Prayer: Thank you, oh Lord, that we are your instruments of righteousness; because of your righteousness, salvation and love!

April 11 Music

Scripture Text: I Corinthians 13:1

"Though I speak with the tongues of men and of angels, and have not charity, I am become as sounding brass, or tinkling cymbal."

The Apostle Paul reminds the Church of Corinth that they are instruments of love for God, His Son, and His people. When we sing Reginald Heber's hymn: "Holy, Holy, Holy ", May we sing praises to our God for sending His loving Son of Charity.

Man's Charity: I Corinthians 1:9

The Apostle Paul reminds the Church of Corinth that they are in fellowship with Trinity of love. When we sing John Newton's hymn: "Amazing Grace "May we sing praises to our Faithful God who called us into the fellowship of His Son Jesus Christ Our Lord!

God's Performers: II Corinthians 9:7

The Apostle Paul reminds the Church of Corinth that they have a purpose in giving hearts; not grudgingly. When we play Ludwig Beethoven's composition: "Ode to Joy", May we lift our praises to our Loving God who loves a cheerful giver!

Prayer: Thank you, Oh Lord, that we are your pleasant sounding brass or cymbal as we lift praises for Your love, fellowship and purpose in us!

April 12 Music

Scripture Text: Galations 6: 6

"Let him that is taught in the word communicate unto him that teacheth in all good things."

The Apostle Paul reminds the churches of Galatia to communicate what God taught them through His Son and His Spirit. When we sing Edward Perronet's hymn: "All Hail The Power", May we join in song; in communicating the power of Jesus' name!

Man's Power: Galations 1: 10

The Apostle Paul reminds the churches of Galatia how servants of Christ, persuade and seek to please God. When we sing prayerfully Issac Watts' hymn: "Jesus Shall Reign", May praise God for the power of Jesus' kingdom!

God's Performers: Galations 5:22

The Apostle Paul reminds the churches of Galatia how his "brethren" should walk in the Spirit of the Lord. When we sing prayerfully Charlotte Elliot's hymn: "Just As I Am", May we communicate love, joy, peace, longsuffering, gentleness, goodness, faith, meekness, and temperance (the fruit of the Spirit)!

Prayer: Thank you, Oh Lord, that we are your communicators ready to seek, to please, and to walk in the Spirit of the Lord!

April 13 Music

Scripture Text: Ephesians 5:19

"Speaking to yourselves in psalms and hymns and spiritual songs, singing, and making melody in your heart to the Lord ..."

The Apostle Paul encouraged the saints of Ephesus to praise God according to His will. When we sing Walter Dix's hymn: "As With Gladness Men of Old", May we communicate joyful praises to the Lord our earthly king!

Man Speaks: Ephesians 2:8

The Apostle Paul encouraged the saints of Ephesus to speak of their salvation by grace, through faith; not of ourselves, as it is the "gift of God"! When we sing Charles Wesley's hymn: "O For A Thousand Tongues to Sing" May we communicate joyful praises to the Lord, our gift from God!

God's Performers: Ephesians 6:13

The Apostle Paul directed the saints of Ephesus to stand up for their salvation; protected by God's armor. When we sing George Duffield's hymn: "Stand Up For Jesus", May we communicate sincere praises to our Captain; our Christ!

Prayer: Thank you, O Lord, that we can make melodies in our heart!

April 14 Music

Scripture Text: Philippians 4:4

"Rejoice in the Lord alway: and again I say, Rejoice!

The Apostle Paul and Timotheus, servants of Jesus Christ encourage the saints of Philippi to rejoice in the Lord! When we sing Fanny Crosby's hymn: "He Hideth My Soul", May we express our joy towards Jesus; Great Redeemer!

Man's Joy: Philippians 3:14

The Apostle Paul and Timotheus encourage the saints of Philippi to find their joy; "the prize of the high calling of God in Christ Jesus." When we sing Isaac Watts hymn: "When I Survey the Wondrous Cross", May we find joy in Jesus; Divine Redeemer!

God's Performers: Philippians 4:11

The Apostle Paul and Timotheus encourage the saints of Philippi to be content in "whatever state"; as they have learned. When we sing Reverand J.H. Sammis' hymn: "Trust and Obey", May we find happiness in Jesus; Glorious Redeemer!

Prayer: Thank you, Oh Lord, that we can rejoice in the "survey" of Christ sacrificing His life for us!

April 15 Music

Scripture Text: Colossians 3:23

"And whatsoever ye do, do it heartily, as to the Lord, and not unto men."

The Apostle Paul and Timotheus wrote to the saints and faithful brethren "giving thanks" and "praying always". When we sing The Salvation Army Songster W. J. Brand's chorus: "The World Is Needing Us", we pray to the Trinity with faith!

Man's Music: Colossians 2:6,7

The Apostle Paul and Timotheus wrote to the saints and faithful brethren encouraging them to "receive, walk, be rooted and built up! When we sing J. Rowe's chorus: "I Walk With the King", we pray to the Trinity with praise!

God's Performers: Colossians 4:6

The Apostle Paul and Timotheus wrote to the saints and faithul brethren encouraging them to "speak with grace and seasoned with salt"! When we sing The Founder of The Salvation Army; William Booth's hymn: "O, Boundless Salvation", we pray to the Trinity with love!

Prayer: Thank you, Oh Lord, for your boundless salvation through your Son Saviour and King of the World!

April 16 Music

Scripture Text: I Thessalonians 3: 2

"... and sent Timotheus, our brother and minister of God, and our fellowlabourer in the gospel of Christ, to establish you, and to comfort you concerning your faith."

The Apostle Paul sent Timotheus to comfort the souls of the fellow labourers (church of Thessalonians) of their faith in the gospel of Christ. When we sing Bishop Phillips Brook's Christmas Hymn: "O Little Town of Bethlehem", we meet to celebrate Jesus' birth!

Man's Comfort: I Thessalonians 4: 23

The Apostle Paul sent Timotheus to comfort the souls of the fellow labourers (church of Thessalonians) of sanctification; "preserved blameless" unto the coming of our Lord Jesus Christ! When we sing The Salvation Army General; E. C. Booth's Hymn: "The World For

God", we meet to celebrate Jesus' salvation!

God's Performers: II Thessalonians 3:1

The Apostle Paul sent Timotheus to comfort the souls of the fellow labourers (church of Thessalonians) for a "free course" of the Lord's gospel. When we sing S. Henry's chorus of faith: "He Knows", we meet to celebrate Jesus' life!

Prayer: Thank you, Oh Lord for comforting our souls, freely, through your faith and sanctification of your "labourers".

April 17 Music

Scripture Text: II Timothy 1: 13

"Hold fast the form of sound words, which thou hast heard of me, in faith, and love which is in Christ Jesus."

The Apostle Paul writes to Timothy (whom He calls "son") and gives advise in faith and love which Christ Jesus teaches us. When we sing J. Oatman Jr.'s hymn: "Count Your Blessings", we hold fast each word of sound blessing from our Lord of sound surprises!

Man's Sound Words: I Timothy 2: 1

The Apostle Paul writes to Timothy and "exhorts" that for all men there will be: supplications, prayers, intercessions, and giving of thanks! When we sing C.A. Miles' hymn: "Beulah Land", we hold fast each word of sound blessing from our Lord of sound bounties!

God's Performers: II Timothy 2:15

The Apostle Paul writes to Timothy and advises that he study as a workman"...."rightly dividing the word of truth". When we sing The Salvation Army Colonel E.H. Joy's chorus: "I Believe In The Word of God", we hold fast each sound word of blessing from our Lord of sound promises!

Prayer: Thank you, Oh Lord, for guiding us in the study of the sound, true promises in Your Holy Bible!

April 18 Music

Scripture Text: Titus 3: 8

"This is a faithful saying, and these things I will that thou affirm constantly, that they which have believed in God might be careful to maintain good works. These things are good and profitable unto men."

The Apostle Paul writes to Titus (whom he calls "son") and gives advise after appointing Titus as Bishop of Crete. His advise includes a reminder that bishops are stewards. When we sing A.A. Pollard's chorus: "Have Thine Own Way, Lord", we are ready to be His stewards and sing faithful words to our God of faithful sayings !

Man's Faithful Saying:

Titus 1: 7,8

The Apostle Paul writes to Titus and exhorts him to be blameless and not selfwilled, but a lover of hospitality. When we sing The Salvation Army Major G.P. Ewens' chorus: "Living Beneath the Shade", we are ready to enjoy full salvation and sing faithful words to our God of faithful sayings !

God's Performers:

Titus 2: 13

The Apostle Paul writes to Titus and advises that he look for hope and appearance of the "great God and our Saviour Jesus Christ". When we sing E. W. Blandly's chorus: "Where He Leads Me", we are ready to "follow", to "go with" our God of faithful sayings..." all the way" !

Prayer: Thank You, Oh Lord for leading us to look for You and follow!

April 19 Music

Scripture Text: Philemon 10, 11

"I beseech thee (Philemon) for my son Onesimus, whom I have

begotten in my bonds; which in time past was to thee unprofitable, but now profitable to thee and to me..."

The Apostle Paul writes to Philemon (fellow-labourer) and advises him to allow other servants of God another chance to be "profitable". When we sing Mrs. Heathcote's chorus: "I'll Follow Thee", we follow our Lord; "deny never" because of our Lords' profitable grace!

Man's Profitable Words:

Philemon 17

The Apostle Paul writes to Philemon and advises him to receive Onesimus as a "partner".

When we sing The Salvation Army Colonel Pearson's chorus: "Lead Me Higher", we have "fellowship" with our Lord because only our Lord can "cleanse" with His profitable grace!

God's Performers: Philemon 1, 2

The Apostle Paul writes to Philemon and greets "fellow prisoners" of the Lord. When we sing S.E. Cox's chorus "Swing Wide The Door", we are prisoners of the Lord because we only obey our Lord who is the "King of Kings" and "shelters" us with His profitable grace!

Prayer: Thank You, Oh Lord for sheltering us; Your prisoners!

April 20 Music

Scripture Text: Hebrews 12: 1

"Wherefore seeing we also are compassed about with a great cloud of witnesses, let us lay aside every weight, and the sin which doth so easily beset us, and let us run with patience the race that is set before us..."

The Apostle Paul writes to a group of witnesses; the Hebrews. He advises them to lay aside all that hinders us from running the race set by our Lord Jesus Christ.

When you sing praises to God; have you ever tried to race through the alphabet while praising Him? Try these spiritual and secular songs:

Amazing Grace and America, Because He Lives and Born Free, Count Your Blessings and Climb Every Mountain, Do Lord and Down In The Valley, Everywhere He Went and Everything Is Beautiful, Faith Of Our Fathers and Friendship... Friendship. Go Tell It On The Mountain and God Bless America, Heaven Came Down and Have Yourself a Merry Little Christmas Into My Heart and It's A Small World After All Jesus Loves Me and Joy To The World

Keep On Believing and Knock Three Times Let The Lower Lights Be Burning and Let There Be Peace More About Jesus and Morning Is Broken No Never Alone and Now The End Is Near Over The Sea and Oh My Darling, Clementine

Prayer Gently Lifts Me and Please Release Me Quit The Field Never and Que Sera Read Your Bible and Reach Out And Touch Sing On In Sunny Days and Skip To My Lou Teach Me How To Love Thee and Too-la Roo-la Roo-la Until Then and Up, Up And Away

Victory In Jesus and Volare What A Friend We Have In Jesus and When You Wish Upon A Star 'X'cept I Am Moved With Compassion and 'X'ccentuate The Positive Yesterday, Today, Forever and Yesterday's Gone Zaccheus Was A Wee Little Man and Zippity Doo Daa!

Prayer: Thank You, Oh Lord for the songs we can sing on Your Highways!

April 21 Music

Scripture Text: Ephesians 5:19

"Speaking to yourselves in psalms and hymns and spiritual songs, singing and making melody in your heart to the Lord..."

The Apostle Paul wrote to the Church of Ephesus and encouraged them to share their God given wisdom by singing and making melody. I am inspired by God, and how in His infinite wisdom he allowed Hischildren to present to His world melodies for the heart!

When we sing: Oh, Danny Boy; we sing a familiar tune: Londonderry

Air. The Salvation Army Lieutenant Colonel A.R. Wiggins wrote new lyrics to this familiar tune: "If On My Soul." Both sets of lyrics with this inspiring melody allow God's family to call His children to "come back" and promise to God: "to live to do Thy holy will!

When we sing: "Row, Row, Row Your Boat", we sing a familiar tune: childhood ditty! Perhaps you are familiar with the lyrics to this same tune in the chorus: "Jesus Never Fails "(annonymous). Both choruses with this inspiring melody allow God's family to command His children to "row gently" and praise His Son: "I'm glad, so glad, Jesus never fails" !

When we sing: "Silent Night" as one of our Christmas Carols we are reminded how this is sung in so many languages and in so many countries! Perhaps you have heard the lyrics to this same tune in the chorus: "Wonderful Love" (annonymous). Both choruses with this inspiring melody allow God's family to celebrate as His children the holy birth of His Son Jesus and His wonderful love: "filling us thrilling us" !

Prayer: Thank You, Oh Lord for the melodies we can make sing from our hearts to You!

April 22 Music

Scripture Text: Revelation 1: 1

"The Revelation of Jesus Christ, which God gave unto Him , to show unto His servants things which shortly must come to pass; and He sent and signified it by His angel unto His servant John..."

St. John The Divine wrote the final book of The Holy Bible; The Revelation of Jesus Christ. John encourages his readers by showing (advertising) the coming of the Lord. John's advertisement can be compared to a few commercials of today:

The first advertisement shows a young girl squeezing bright yellow mustard on her sandwich and singing "You Are My Sunshine" ! The bright sunlight of the Revelation of Jesus Christ is sung about by singing: "There Is Sunshine In My Soul Today"! Let us become His

Sunbeams (name for young girls' troop within The Salvation Army Church) !

In the second advertisement we hear the words to a familiar ditty: "Head and Shoulders" and notice this is also the name of a bottle of lotion for dry skin! The soothing word of The Revelation of Jesus Christ is sung aboutby singing: "There Is A Balm In Gilead" ! Let us become His League of Mercy (name for church members of The Salvation Army who visit in homes and institutions) !

In the third advertisement we witness children and adults putting on bandaids and singing a cheerful ditty: "I am stuck on bandaids...". The salvation of The revelation of Jesus Christ is sung about by singing: "Oh, Boundless Salvation" ! Let us become His Junior or Senior Soldier (name for church members and servants of The Salvation Army Church) !

Prayer: Thank You, Oh Lord, for the commercials, the ads that show Your Revelation...Your Coming and our being ready for You!

April 23 Music

Scripture Text: Psalm 96: 1, 1

"O sing unto the Lord a new song; sing unto the Lord, all the earth."

The Psalmist David wrote and advised us to sing new song. David created new songs daily and they could easily be included in a Musical for Our Lord ! David's Musicals can be compared to those of today:

In the first Musical: "The Sound of Music "we hear about the hills being alive with Music and join in naming our favorite things! We can daily praise our Lord with sounds of Music by singing: "Sing, Sing, Sing "!

In the second Musical: "The Lion King" we hear about the jungle animals led by the mighty lion who is found sleeping and resting ! We can daily praise our Lord with mighty "roars" by singing: "Majesty" !

In the third Musical: "Oklahoma" we hear that this is the place! We can daily praise our Lord with all kinds of singing in all kinds of places by singing: "Jesus Shall Reign" !

Prayer: Thank You, Oh Lord for sharing with us your heavenly Musical sung by Your Choir of Angels !

April 24 Music

Scripture Text: Psalm 111: 1

"Praise ye the Lord, I will praise the Lord with my whole heart, in the assembly of the upright, and in the congregation. "

The Psalmist David encourages again to praise the Lord for an audience...congregation. David performed with instruments that brought forth praises to His Lord. David's instrumental pieces can be compared with those of today:

Our first instrumental piece is "The Entertainer" with a strolling tune, followed by the picking up of a quicker pace, and with a rushing finale! May we join in the congregation that celebrates our "Powerful Performers...The Trinity. Let us stroll to the tune of our Trinity; pick up the pace, and rush to our Trinity by singing: "Holy, Holy, Holy "!

Our second instrumental piece is "Chariots of Fire" with an anticipating tune, followed by the picking up of a confident tone, and with a triumphant finale! May we join in the assembly that races toward the Trinity; anticipate with confidence the coming of our Trinity by singing: "Swing Low, Sweet Chariiot" !

Our third instrumental piece is "String of Pearls" with an up-beat tune, followed by repetitive string of notes, and with an attractive finale! May we join in appearing before our Trinity by singing: "Bright Jewels" !

Prayer: Thank You Oh Lord, for allowing us to come to you with tones of anticipation, attractiveness and pleasing to You!

April 25 Music

Scripture Text: Psalm 100: 1, 2

"Make a joyful noise unto the Lord, all ye lands. Serve the Lord with gladness: come before His presence with singing. "

Once again the Psalmist David encourages us to be joyful and we serve and come into our Lord's presence. David sang anthems to His Lord. David's anthems can be compared to those of today:

Our first anthem is "Holy, Holy, Holy "and early in the morning our praises rise to our God; King of Kings. We join the choir of angels in singing: "Handel's Messiah" as we serve and come before Him daily!

Our second anthem is "The Star-Spangled Banner" and by the dawn's early light we praise our God for blessing America! We join the crowds of fans in singing: "God Bless America" as we serve and come before Him!

Our third anthem is "The Armenian National Anthem" and by the proud words of praise to our God for allowing Armenia to fly its' yellow, red, and blue colored flag for its newly formed country! We join the crowds of citizens in singing: "You're A Grand Ole Flag" as we worship and serve His world!

Prayer: Thank You Oh Lord, that we can sing anthems of praise to You for the freedom You so freely gave to us!

April 26 Music

Scripture Text: Psalms 103: 1

"Bless the Lord, oh my soul and all that is within me, bless His holy name."

The Psalmist David sang blessings to his Holy Lord. Today we sing many blessings recorded in the Holy Bible:

We sing blessings to our God at banquets: Song of Solomon 2: 4 As we sit to partake at God's 'banqueting house', May we ask God to be present at our table as we partake of His Harvest. Let us not forget to sing blessings or say grace at each God given banquet !

We chant blessings to our God at ceremonies: Numbers 6: 24-26 As we rise from partaking as God's 'blessed children', May we ask God to be gracious in our families as we partake of His Peace. Let us not forget to sing blessings or say our vows at each God created ceremony !

We sing blessings to our God in prayer: Psalm 103: 1 As we start each new day we bless God with our souls and with all that is within our bodies as we partake of His Holy Name. Let us not forget to sing blessings or recite a prayer each God inspired day!

Prayer: Thank you oh Lord, that we can sing blessing of Your love, peace and holiness.

April 27 Music

Scripture Text: Psalm 98 : 1

"Oh, sing unto the Lord a new song; for He hath done marvellous things: His right hand, and His holy arm, hath gotten Him the victory."

The Psalmist David wrote and sang new songs. He wrote as a Shepherd, and as the King of Israel, David gave thanks to his Lord!

I have written poetry that came with a melody! Let me expound on three of these poems inspired my my Lord:

"In The Beginning"

In the beginning God created the heavens and the earth. In the beginning of this new year allow God's creation to give re-birth. Genesis 1:1

In the beginning was the 'word' and the 'word' was with God. In the beginning of each new day allow God's word to be understood. John 1:1

Says the Lord: "I am the (Alpha) beginning and the Omega) end. Begin each new moment by allowing God's love and power to blend! Revelation 22:13

"Believe"

Let not your heart be troubled my friends. Believe in God and all that He sends. He sends His loving care through family and friends. He sends His happiness through Jesus His Son! Believe that your heart need not be troubled my friends. Believe in God and all that He sends! John 14:1

What Does The Lord Require?

What does the Lord require of you? What does the Lord require of you? The answer is found in the Holy Bible; Chapter 6 of Micah, verse 8! What do you do but to do justly, what do you love but to love mercy. How do you walk, but to walk humbly with thy God! Micah 6: 8

Prayer: Thank You Lord, for inspiring me to write poetry and songs!

April 28 Music

Scripture Text: Philippians 4: 4

"Rejoice in the Lord alway: and again I say, Rejoice. "

Apostle Paul writes to the saints of Philippi. He encourages the Philipians to rejoice alway. I recognize today's scripture text being put to Music and I have heard the text sung in a round like "Row, Row, Row Your Boat". What a good way to memorize scripture! What a good way to spread the joy!J

"J" in the word joy stands for Jesus! Apostle Paul encourages his readers to sing praises; rejoice in the Lord. Jesus must be first! We sing about His birth, His ministry, His sacrifice, His death, His Resurrection, and His coming again! Rejoice in your Lord alway! Sing to Jesus a familiar Christmas Carol or an Easter Hymn such as "Joy To The World" Read Philipians 4:1.

"O" in the word joy stands for others!

Apostle Paul encourages his readers to sing praises; rejoice in the Lord and others. Others must be second! We sing at birthdays, special events, graduations, milestones, funerals, and memorials. Rejoice with others alway! Sing with others a familiar anthem, or hymn such as "Holy, Holy, Holy "! Read Philipians 4: 2,3.

"Y" in the word joy stands for yourself! Apostle Paul encourages his readers to sing praises; rejoice in the Lord and yourself. You must be last! You sing at your own birthday, special events, games, graduations, milestones, and allow others to rejoice in the Lord at your funeral and memorial. Rejoice daily and alway! Sing alone to your Lord the familiar Consecration Song: "Take My Life "! Read Philipians 4: 5

Prayer: Oh, Lord, I rejoice and give thanks to You! We rejoice alway!

April 29 Music

Scripture Text: Revelation 18: 22

"And the voice of harpers, and Musicians, and of pipers, and trumpeters, shall be heard no more at all in thee..."

St. John The Divine wrote the revelation of Jesus Christ, which God gave to him. He was inspired by God to tell others what was to come. He wrote specifically to seven churches of Asia. In the eighteenth chapter, John is sharing his vision of one of the seven angels warning him of the judgment; the destruction of the powerful kingdom of Babylon... Revelation 18: 10. The voice of harpers and Musicans of God's orchestra; of His Heavenly Kingdom, resound clearly and way above the voices of wickedness from any earthly kingdom!

John wrote that God will put a stop on merchandise of merchants,crafts of craftsmen, ships of shipmasters, millstones of builders, or lights from candles, or voices of the bride and the groom of weddings in the great city of Babylon .. Revelation 18: 22-23. The voice of pipers of God's orchestra; of His Heavenly Kingdom, rise majestically way above the voices of pride and jealousy from any earthly kingdom!

St. John The Divine writes of the destroyed Babylon; the weeping and mourning, the desolation, blood and violence. The sound of the millstone would be stopped; Music to the ears of any builder! ...Revelation 18: 21 & 24. The voice of trumpeters of God's orchestra; of His Heavenly Kingdom, echo strongly around the walls of destruction and evil from any earthly kingdom!

Prayer: Thank you, Lord for your heavenly orchestra; which resounds throughout your entire kingdom!

April 30 Music

Scripture Text: Psalm 89: 1

"I will sing of the mercies of the Lord for ever: with my mouth will I make known thy faithfulness to all generations."

The Psalmist David continues to be recognized for His 150 Psalms. He was used to singing daily of his God's mercies.

Music is known to soothe the soul, calm the body, and clear the mind. My sister Sue would agree with me that Music surrounded our farm family, and we each had our own way of expressing ourselves concerning the mercies of our God.

Sue's illustration for April will be worth a score of Music!

Prayer: Thank You Lord, for Your earthly illustrators to help us picture Your mercies and faithfulness to all generations.

May 1 Bouquets

Scripture Text: Genesis 1: 11

"And God said, Let the earth bring forth grass, the herb yielding seed, and the fruit tree yielding fruit after His kind, whose seed is in itself, upon the earth: and it was so."

The Prophet Moses writes in his first book about God's creation of earth and how on the second day He included grass, herbs, flowers, blossoms, and fruit, whose seed was after His kind. God saw that it was good! Genesis 1: 12 God allows us to gather Bouquets created after His seed!

Moses continues to record the account of God's creation of earth and how on the third day He included light for the earth's plants! On the fourth through the sixth day, God included in His creation fowl, creatures, and man to be fruitful and multiply; all made in His image, after His image. Genesis 1: 27 God allows us to multiply Bouquets created after His seed!

The Prophet Moses recalls how God rested the seventh day and then brought to Adam all the creatures and plants He created; giving him the task of tending them and giving them names! Genesis 2:19 God allows us to tend and name Bouquets created after His seed!

Prayer: Dear God, please accept the first bouquet of May flowers brought from April showers!

May 2 Bouquets

Scripture Text: Genesis 3: 18

"Thorns also and thistles shall it bring forth to thee; and thou shalt eat the herb on the field..."

Moses recalls the account of how Adam and Eve had eaten from the tree of forbidden fruit. As a consequence, God would allow thorns and thistles among the herbs they would eat.

Thorns: Perhaps Adam and Eve picked a bouquet of roses or blossoms from a thorn apple tree. Either bouquet would have thorns. No one likes to have a thorn in their foot or hand! Jesus wore a crown of thorns...perhaps from a bouquet of roses or from blossoms from a thorn apple tree. Either bouquet contain sharp thorns. Not one of us would have taken Jesus' place and worn the crown of thorns on our heads.

Thistle: Perhaps Adam and Eve picked a bouquet of light purple blossoms from the thistles. The thistle would have prickly stems. No one likes to handle or step on prickly thistles! Perhaps within Jesus' crown of thorns there were traces of purple blossomed thistle with it's prickly stems. Not one of us would have taken Jesus' place and worn the crown of thorns and thistles on our heads, or walked along the prickly path to calvary .

Herbs: Perhaps Adam and Eve picked a bouquet of herbs with their variety of odors. The herbs would include plants that would easily form a thicket where an animal could easily be entangled. No one likes to get tangled in a thicket! Today, let us reflect on how in our daily lives we can easily form a thicket where sin could easily be entangled. Not one of us would be able to free ourselves without the help through salvation by our Saviour, Jesus Christ!

Prayer: Dear God, please accept this beautiful bouquet of thorny roses, lavender thistles of prickly stems and the entangled herbs of the field as our thanks to You for sending your Son, Jesus Christ to be our Saviour!

May 3 Bouquets

Scripture Text: Genesis 8: 11

"And the dove came in to him in the evening; and lo, in her mouth was an olive leaf plucked off: so Noah knew that the waters were abated from off the earth."

Moses gives an account of Noah on the ark, waiting for the first sign of land after the flood. He sent a dove to bring back any signs of plants for that would mean land, which would mean life of plants! Moses becomes relieved when the dove returns to the ark with an olive leaf! One of the first things he and his family would do upon stepping on land is to gather enough olive leaves to make a bouquet! We are reminded of the impact of gathering and displaying of leaves:

Fig leaves were gathered by Adam and Eve to cover them from the elements of nature and from their sinful nature. Jesus was covered by cloth from elements of nature and with natural herbs for His body to be preserved for our salvation! We try to cover up our sin by gathering excuses (some as visible as the size of a fig leaf!), when we should instead be gathering God's fruit hidden beneath those huge leaves!

One solitary olive leaf was presented to Noah by a dove as a sign that the destruction of land from the flood was by God. He reminds us that the same power He uses to destroy is God's way of pruning! We try to prevent sin from entering our lives (some as subtle as the size of an olive leaf!), when we should instead be giving back to God the fruit hidden beneath those small leaves!

The flood waters surrounding Noah's ark would by God's power slowly soak back into the ground, evaporate from the wind and the sun. We are reminded that the same wind(invisible) and the same sun (visible) contain the power to prepare the land for future gardens and fields. We try to clear ourselves from sin (some as subtle as the dried leaves scattering upon the land!), when we should instead be gathering the fruit hidden beneath those colorful leaves!

Prayer: Dear God, accept this bouquet of colorful leaves that you allow to fall from your plants or cling to the vine or stem as our thanks to your Son; Saviour Jesus Christ for wearing a crown for our salvation!

May 4 Bouquets

Scripture Text: Genesis 37: 7

"For, behold, we were binding sheaves in the field and, lo, my sheaf arose, and also stood up right; and behold, your sheaves stood round about, and made obeisance to my sheaf."

Moses continues to record the names of dukes and kings as well as recalling the generation of Jacob and how they were strangers in the land of Canaan. The older sons of Jacob were also strangers to their youngest brother's dreams (they were already jealous of their father's 'favoritism' toward Joseph). One such dream was that of Jacob's sons binding sheaves:

Prior to bringing in the sheaves, they have to be gathered. When the sheaves are standing tall and clearly ready for harvest, they become a bouquet of stalks. There will be a sturdy, upright stalk to support the others that appear to bow before it. We recognize that Joseph would be the sturdy, the upright to support his own jealous brothers; and that they would bow before him. We are reminded that Jesus Christ stood sturdy; upright on the cross to support His sinful brothers; and that we would all bow before Him!

Prior to bringing in the sheaves, they have to be bound. When the sheaves become a bouquet of stalks they have to be tied together to prepare them for gathering. We recognize that Joseph would be closer to his brothers and that all of Jacob's sons would gather around Joseph. We are reminded that Jesus Christ stood among His brothers as He gathered His Father's (God's) sinful children; and that we bow before Him!

The time for gathering of the sheaves has arrived! When the bouquet of stalks are gathered in the arms of the harvester they bow in obedience. We recognize that Joseph would gather his jealous brothers along with an entire nation that would bow before him. We are reminded that our Lord Jesus Christ gathered His sinful brothers and that we bow before Him!

Prayer: Dear God, accept this harvested bouquet of sheaves that you allow to be bound together as out thanks to Your Son, Jesus Christ who was tied on the cross for our salvation!

May 5 Bouquets

Scripture Text: Exodus 2: 3

"And when she could not longer hide him, she took for him an ark of bulrushes, and daubed it with slime and with pitch, and put the child therein; and she laid it in the flags by the river's brink. "

Moses, in his second book recalls his own birth and upbringing! He would be found among the bulrushes; the flags by the banks of a river in Egypt. He would be hidden because sons were to be cast into the river while daughters would be saved. The plants of the river would save baby Moses' life!

The bulrushes stood firm and helped protect the lives of many small creatures of the river. Moses would be one of those creatures protected! He would be hidden until the right "guardian" would come to save him! We are reminded that God called His Son to meet His sinful creatures hiding because we need to be saved. The bulrushes would be carefully separated to reveal us to our Saviour, Jesus Christ!

Some of the bulrushes would be daubed with slime and pitch to build an ark. Slippery, sticky residue would be the 'glue' used to build protection from the powerful forces of the river! We are reminded that God allowed the persecutors of our Christ to daub hyssop upon our Jesus who became the Saviour!

The ark for baby Moses would be placed near the brink (bank) of the river. Gentle waves would lap along the edges of the ark without the strong winds forcing it from the flags (picture plants with thick stalks and wide leaves!). We are reminded that God allowed the protectors of our Jesus to cover Him with cloth protecting our Saviour so He could save us from the strong winds of sin!

Prayer: Dear God, I present to you a bouquet of bulrushes to thank Your Son, Jesus Christ for being wrapped in swaddling clothes at His birth and to fulfill Your will that He save us from our sins!

May 6 Bouquets

Scripture Text: Joshua 24: 26

"And Joshua wrote these words in the book of the law of God, and took a great stone, and set it up there under an oak tree, that was by the sanctuary of the Lord."

Joshua, after the death of Moses made a covenant with God as he gathered the tribes of Israel and asked them to choose the gods of their fathers or his God of their fathers. The covenant was placed under an oak tree. The leafy and thick branches of an oak not only hide the fruit but provide a welcoming shade from the heat of the day and a welcoming shelter from the winds and rains! A bouquet of oak leaves and acorns signify the strength of such a mighty tree!

Perhaps Joshua placed his covenant to God under the oak tree while it was bearing the leaves and seeds of Spring and Summer! The shade of the mighty oak shelters with its numerous Bouquets of leaves and signs of acorns is welcome during the windy days of Spring and the hot days of Summer!

Perhaps Joshua placed his covenant to God under the oak tree while it was showing and losing the leaves and seeds of Autumn and Winter. The thick branches of the mighty oak allow the numerous Bouquets of leaves and acorns to linger longer on the oak than on the ash or the maple. The oak welcomes us during the warm or cool days of Autumn and the windy cold days of Winter!

We are reminded of God's Son, Jesus Christ's majestic presence from season to season!

Prayer: Dear God, I present to you a bouquet of oak leaves and acorns, to thank your Son, Jesus Christ being our majestic King!

May 7 Bouquets

Scripture Text: Ruth 1: 22

"So Naomi returned, and Ruth the Moabitess, her daughter in law, with her, which returned out of the country of Moab: and they came to Bethlehem in the beginning of barley harvest. "

Ruth had just said to Naomi: '...Whither thou goest, I will go; and where thou lodgest, I will lodge: thy people shall be my people, and thy God my God...' This oath would include going to the field and gleaning ears of corn. Ruth would be gathering the grain of the field. There would be Bouquets of ripened barley still clinging to the stems and the ripened corn still clinging to the stalks. The famine of the land would be subdued by the fruits of the field!

Ruth joined the gleaners of the barley and the corn. The gleaners worked after the reapers. God not only provided the reapers and the gleaners to harvest the bouquet of the fruits of the field but also two strangers to sit together among the reapers at mealtime.

Ruth would join Boaz (the owner of the field where she gleaned). God provided them with a meeting place where the Bouquets of the fruit of the field would be winnowed'. When Ruth returned to Naomi, she carried in her vail six measures of barley. God provided Ruth with a bouquet from the harvest to bring back to Naomi who would witness Boaz taking Ruth as his wife.

We are reminded of how God's Son Jesus Christ's ministry within the fields of grain and how we can glean Bouquets from the harvest!

Prayer: Dear God, I present to you a bouquet of the grains of the field, to thank you for Your Son Jesus' ministry and harvesting within Your Kingdom!

May 8 Bouquets

Scripture Text: I Samuel 17: 17

"And Jesse said unto David his son, Take now for thy brethren an ephah of this parched corn, and these ten loaves, and run to the camp to thy brethren..."

The youngest son of Jesse, the keeper of the sheep, is called from the fields of natural Bouquets of flowers and grain for the sheep. He is given the job to deliver food to his older brothers who are called to help protect the land.

David would be running to the camp of his brothers with a bag of parched corn to present provisions for them. We are familiar with the rest of the story! God provides David with five smooth stones that would be this shepherd lad's way to defeat the giant, Goliath of the Phillistines: "I come in the name of the Lord of hosts...for the battle is of the Lord's" (17: 47)

David would put his hand in the bag that once contained the bouquet of parched corn provided to his brothers. One stone, one pull of the sling...God prevailed as Goliath fell to the ground, defeated, killed by one aim of a stone to his forehead!

We are reminded of how Jesus Christ fed the five thousand hungry people by providing one lad with loaves made from the harvested Bouquets of grain!

Prayer: Dear God, I present to you a bouquet of grains from Your fields, to thank You for Your Son Jesus' miracles and His provisions for Your Kingdom!

May 9 Bouquets

Scripture Text: II Chronicles 9: 1

"And when the queen of Sheba heard of the fame of Solomon, she came to prove Solomon with hard questions at Jerusalem, with a very great company, and camels that bare spices, and gold in abundance, and Precious Stones: and when she was come to Solomon, she communed with him of all that was in her heart."

Solomon as King of Israel would be greeted by Queen of Sheba who was impressed by his leadership, his wisdom, and his creation of a house for his God. She made sure she included spices with the gold and Precious Stones. Perhaps there were Bouquets of the precious spices to provide a pleasant odor or taste within the temple built for the Lord God! We are reminded that at Jesus' birth and at his death there was the presentation of spices to give homage to the Saviour of the world.

The Queen of Sheba would be recognized as a leader with her wisdom to grow and harvest spices in abundance to present to Solomon' immense temple for God. She made sure he had variety and a sufficient supply. Perhaps the Bouquets of abundant spices provided worshippers of God a gift for their majestic God! We are reminded that at Jesus' feet a beloved follower poured her expensive perfume to give homage to the Christ of the world.

Prayer: Dear God, I present to you a bouquet of spices from your gardens, to thank Your Son, Jesus' for presenting Himself in abundance such as harvested spices.

May 10 Bouquets

Scripture Text: Matthew 18: 3

"...Verily, I say unto you , Except ye be converted, and become as little children, ye shall not enter into the kingdom of heaven."

Matthew, the first gospel writer of the New Testament quoted words spoken by Jesus to his disciples. They had just asked Him who is the greatest in the kingdom of heaven. His answer is the little children.

We are reminded that little children are yet innocent, not so easily swayed by the values of the world and depend on their mothers. Their many needs are met by their mother and they show love toward her without any limitations!

No wonder there is a flower included in many Bouquets presented to our mothers that is called "Baby's breath"!

A bouquet with Baby's Breath has a subtle, gentle beauty. Often the father or the baby's siblings help this little infant in celebrating Mother's Day. On that special day we are as a little child; innocent, dependent on others to show love.

A bouquet with Baby's Breath has delicate, pure white colors. Often the father or the baby's siblings help this little infant in sharing Mother's Day. On that special day we are as a little child; trusting, a florist to make the special delivery.

We are reminded of how Jesus as an infant was dependent and innocently trusted His mother to prepare Him for the kingdom of heaven. He would share with His father and sibling the pure, delicate, beauty of love that only a mother could give.

Prayer: Dear God, I present to You a bouquet of Baby's Breath to thank Your Son, Jesus who encouraged His Disciples to be as little children as they recognize their dependence on their mother.

May 11 Bouquets

Scripture Text: Matthew 18: 4

"Whosoever therefore shall humble himself as this little child, the same is greatest in the kingdom of heaven."

Jesus continues to teach us the innocence of little children and encourages us to be as humble as them! There is no hesitation as they show their love toward the family everyday!

As we continue to honor our mothers, let us be reminded of the innocent child's show of love when the mother is presented with a fistful of bright yellow blossoms. We chuckle at these smelly and stained fists holding a bouquet of weeds; dandelions!

A bouquet of dandelions are bright yellow; one of the primary colors so easily recognized all around a child's world: the sun, the stars, and the moon! We are reminded that Jesus even as an infant would be surrounded by bright yellow and recognized all around the world: the Star in the East that hovered over His Mother, Mary and His Father, Joseph.

A bouquet of dandelions are smelly and stain our hands; one of the primary sins so easily surrounding a child's world; hate,jealousy, and wrong-doings. We are reminded that Jesus even as an infant would be surrounded by ugly stains and recognized all around the world: the smelly and stain manger that surrounded His Mother and Father.

Prayer: Dear God, I present to You a bouquet of dandelions of bright yellow (with its offensive odor and stain) to thank You for your

Son, Jesus being born a saviour in an offensive smelly and stained manger.

May 12 Bouquets

Scripture Text: Matthew 18: 10

"Take heed that ye despise not one of these little ones; for I say unto you, that in heaven their angels do always behold the face of my Father which is in heaven."

Jesus called a little child and set him in the midst of the disciples. He continued to advise His disciples by exhorting them to heed and despise (hate) not these little ones. There is no question that each little life is being guarded, by God and His angels in heaven. Any loving mother would allow God's protection for her little children! Notice how many mothers have received from their little children (young and older!) a bouquet of flowers with a bright yellow center, and pure white petals; the daisy!

Each daisy in this bouquet has a bright yellow center. How can a mother despise any of her children if she has allowed her Heavenly Father to protect them. Mother Mary recognized that her baby boy, Jesus would be presented not only to her but to the whole world as the bright, yellow light; the center of God's heaven!

Each daisy in this bouquet has pure white petals. How can a mother despise any of her children is she has allowed her Heavenly Father to prepare them. Mother Mary recognized that her baby boy, Jesus would be presented not only to her but to the whole world as pure, unblemished child; the greatest in God's heaven!

Prayer: Dear God, I present to you the daisy pulled from a bouquet of these bright yellow and pure white flowers to thank Your Son Jesus teaching each mother to choose to love or to love not each bright, and pure child presented and prepared by His Heavenly Kingdom!

May 13 Bouquets

Scripture Text: Song of Solomon 2: 1

"I am the rose of Sharon, and the lily of the valleys."

The book of Solomon is his song of songs. He sings of love... remembered more than wine (1:4). He sings that he is the rose of Sharon...a flower that signifies the great love that is remembered more than wine! His kingdom would be ruled with such great love!

We are reminded of the impact from the aroma and beauty of a single rose! We celebrate around this time of year; Mother's Day, and often present our dear mothers with a single rose to remember her great love for her children!

God allowed Jesus' mother to be recognized as Mother Mary and is remembered for her single love through her son, Jesus shows His great love for God's children!

King Solomon, the Lily of the Valleys; invited his people to witness how he ruled his kingdom with glory and majesty. He compares himself to a lily that grows among the thorns and is remembered for His great love through His father, God.

May we be reminded as we recognize our Mother on her special day; present her with a yellow rose that symbolizes courage and a white lily that symbolizes purity.

Prayer: Dear God, I present you a bouquet of roses and lilies as my way of thanking You for sending Your Son to be our "Rose of Sharon", the Lily of the Valley, and our Saviour!

May 14 Bouquets

Scripture Text: Isaiah 27: 3

"I the Lord do keep it; I will water it every moment: lest any hurt it, I will keep it night and day. "

The Prophet Isaiah's vision includes the exhortation to repentance and the coming of Christ's kingdom. Isaiah warns nation after nation to repent from their evil ways and preaches of God's care and provision of His nations. Included in God's care of every nation is His tending the gardens, forests, fields and vineyards. He provides beautiful Bouquets!

In today's devotional we will expound on God's care of His vineyard: God keeps (tends) His vineyard; causing the plants to take root, blossom and bud. (27:6). God's vineyard bouquet is being prepared! We are reminded of how God sent His Son, Jesus to be our Saviour. We recall how Jesus testifies that He is the vine and we are His tender branches! (John 15: 15: 5)

God waters His vineyard; causing the plants to bear fruit. God's vineyard is ready for harvest! We gather the colorful grapes with hues of brown, green, red, white and purple. We are reminded of how God sent His Son, Jesus to be our Saviour. We recall how Jesus testifies that the gift of God when we thirst is living water! (John 4: 10)

Prayer: Dear God, I present to You a fruit bouquet of grapes from Your vineyard to thank Your Son, Jesus for being the vine!

May 15 Bouquets

Scripture Text: Isaiah 29: 17

"Is it not yet a very little while, and Lebanon shall be turned into a fruitful field, and the fruitful field shall be esteemed as a forest? "

The Prophet Isaiah continues to share his vision of the judgment of God. He not only tends the vineyard but also provides for the field and the forest.

God provides fruit Bouquets from the field! The provided fruit of the field grows on vines. Picture tomatoes, and melons in abundance! Picture bright, colorful fruit! We are reminded that we are God's fruit; formed from the strong healthy vine (which represents His Son, Jesus). Do we allow God and His Son, Jesus to be gardeners of our fields (our lives)?

God provides nuts and fruit Bouquets from the forest. The provided fruit of the forest grows on twigs. Picture the nuts, and berries in abundance! Picture small, healthy fruit! We are reminded that we are God's fruit; formed from the small but mighty twig (which represents His Son, Jesus). Do we allow God and His Son, Jesus to be rangers (guardians) of our forests (our lives)?

Prayer: Dear God, I present to You a bouquet of fruit of the field and of the forest to thank Your Son, Jesus for being our gardener of our fields and guardian of our forests!

May 16 Bouquets

Scripture Text: Isaiah 51: 3

"For the Lord shall comfort Zion: He will comfort all her waste places; and He will make her wilderness like Eden, and her desert like the garden of the Lord; joy and gladness shall be found therein, thanksgiving, and the voice of melody."

The Prophet Isaiah speaks of the restoration of God's kingdom and includes the exhortation to follow after righteousness. God provides His followers comfort from the wilderness and desert. He creates gardens like Eden and like the garden of the Lord.

Only God can provide us comfort from the wilderness of our lives. His provision continues from the beginning of creation! Adam and Eve were the first recipients of God's comfort from all the wandering aimlessly through forests. God provided His Son, Jesus to be that "light" to permeate the dense floors of the forest! Let us follow God's Son through the dense forests that bear the fruits of God's gardens!

Only God can provide us comfort from the deserts of our lives. His provision continues from the birth of His Son! Jesus' was the first recipient of God's comfort from all the wandering aimlessly through deserts. God provided His Son, Jesus to be that "way" to cross through the dried floors of the desert! Let us follow God's Son through the dried deserts that bear the fruits of the one and only Garden of the Lord!

Prayer: Dear God, I present to you Bouquets of flowers from

Your deserts, to thank Your Son, Jesus for leading us through the wildernesses of our lives!

May 17 Bouquets

Scripture Text: Matthew 6: 28

"And why take ye thought for raiment? Consider the lilies of the field, how they grow; they toil not, neither do they spin..."

Jesus saw the multitudes of people from Galilee, from Decapolis, from Jerualem, from Judaea, and from beyond Jordan. He went up into a mountain. Christ spoke to His followers (disciples) the words we still continue to read: The Sermon On The Mount. He included His many Beatitudes, His instructions for the disciples to be the Salt, the Light, Communicators, Prayers, Servants and Recipients of God's Field!

Jesus has His disciples consider the lilies of the field and how His Heavenly Father has "arrayed" them; "fed" them and "clothed" them. No wonder lilies are so beautiful and delicate.

Lilies of the field grow; multiply under the elements of the weather. So God meets our needs to grow; as we multiply for His Field (Kingdom); multiply under the elements of the weather. We are reminded of Jesus' display of wisdom under the elements of the weather upon the sea, mountaintop or in the valley.

Lilies of the field toil not; showing beauty amidst signs of turmoil. So God meets our needs to grow as we show beauty for His Kingdom; show beauty amids signs of turmoil. We are reminded of Jesus' display of beauty amidst the turmoil of the cross.

Lilies of the field spin not: displaying strength amidst other plants. So God meets our needs to grow as we display strength for His Kingdom; display strength amidst other people. We are reminded of Jesus' display of strength amidst His Father's people as He rose from the grave.

Prayer: Dear God, I present to you a bouquet of lilies, to thank

Your Son, Jesus Christ; the Lily of the Valley for showing His inner beauty and strength to be our Saviour.

May 18 Bouquets

Scripture Text: Mark 4: 8

"And other fell on good ground, and did yield fruit that sprang up and increased; and straight forth, some thirty, some sixty, and some an hundred."

Jesus taught His disciples by the seaside. He taught by parables and doctrines. This particular parable was about the sower who went out to sow seeds. Some seeds never made it under the earth. Other seeds grew but in shallow ground. They never grew to bear fruit due to being choked by weeds. Finally, some seeds fell on good ground. They brought forth fruit...enough to make a bouquet....some thirty, some sixty, and some hundred.

Jesus was teaching how His disciples could yield fruit for His Kingdom even by thirty. I can picture a small orchard containing a bouquet of thirty fruit trees with their aromatic blossoms enticing us to watch for the yielding of fruit. We are reminded to yield fruit for God's Kingdom; joining His Son in being aromatic blossom enticing the world to yield fruit on good ground!

Jesus was teaching His disiples how they could yield fruit for His Kingdom even by sixty! I can picture picture a field containing a bouquet of sixty stalks with their colorful fruit enticing us to watch for the harvesting of fruit. We are reminded to yield fruit for God's Kingdom; joining His Son in being colorful fruit feeding the world to join in yielding more fruit on good ground!

Jesus taught the multitudes and His disciples how they could yield fruit for His Kingdom even by an hundred! I can picture a field containing a bouquet of an hundred slender stems with their tender, white blossoms enticing us to show God's glory! We are reminded to yield to God's glory for His Kingdom; joining His Son in being tender, pure blossoms displaying to the world what can be yielded on good ground!

Prayer: Dear God, I present to you Bouquets of thirty, of sixty, or of an hundred to thank Your Son, Jesus Christ for His ministry contained seed that yielded fruit by the millions!

May 19 Bouquets

Scripture Text: Luke 24: 1

"Now upon the first day of the week, very early in the morning, they came unto the sepulchre, bringing the spices which they had prepared, and certain others with them."

The Physician Luke records the burial of His dear Saviour, Jesus Christ. Bouquets of spices had been prepared by His followers. Others that followed included Mary Magdalene, Mary, the mother of James, Joanna, and other women (24:10).

The bouquet of spices were prepared by Jesus' followers; including Mary Magdalene who had prepared a precious ointment to wash her Lord, Jesus' feet. Just like the precious ointment prepared for Jesus before He died on the cross, the bouquet of spices prepared for Him at the tomb would be aromatic and be used for preservation. I am reminded that our daily lives should include the preparation of a bouquet of spices that reveal to others that we are one of Jesus' followers!

The bouquet of spices were carried by Jesus' followers; including Mary the mother of James who had carried a special child who would sit at Jesus' feet. Just like the precious spices prepared for Jesus before He was born in Bethlehem, the bouquet of spices prepared by the wisemen would be aromatic and be used for adoration. I am reminded that our daily lives should include the carrrying of a bouquet of spices that reveal to others that we are one of Jesus' admirers!

The bouquet of spices were brought by Jesus' followers; including Joanna who with other followers witnessed that the stone in front of the sepulchre was rolled away. The precious bouquet of spices prepared for the preservation and in adoration of their Lord, Jesus

Christ was carried to the tomb. But, what happened to them when the tomb was found empty? We can only imagine! I am reminded that our daily lives should include the bringing of a bouquet of spices with other followers to our Lord, and Saviour, Jesus Christ as we wait for His return!

Prayer: Dear God, I present to you a bouquet of spices, to thank Your Son, Jesus Christ for His life, death and resurrection as Saviour for Your whole world!

May 20 Bouquets

Scripture Text: John 15: 1

"I am the true vine, and my Father is the husbandman."

Jesus answered many questions from His followers and today's scripture text is part of His answer to a question asked by Judas (not Iscariot): ' Lord, how is it that thou wilt manifest thyself unto us, and not unto the world?'

Jesus includes the promise of the Comforter (Holy Spirit) to those who come to His Father, God in love, peace, and obedience. He compares Himself to a vine tended by His Father God that will bring forth fruit from the many branches. Included in our God's position as husbandman is the taking away, bearing of, and purging of the branches.

Jesus states that He is the vine and we are the branches. God will take away some of the branches. If we do not bear fruit for His vineyard (kingdom) God will allow us to be taken away just like a dried up branches not receiving what is needed to bear fruit. God sent His Son, Jesus to present to us His love. Why do we not stretch forth as part of God's kingdom?

Jesus states that He as the vine allows us; His branches to bear fruit. God will bear His vineyard with fruit. If we become His fruit May our bouquet include the presenting of our Saviour's peace! What beautiful bouquet can be be a part of for God's kingdom?

Jesus states that He is the obedient vine and as His branches we depend on His support from the forces of nature and humans! God, as the husbandman allows for strong winds, heavy rains, gently breezes, soaking sunshine to be a part of the preparation. What is within our bouquet being presented to God in adoration of His Son, Jesus and for His kingdom?

Prayer: Dear God, I present to you a bouquet of fruit to thank Your Son, Jesus our Saviour who we can cling to in preparation for the coming of Your Kingdom!

May 21 Bouquets

Scripture Text: Esther 9: 28

"And these days should be remembered and kept through out every generation, every family, every province, and every city; and that these days of Purim should not fail from among the Jews, nor the memorial of them perish from their seed. "

Esther had become the Queen and was allowed to make petitions before the King Ahasuerus. She recognized the importance of writing invitations and sending letters to the Jews under the authority of their leader Mordecai. She included within her decree words of peace and truth. (9: 30) These days would be remembered and there would be fasting and feasts; memorials.

For today's devotional we will begin the study of monthly memorials (holidays) that are remembered for their words of peace and truth. Each monthly memorial will have a flower that represents a day to remember.

January's flower is the Carnation or the Snowdrop. A bouquet of these flowers would be gathered for the rememberance of Epiphany which is a celebration observed twelve days after Christmas. We are reminded that January 6th is a day to remember peace onearth through the birth of our Lord, Jesus, and for His truth (good will)toward all men.

February's flower is the Violet or the Primrose. A bouquet of these would be gathered for the rememberance of Saint Valentine which is a observed on the fourteenth of the month. We are reminded that February 14th is a special day to remember love on earth through the earthly life of our Lord, Jesus, and for His love (agape) toward all men.

Prayer: Dear God, we present to you a bouquet of Carnation, Snow-drop, Violets and Primrose to thank Your Son Jesus for His birth, and life of peace, truth and love.

May 22 Bouquets

Scripture Text: Isaiah 9:6

"For unto us a child is born, unto us a son is given: and the government shall be upon his shoulder: and his name shall be called Wonderful, Counseller, The Mighty God, The everlasting Father, the Prince of Peace."

The Prophet Isaiah's vision included what he saw concerning Judah and Jerusalem and their influence within the kingdom of God. We are reminded of the names given to our Lord, Jesus Christ.

Today we continue to remember names of holidays and the names of Bouquets of flowers representing two more months of the year:

March's flower is the Jonquil, or Daffodil, or Narcissus. A bouquet of these flowers would be gathered for the rememberance of Saint David,n which is a celebration observed on the first of the month. We are reminded that March 1st is a special day to remember the saints before us who honored the life, death and resurrection of our Lord Jesus; His sacrifice for all men.

April's flower is the Sweet Pea, or Daisy. A bouquet of these flowers would be gathered for Easter which is a celebration observed either this month or in March. We are reminded that Easter Week is a special time when our Risen, Lord, and Saviour Jesus Christ blesses us with His sweet, bright and pure presence!

Prayer: Dear God, we present to You a bouquet of Jonquil,

Narcissus, Daffodil, Sweet Pea and Daisy, to thank Your Risen Son Jesus Christ for His blessed resurrection.

May 23 Bouquets

Scripture Text: Matthew 6: 28

"And why take ye thought for rainment? Consider the lilies of the field and how they grow; they toil not nor do they spin..."

One of Jesus' Disciples; also recognized as a Tax Collector quotes from one of His words of wisdom included in His Sermon on The Mount, (Beatitudes). We are encouraged to compare our lives with His and what our motives should include. We recognize two more months and their flowers:

May's flower is the Lily of the Valley. A bouquet of these flowers would be gathered for Mother's Day which is a celebration recognized the second Sunday of the month. We are reminded on Mother's Day the sacrifice of our Lord Jesus' Mother; Mary and how she gave her only son who would be called the Lily of The Valley.

June's flower is the Rose. A bouquet of these flowers would be gathered for Father's Day which is a celebration recognized the third Sunday of the month. We are reminded on Father's Day the wisdom of our Lord Jesus' Father; Joseph and how he taught his only son to be a carpenter. Joseph gave his only son who would be hung on a wooden cross for our salvation.

Prayer: Dear God, we present to you a bouquet of Lily of the Valley and Roses to thank Your Son for sacrificing His life for Your World!

May 24 Bouquets

Scripture Text: John 8: 31, 32

"Then said Jesus to those Jews which believed on Him, 'If you continue in my word, then are ye my disciples indeed: and ye shall know the truth, and the truth shall make you free.' "

Saint John records the words that Jesus spoke in the temple; in the treasury. Jesus' hour was yet to come and no man laid hands on Him. He spoke to the Jews who believed; trusted in Him. They were commanded to continue in His word; be His disciples. We recognize two more months and their flowers.

July's flower is the Larkspur or the Water Lily. A bouquet of these flowers would be gathered for Independence Day which is a celebration recognized on July 4th. We are reminded on July 4th of the freedom that is ours when we continue studying the Holy Bible by land or by sea!

August's flower is the Gladiolus or the Poppy. A bouquet of these flowers would be gathered on Friendship Day which is recognized the first Sunday of August. We are reminded on Friendship Day of the truth that sets us free due to our Saviour Jesus Christ's sacrifice during an ongoing war against sin.

Prayer: Dear God we present to you a bouquet of Larkspur, Water Lily, Gladiolus, and Poppy to thank Your Son; the Saviour of the whole world; setting us free from the wars of sin.

May 25 Bouquets

Scripture Text: I Peter 1: 7

"That the trial of your faith, being much more precious than of gold that perisheth, though it be tried with fire, might be found unto praise and honour and glory at the appearing of Jesus Christ..."

The Apostle Peter writes to "scattered strangers" about the hope found in the resurrection of Jesus Christ. He advises this "elect" the ongoing trials of faith. We continue comparing our faith to the flowers of the next two months.

September's flower is the Aster or the Morning Glory. A bouquet of these flowers would be gathered on Grandparents Day which is celebrated on the first Sunday of September. On this special day we are reminded of the faith of our fathers and of our Heavenly Father's Son being our Morning Glory rising toward the heavens.

October's flower is the Calendula or the Marigold. A bouquet of these flowers would be gathered on Columbus Day which is recognized on the second Monday of October. On this historical day we are reminded of the faith of our discoverers and of our Heavenly Father's Son showing forth the preciousness and brightness such as we see in the blossom of the Marigold.

Prayer: Dear God we present to You a bouquet of Aster, Morning Glory, Calendula, and Marigold to thank to thank Your Son, shining forth in glorious and shining faith as the resurrected Saviour for the whole world.

May 26 Bouquets

Scripture Text: Philippians 4: 19

"But my God shall supply all your need according to his riches in glory by Christ Jesus."

The Servant Paul along with Timotheus writes to the bishops and deacons at Philippi. The fellowship of believers can be compared to the flowers that will be mentioned for the last two months of the year.

November's flower is the Chrysanthemum. A bouquet of these flowers would be gathered on Thanksgiving Day which is recognized on the third Thursday of November. On this historical day we are reminded of our daily needs being met by our Heavenly God, Saviour Jesus, and The Holy Comforter.

December's flower is the Narcissus or the Holly. A bouquet of these flowers would be gathered on Christmas Day which is recognized every 25th of December. On this special day we present gifts, receive gifts and are reminded of the most precious gift from our Heavenly Father; His Only Son, and with guidance of the Holy Ghost.

Prayer: Dear God, we present to you a bouquet of Chrysanthemum, Narcissus and of Holly to thank Your Son Jesus for meeting our needs and being the most precious gift for the world.

May 27 Bouquets

Scripture Text: Micah 5: 7

"And the remnant of Jacob shall be in the midst of many people as a dew from the Lord, as the showers upon the grass, that tarrieth not for man, nor waiteth for the sons of men."

The Minor Prophet Micah recorded his vision concerning what he saw for Samaria and for Jerusalem; peace in the last days, and the birth and coming of Christ. Micah's vision includes some illustrations of how important the dew and showers from the Lord is to the fields.

Sometimes we gather Bouquets of flowers from God's fields or gardens just after the refreshing dew of the morning. We are His people who need to be refreshed daily by the dew we see as we walk through His gardens or fields of flowers. May we allow the gentle refreshing of our lives each day so freely given to us by God.

Sometimes we gather Bouquets of flowers from God's forests, gardens, or fields just after the refreshing showers of the day. We are His people who need to be refreshed by showers of rain we see, hear and often run through His gardens, forests and fields. May we allow the intense refreshing of our lives each day so freely given to us by God.

Prayer: Dear God we present to You a bouquet of refreshed flowers to thank Your Son for gently refreshing His followers as the gentle dew and for intense showers.

May 28 Bouquets

Scripture Text: Mark 4: 28

"For the earth bringeth forth fruit of herself; first the blade, then the ear, after that the full corn in the ear. "

One of the Gospel writers; Mark records the words of parables from Jesus that spoke of comparisons of nature; plants, with our daily challenge to live as He desires.

Sometimes we gather Bouquets of flowers from God' soft earth of the desert, field, mountain, or shoreline. First the blades of grass, then the stems to support the buds and the full blossom. God sent His Son, Jesus to be our support in time of need.

Sometimes we gather Bouquets of flowers from God's hard earth ot the desert, field, mountain, or shoreline. First the visible roots so close to the earth's surface, then the stems struggling to produce buds that eventually come to full bloom. God sent His Son, Christ to be our example in time of witnessing.

Prayer: Dear God I present to you a bouquet of flowers to thank Your Son for being from the root of Jesse and becoming the Lily of the Valley!

May 29 Bouquets

Scripture Text: Exodus 12: 14

"And this day shall be unto you for a memorial; and ye shall keep it a feast to the Lord throughout all generations; ye shall keep it a a feast by an ordinance for ever. "

The Prophet Moses and Aaron spoke to the people of Egypt about God's passover. This day would be a feast to the Lord and a memorial. for those lives spared for the freedom of others. On this day (May 29th), we May be celebrating Memorial Day.

We celebrate Memorial Day by attending parades or picnics. We notice the display of the american flag of red, white, and blue. We notice the wearing of these patriotic colors. Memorial Day gatherings need to start with a salute and thank you to our God for sending His Son to spare His life for our freedom. We honor the fallen soldiers and remember their families and loved ones in prayer.

We celebrate Memorial Day by attending special services. We notice the gathering of people with Bouquets of red, white, and blue flowers (including the poppy or carnation) displaying gratitude. Memorial Day services need to start with a salute and thank you to our God for sending His Son to return again for our freedom. We honor the humble soldiers as they remember other families and loved ones in prayer.

Prayer: Dear God, I present to you a bouquet of poppies and carnations to thank Your Son, our Risen Christ for His comfort and grace.

May 30 Bouquets

Scripture Text: Ephesians 5: 9, 10

"(For the fruit of the Spirit is in all goodness and righteousness and truth:) Proving what is acceptable unto the Lord."

The Apostle Paul wrote to the Church of Ephesus encouraging them to receive the power of the Holy Spirit (Acts 1:8) and present themselves acceptable unto the Lord (Romans 12). The Christians were encouraged to present the fruit of the Spirit. They were to present themselves as a bouquet of goodness, righteousness and truth.

Goodness is the bunch of grapes in a fruit bouquet. Their colors range from green, purple to red. They taste either sweet or tart. A grape can be the size of a tiny pea or the size of a marble. They grow together in goodness to form a bunch of acceptable fruit for the vineyard. We are reminded as were the early Christians to grow together in goodness for the Holy Spirit and for the building of God's vineyard.

Righteousness is the handful of apples in the fruit bouquet. Their colors range from red, yellow, to green. They taste either sweet or tart. An apple can be the size of a golf ball or the size of a baseball. They grow together in righteousness to form a handful of acceptable fruit for the orchard. We are reminded as were the early Christians to grow together in righteousness for the Holy Spirit and for the expansion of God's orchard.

Truth is the bunch of bannas in the fruit bouquet. Their colors range from green, yellow, to brown. They taste best when slightly firm and not mushy from becoming over ripened. They grow together in truth to form a bunch of acceptable fruit for the jungle. We are reminded as were the early Christians to grow together in truth for the Holy Spirit and for the expansion of God's jungle.

Prayer: Dear God, I present to you a fruit bouquet of grapes, apples and bananas to thank Your Son Jesus becoming our example of goodness, righteousness, and truth within Your kingdom.

May 31 Bouquets

Scripture Text: Revelation 21: 2

"And I John saw the holy city, new Jerusalem, coming down from God out of heaven, prepared as a bride adorned for her husband."

Saint John wrote of the revelation of Jesus Christ. Within His writings John introduces himself as a servant of his Saviour and recognizes the similarity of the new Jerusalem to a wedding. Today, I recognize my parents anniversary date!

My sister Sue joins me by presenting May's theme; Bouquets through another of her illustrations.

Prayer: Dear God, I give You thanks for all the " Bouquets" my sister Sue had been able to share as she walks daily in Your presence.

June 1 Precious Stones

Scripture Text: Genesis 1: 10

"And God called the dry land Earth; and the gathering together of the waters called He seas: and God saw that it was good."

The Prophet Moses begins his first book with God's creation of the earth.

We read within the first chapters of Genesis how dependent the land and water are on each other. The land of precious gems is dependent on the rivers moisture!

Gold is the first precious gem mentioned in Moses' account of God's Creation; Genesis 2: 11.

Within the garden of Eden there was a river with four heads. One such head covered the land of Havilah; and the gold of that land was good. We are reminded of how any hard-working miner does not want to end up finding "fools' gold" ! They would rather find the real gold! Unfortunately the real, good gold that God created was used to form idols (images) that were worshipped rather than God. May we worship our God with lives as pure as gold.

The second precious gem mentioned in Moses' account of God's Creation is the Bdellium; Genesis 2: 12. This gem was found in the same river as the gold. We are reminded of how any hard working tiller of the land would find Bdellium as a gem of the field (suggested to be vegetable gum) or of the sea (suggested to be pearls). Unfortunately Bdellium was found in the building of temples made for the worshipped golden idols. May we worship our God with lives as productive as bdellium.

There is a third gem mentioned in Moses' account of God's Creation: the onyx stone. The onyx is of milk white and black colors and is in the same river as the Bdellium and the gold.

We are reminded of how any hard working gardener of the land would find onyx as a transparent gem of the field or a translucent mixture of the river. Unfortunately onyx would be found in the building of altars made for the worshipped golden idols. May we worship our God with lives as transparent and translucent as the onyx.

Prayer: Dear God, we present to You precious gems of your creation as tokens of our appreciation of Your Son, Jesus Christ becoming our pure, productive and transparent Saviour.

June 2 Precious Stones

Scripture Text: Genesis 8: 20

"And Noah builded an altar unto the Lord; and took of every clean beast, and of every clean fowl, and offered burnt offerings on the altar."

The Prophet Moses gives the account of Noah and the Flood. After surviving the major flooding of the earth and placing his feet back on the land, Noah built an altar to the Lord, took of God's creatures and worshipped God by offering a sacrifice.

Moses does not desribe the altar to the Lord, but we can imagine the stone from the dry land was part of the building of the altar. Perhaps we could picture a line of animals being used according to their strength to help move rocks and stones for the building of the altar. We are reminded of the miraculous removal of the massive stone from Jesus' tomb so that He could help move the rocks and stones for the building of God's Kingdom. May we be builders of God's Kingdom by presenting ourselves as Precious Stones within the building of His kingdom.

Moses took more time in describing the gathering of the beasts and fowls of the earth, so we can picture cattle, fowl, and creeping things. These creatures were gathered as survivors of the major flood to provide sacrifices to God. We are reminded of the miraculous sacrifice of Jesus so He could help fulfill the salvation of God's Kingdom. May we be gathers for God's Kingdom by sacrificing our precious gems of time and talent for the Kingdom Of God.

Moses wrote a desciptive account of the burnt offerings on the altar and how the Lord smelled a sweet savour, and no more would the ground be cursed (8:21). Noah would be blessed by God We are reminded of the sweet smelling savour of Jesus who became the sacrifice for the coming of God's Kingdom. May we be blessings for God's Kingdom by presenting our lives as sweet and pleasant.

Prayer: Dear God, we present to you Precious Stones of Your re-creation during the major flood of Noah's time to thank You for Your Son Jesus who presents us with precious gems of blessings daily.

June 3 Precious Stones

Scripture Text: Genesis 13: 2

"And Abram was very rich in cattle, in silver, and in gold."

The prophet Moses introduces us to Abram who with his family went into the land of Canaan and journeyed on toward Egypt because of a major famine (12: 10). The substance of the land was so great that Abram went in one direction and Lot the other (13:11). He is given more land by God and gives thanks by building an altar unto the Lord (13:18).

Abram was rich in cattle. The land had to be fertile and provide for the cattle. God protected Abram from a major famine just as He protected His infant Jesus by providing the beasts of the field to surround Him at the manger. May we recognize how rich we are in God's Kingdom because of His Son, Jesus, the Precious Saviour of the entire world.

Abram was rich in silver. God provided Abram with river banks just as He provided His human Jesus with the precious rocks of the land to surround Him at the tomb. May we recognize how rich we are in God's Kingdom because of His Son, Christ, the Pure Redeemer of the entire world.

Abram was rich in gold. God directed Abram as he walked the

length and breadth of the land (13:17) just as He provides His divine Jesus with the Precious Stones of the temple to honor Him. May we recognize how rich we are in God's Kingdom because of His Son, Christ, the Perfect Price for the entire world.

Prayer: Dear God, we present to You, the Precious Stones of Your land to thank Your Son, Jesus Christ for being our Precious Saviour, Pure Redeemer and Perfect Price for the coming of Your Kingdom.

June 4 Precious Stones

Scripture Text: Genesis 28: 10, 11

"And Jacob went out from Beersheba, and went toward Haran. And he lighted upon a certain place, and tarried there all night, because the sun was set; and he took of the stones of that place, and put them for his pillow, and lay down in that place to sleep."

The Prophet Moses gives an account of Jacob following his father Issac's instructions to leave the land of Canaan. We read of how Jacob took of the stones of a certain place and put them for his pillows. He has a dream and sees a ladder that stretches from earth to heaven and with angels descending and ascending (28: 12).

The stones served as pillows for sleep. Jacob was getting much needed rest. He had deceived his father, and obtained the blessing that was for his twin; Esau. He had to flee from Canaan the stone that served a purpose for Jesus who needed much sleep. and was following his father's wishes. Perhaps this was one of the first days away from the threats of Esau that Jacob was able to get much needed rest. We are reminded of He had been hung on the cross, after a cruel beating and for our salvation. There was a huge tomb stone where Jesus laid; away from the threats of the soldiers and the helplessness of His family and disciples. May we follow the example of our Christ (the Rock).

Upon waking up from a dream with the conviction that the Lord was with him, Jacob rose up early in the morning and took the stones that served as pillows for a pillar and poured oil upon the top of it.

We are reminded of the stone that served a purpose for Jesus who needed to be buried. There were members of His family and a circle of disciples that were coming Easter Morning to bring oils to preserve His body. May we follow the example of our Christ (the Redeemer).

Just prior to leaving this place of rest, Jacob made a vow that if God would be with him, provide for him and prepare him to return to his father's house, then the stone would be God's house. We are reminded of how of the stone was rolled away from the tomb and Jesus was not in the tomb. He meets up with of His followers and promises to send them a comforter; the Holy Spirit. May we follow the example of our Christ (the Risen).

Prayer: Dear God, we present to You Precious Stones to thank You for Your Son, Christ the Rock, Redeemer and the Risen.

June 5 Precious Stones

Scripture Text: Exodus 35: 5

"Take ye from among you an offering unto the Lord: whosoever is of a willing heart, let him bring it, an offering of the Lord; gold, and silver, and brass..."

The Prophet Moses recalls about his leadership and how he gathered all the congregation of the children of Israel and included the bringing of offerings to the tabernacle of God. The invitation for this gathering was for those of a willing heart; willing to offer gold, silver, and brass.

The gold offered would be used for the tabernacle with its ark and the mercy seat. This precious gold would serve as the building of God's house so future generations would have a place to worship. We are reminded that Jesus spent time in the tabernacles of gold, built for a place to worship God. May we be willing to bring an offering of gold to God.

The silver offered would be used for the garments and jewelry. This precious silver would serve as the adorning of God's house so future generations would come willing to worship in God's house.

We are reminded that Jesus spent one time in the temple correcting individuals who were exchanging silver inappropriately in God's house. May we be proper as we offer silver to God.

The brass offered would be used for the altar and the vessels. This precious brass would serve as the place for sacrifices for God so future generations would come willing to present a way to worship in God's house. We are reminded that Jesus presented himself as the only offering, sacrifice, the only way for worshipping God. May we be willing to sacrifice our brass to God.

Prayer: Dear God, we present to You gold, silver, and brass, to thank You for Your willing, proper sacrifical Saviour.

June 6 Precious Stones

Scripture Text: Joshua 4: 2, 3

"Take ye twelve men, out of the people, out of every tribe a man, and command ye them, saying, Take you hence out of the midst of Jordan, out of the place where the priests' feet stood firm, twelve stones and ye shall carry them over with you, and leave them in the lodging place, where ye shall lodge this night."

Joshua was Moses' minister who would follow him as the leader for the tribe of Israelites. He was directed to cross the Jordan River. He would have twelve of his men standing in the river where a miraculous event would take place; the parting of the river to make a safe path for crossing. Upon the completion of a safe crossing, twelve stones would be brought along.

The twelve stones from the Jordan would be carried as a memorial unto the children of Israel for ever (4:7). A stone would be pushed in front of Jesus' tomb as a memorial unto the children of God for ever. We are reminded of our Saviour's love for us because of a single, precious stone.

The twelve stones would be left in the lodging place of the twelve chosen men carrying them across Jordan. A stone would be left by Jesus' empty tomb and His loved ones would carry the news back to

Jerusalem. We are reminded of our Saviour's love for us because of His twelve disciples carrying and passing along the memorial unto the children of Israel for ever.

Prayer: Dear God, we present to You Precious Stones to thank Your Saviour, Jesus for sacrificing His life and passing along the memorial of Israel.

June 7 Precious Stones

Scripture Text: I Samuel 17: 40

"And he took his staff in his hand, and chose him five smooth stones out of the brook, and put them in a shepherd's bag which he had, even in a scrip; and his sling was in his hand: and he drew near to the Phillistine."

I Samuel is also called the First Book of the Kings. We read in chapter 17 the story of the boy shepherd, David and how he went to battle against the Phillistine Giant, Goliath. He only needed one of those five stones to defeat the army of the Phillistines.

The one precious stone from his shepherd's bag would make David a champion. We read that the stone sunk into the giant's forehead and he fell upon his face to the earth. When the Philistines saw their champion was dead, they fled. We are reminded that when some of the followers of Christ saw their King was dead, they fled. Do we run away from our Saviour and King?

The one precious stone would be seen by those who saw the head of Goliath including King Saul. King Saul witnessed David and asked whose son he was. David, from Bethlehem would become friends with King Saul's son Jonathan. David was accepted as leader over the men of war. We are reminded that when the followers of Christ saw that their King returned, they worshipped Him. Do we run daily to worship our Saviour and King?

One precious stone and some arrows would become a sign for David in saving his own life. King Saul sent his son Jonathan to bring back David, with intentions to kill him. Jonathan had him hide behind a stone and receive a sign by the landing of arrows whether to return or stay away from Saul's threat. We are reminded that the followers of Christ witnessed Jesus returning to heaven. Do we live each day in faith of His return as Saviour and King?

Prayer: Dear God, we present to You a precious stone to thank You for Your only begotten Son for being our Saviour and King.

June 8 Precious Stones

Scripture Text: I Kings 18: 31, 32

"And Elijah took twelve stones, according to the number of the tribes of the sons of Jacob, unto whom the word of the Lord came saying, Israel shall be thy name: And with the stones he he built an altar in the name of the Lord: and he made a trench about the altar, as great as would contain two measures of seed."

I Kings is also called the Third Book of Kings. In this book is recorded the Prophet Elijah's challenge to those worshipping Baal instead of God.

Included in this challenge is the gathering of twelve stones. Thus this tradition continues to serve as a memorial for Israel . May we be willing to follow tradition of gathering our talents in service to our King and Saviour.

The challenge became intense as four barrels of water were upon the altar of twelve stones, upon the sacrifice, upon the wood, three times and the water filled the trench. May we be willing to follow orders for an intense challenge while serving our King and Saviour.

The sight of fire consuming the sacrifice, the wood, the stones, the dust and the water caused the prophets of Baal to fall on their faces and proclaim that the Lord is the God. May we be willing to be witnesses of the fire of God (through His Holy Spirit), and come proclaiming that the Lord is the God.

Prayer: Dear God, we present to you gathered Precious Stones in building an altar where we can be consumed by the fire of His Holy Spirit.

June 9 Precious Stones

Scripture Text: II Chronicles 9: 1

"And when the queen of Sheba heard of the fame of Solomon, she came to prove Solomon with hard questions at Jerusalem, with a very great company, and camels that bare spices, andgold in abundance, and Precious Stones: and when she was come to Solomon, she communed with him of all that was in her heart."

Queen of Sheba came to Solomon with gold in abundance and believed not until she came and communed with him. We are reminded that King Solomon already had gold in abundance. When Queen of Sheba saw with her own eyes the house he had built and heard him speak with wisdom, she presented King Solomon with an hundred and twenty talents of gold towards the building of God's house. We are reminded that God's Son; King of the Jews was presented at His birth gold. When we go to God our Father who rules the whole world, do we come with our talents of gold?

Queen of Sheba communed with King Solomon and presented him with Precious Stones. She gave her blessing toward his Lord, God and for his throne as King of Israel. As she prepared to leave, Sheba took her own servants and went to her own land, knowing her Precious Stones would enhance thebeauty of God's house. We are reminded that God's Son; King of the Jews already had all the treasures including Precious Stones to enhance the beauty of God's house. When we go to God our Father who rules the whole world, do we come with our earthly treasures including Precious Stones?

Prayer: Dear God, we present to You Precious Stones to thank You for your Son, for giving His precious life for our salvation.

June 10 Precious Stones

Scripture Text: Proverbs 1: 1-2

"The proverbs of Solomon, the son of David, king of Israel; To know wisdom and instruction; to perceive the words of understanding..."

Let us consider the book of Proverbs as pearls of wisdom:

Our first pearl of wisdom is found in Proverbs 1: 8, 9; "My son, hear the instruction of thy father, and forsake not the law of thy mother: For they shall be an ornament of grace unto thy head, and chains about thy neck. "Wisdom is compared to treasured ornaments and chains. Thus our father's instruction and our mother's law serve as valuable advice.

Our second pearl of wisdom is in Proverbs 2: 3. 4; "Yea , if thou criest after knowledge, and liftest up thy voice for understanding; If thou seekest her as silver, and searchest for her as for hid treasures..." Wisdom is compared to silver and other hid treasurers.

Our third pearl of wisdom is in Proverbs 3: 5, 6; "Trust in the Lord with all thine heart; and lean not unto thine own understanding, In all thy ways acknowledge him, and he shall direct his paths." Wisdom is not of our understanding and only the Lord can lead us down the path of gold.

Prayer: Dear God, we present to You Precious Stones; pearls of wisdom to thank You for Your Son of knowledge and understanding.

June 11 Pearls of Wisdom

Scripture Text: Proverbs 4: 5

"Get wisdom, get understanding: forget it not; neither decline from the words of my mouth."

King Solomon continues to give advice with his wisdom:

Today's first pearl of wisdom is found in Proverbs 8: 11; "For wisdom is better than rubies; and all the things that May be desired are not to be compared to it. "We are reminded to get wisdom and recognize its worth above all Precious Stones.

Today's second pearl of wisdom is found in Proverbs 10:4: "He becometh poor that dealeth with a slack hand: but the hand of the dligent maketh rich." We are reminded to extend a hardworking hand to receive the riches of God's Kingdom filled with Precious Stones.

Today's third pearl of wisdom is found in Proverbs 15: 16: "Better is little with the fear of the Lord than great treasure and trouble therewith. "We are reminded to be content with little treasures and fear our awesome God who provides us with Precious Stones according to what we need.

Prayer: Dear God, We present to You Precious Stones to thank Your Son, Jesus who accepts us with our few treasures and as we gradually gain His wisdom.

June 12 Precious Stones

Scripture Text: Proverbs 17: 3

"The fining pot is for the silver, and the furnace for gold: but the Lord trieth the hearts."

May the Lord with His infinite wisdom as He tries our heart teach us wisdom that refines as silver and is molded as gold.

Our first pearl of wisdom to refine and mold us is Proverbs 20:15; "There is gold, and a multitude of rubies: but the lips of knowledge are a precious jewel." May we be reminded that the wisdom spoken by God, His precious jewel (Jesus) and through His Holy Spirit are spoken as precious jewels.

Our second pearl of wisdom today is Proverbs 22: 1; "A Good name is rather to be chosen than great riches, and loving favour rather than silver and gold." We are reminded that we have three good names: God, Jesus and The Holy Ghost. We choose them over great riches and love them rather than silver and gold.

Our third pearl of wisdom today is Proverbs 23: 23; "Buy the truth, and sell it not; also wisdom, and instruction, and understanding." May we be reminded that just as we buy Precious Stones, they become our treasured truth to hold and not sell.

Prayer: Dear God, we present to You Precious Stones we bought for a price to thank You for Your Son and how He was brought for a price.

June 13 Precious Stones

Scripture Text: Proverbs 24: 3

"Through wisdom is an house builded, and by understanding it is established."

We continue with the pearls of wisdom. Today wisdom is compared to the building and establishment of an house.

Our first pearl of wisdom today is found in Proverbs 25: 4; "Take away the dross from the silver, and there shall come forth a vessel for the finer. "May we be reminded wisdom is as a refiner; taking away the dullness and building towards a vessel.

Our next pearl of wisdom is found in Proverbs 28: 20; "A faithful man shall abound with blessings: but he that maketh haste to be rich shall not be innocent. May we be reminded that God in His infinite wisdom blesses us in abundance in His time and not for us to be in a hurry to receive.

Our last pearl of wisdom is found in Proverbs 31: 10; "Who can find a virtuous woman ?

For her price is far above rubies. May we be reminded that a woman of virtue receives wisdom from God which is more valuable than Precious Stones.

Prayer: Dear God, we present to You our Precious Stones to thank You for Your faithful, virtuous Saviour of wisdom and power.

June 14 Precious Stones

Scripture Text: Ecclesiastes 2: 8

"I gathered me also silver and gold, and the peculiar treasures of kings and provinces..."

The Preacher Ecclesiastes writes that all is vanity, and generations pass away but the earth abideth forever. Ecclesiastes was also one of the kings over Israel in Jerusalem, and he gave his heart to search out by wisdom concerning all things that are done under heaven. He searched out wisdom concerning treasures on earth. We are familiar with his pearl of wisdom: "To every thing there is a season, and a time to every purpose under the heaven." (3:1)

There is a time to cast away stones ; a time to gather stones. (3:5), We are reminded that Jesus told some of his followers that if they were without sin they could cast the first stone. They learned quickly to cast away the stone rather than to gather this time.

There is vanity for he that loves silver too much. (5:10).

Nor he that loves abundance with increase. We are reminded that Jesus had to cast people out of the temple who loved silver and were not satisfied with what they had as their abundance increased. They learned quickly their greed was not to their benefit!

Time and chance happens to us all. Riches are not just for the men of understanding; nor favor to men of skill. (9: 11) We are reminded that Jesus, a skilled carpenter did not flaunt himself as rich. His many followers would be reminded that we can have times; chances to be rich when we accept His salvation.

Prayer: Dear God, we present to You our Precious Stones to thank You for Your Son, Jesus for making us rich in His love.

June 15 Precious Stones

Scripture Text: Isaiah 28: 16

"Therefore thus saith the Lord God, Behold, I lay in Zion for a foundation a stone, a tried stone, a sure foundation: he that believeth shall not make haste."

The Prophet Isaiah is known to us expecially for his promise of Christ. (9:6) He writes a parable about the kingdom of Christ (11:1), and the fall of Babylon (21: 9). Isaiah writes a song of praise to the Lord God for his confidence in God's strength and dominion over the earthly kingdom (26:13). God is the master builder.

God prepares a foundation in Zion. He lays stone with the tools; line and plummet (28:17). We are reminded of God's infinite wisdom that he shares with us. He allows His people to become His builders. We are reminded of Christ, the son of a carpenter sharing His infinite wisdom. We know one of His names is Rock. Do we allow the Trinity to prepare a foundation?

God lays a stone, a tried stone. He chooses a stone that has been tried, worn by the elements of nature. We are reminded of God's infinite wisdom of choosing His Son to be tried, hung, buried in the earth. We know one of His Son's names was Prince Of Peace. Do we allow the Trinity to use our tried lives?

God lays a sure foundation. He chooses followers of His Son that are faithful. We are reminded of God's infinite wisdom of allowing His Son to be buried, rise again, and join Him in the heavenly kingdom. We know one of His Son's names is Lord. Do we allow the Trinity to lay a sure foundation?

Prayer: Dear God, we present to You Precious Stones to thank You for Your Son, Jesus Christ our Lord, Rock and Prince of Peace.

June 16 Precious Stones

Scripture Text: Jeremiah 18: 6

"O house of Israel, cannot I do with you as this potter? saith the Lord. Behold, as the clay is in the potter's hand, so are ye in mine hand, O house of Israel."

The Prophet Jeremiah was directed by God to go to the potter's house where he would hear God's words. He was continuing to follow God's command: root out, pull down, destroy, throw down, build and plant. (1:10).

God as the potter can destroy a marred vessel. We are reminded of how each one of our lives have been marred. We are aware of how His Son Jesus' life was marred but not by Jesus' doing but by the hands of those who did not trust in the Lord or have hope. May we remain in God the potter's hand: trusting Him even when our lives (His vessels) are being destroyed.

God as the potter can throw down a destroyed vessel. We are reminded of how each one of us have been in a situation where we have been thrown down. We are aware of how His Son Jesus' words were thrown down not by Jesus' doing but by the stopped ears of those who did not trust in the Lord or have hope. May we remain in God the potter's hand; trusting Him even when our lives (His vessels) are being thrown down.

God as the potter can build from a marred and destroyed vessel. We are reminded of how each one of us have had our lives rebuilt. We are aware of how His Son Jesus' power but not by Jesus' doing but by His Heavenly Father. May we remain in God the potter's hand: rebuilt because we have the same powerful Heavenly Father.

Prayer: Dear God, we present to You precious stone; clay to thank Your Son for teaching us how to allow You to be our Heavenly Father and how we must remain in Your hand. You are our Potter. We honor You every day. Happy Heavenly Father's Day!

June 17 Precious Stones

Scripture Text: Ezekiel 34:26

"And I will make them and the places round about my hill a blessing; and I will cause the shower to come down in his season; there shall be showers of blessing."

The Prophet and Priest Ezekiel begins his writings with a vision of a whirlwind, a great cloud, and a fire. He continues with vivid descriptions of creatures with the likeness of men. He cries out for Israel and testifies to his duty as a watchman. He has to speak up when he hears the sounds, sees the warnings, and knows to be a leader for the family of His Heavenly Father. As we remember our earthly Fathers these next few days of devotions May we recognize their role as watchman; looking out for sounds and visions of blessings.

Our earthly fathers need to recognize the sounds of blessings. Ezekiel's duty as watchman recognizes the words of past fathers such as Abraham who became the father of inherited land. (33:24) We are reminded that God, our Heavenly Father sent His Son, Jesus to leave His earthly Father, Joseph, and preach the sounds of blessings. May our ears be open.

Our earthly fathers need to recognize the signs of blessings. Ezekiel's visions are vivid and we recognize the visions of past fathers such as Isaiah who became a watchman for the birth and coming of God's Heavenly Son, Jesus Christ. Jesus would leave His earthly Father, Joseph, and preach the visions of blessings. May our eyes be open.

Our earthly fathers need to share the showers of blessings. Ezekiel shared with those fathers who practiced idolatry, the princes devising mischief, lying prophets, and the inquiring elders (fathers). Unfortunately their role and purpose as a watchman was not of their Heavenly Father. We are reminded that God, our Heavenly Father sent His Son, Jesus, to leave His earthly Father, Joseph and fulfill the role and purpose as Saviour of the whole world.

Prayer: Dear God, we present to you the land of precious stone that receives Your showers of blessings. We thank You for Your Son, Jesus Christ who has become Your example for all the earthly fathers in recognizing and sharing all blessings.

June 18 Precious Stones

Scripture Text: Daniel 1: 9

"Now God had brought Daniel into favour and tender love with the prince of the eunuchs."

Our Heavenly Father brought Daniel, a child of Judah, to stand in King Jehoiakim's palace and teach the learning and the tongue of the Chaldeans (1:4). They were chosen because they "had no blemish, were well favoured, skilful in wisdom, cunning in knowledge, and understanding science. We are reminded that our Heavenly Father brought forth His infant Son who was all-knowing.

Our Heavenly Father brought Daniel into favour of the King's palace to receive a name from the prince of the eunuchs. He was to be called Belteshazzar, and would partake of the King's daily provisions. We are reminded that our Heavenly Father brought forth His youthful Son who was named the Prince Of Peace.

Our Heavenly Father brought Daniel into the tender love of the King's prince of eunuchs to prove that God's provision would suffice. He would be joined by Shadrach, Meshach and Abednego. We are reminded that our Heavenly Father brought His earthly Son to prove that only His provisions would suffice.

Prayer: Dear God, we present to you Precious Stones used to build Your Heavenly Kingdom and to thank You for Your heavenly and earthly Son, Jesus Christ the Lord who is proof that only Your provisions suffice.

June 19 Precious Stones

Scripture Text: Hosea 1: 10

"Yet the number of the children of Israel shall be as the sand of the sea, which cannot be measured nor numbered; and it shall come to pass, that in the place where it was said unto them, Ye are not my people, there it shall be said unto them, Ye are the sons of the living God.

The Prophet Hosea became an earthly father of two sons and a daughter. Unfortunately Hosea and Gomer's children would not exist in the kingdom of the house of Israel, or receive God's mercy within Israel, or be God's people. There would be a change when their Heavenly Father chose to let this come to pass. The number of the children of Israel shall be as the sand of the sea.

God in His infinite power is able to measure or number the sand of the sea. So the children of Israel are as the sand of the sea. In our Heavenly Father's time the children of Israel would become His sons. We are reminded that we are as the sand of the sea, we will be numbered as His sons.

God in His infinite power is able to allow His Son, Jesus Christ to have the same powers in measuring or numbering the sand of the sea.

So the children of God's kingdom are as the sand of the sea. In our Trinity's time all children of the heavenly kingdom will become His sons. We are reminded that we are as the sand of the sea. We will be included in the numbered sons of the living God.

Prayer: Dear Heavenly Father, we present to you precious sand to thank You for the infinite power of Your Trinity Team in numbering us and including us as sons of the living God.

June 20 Precious Stones

Scripture Text: Matthew 2: 11

"And when they were come into the house, they saw the young child with Mary his mother, and fell down, and worshipped him; and when they had opened their treasures, they presented unto him gifts; gold, and frankincense , and myrrh."

Saint Matthew recalls the birth of Jesus Christ and how there were wisemen traveling from the east to Jerusalem; following a star they saw in the east. They were seeking Christ in Bethlehem; where words of prophecy had been written. What sacrifices did these wisemen make to see the prophecy be fulfilled?

The wisemen could have been fathers leaving their own house. They were sacrificing their own time away from their own families. We are reminded that on Father's Day we are thanking our Heavenly Father for earthly fathers and how they sacrifice their time away from their own families; to provide for their needs.

The wisemen could have been fathers traveling to the infant Christ to worship Him. They were sacrificing their own families to join this new young family. We are reminded that on Father's Day we are thanking our Heavenly Father for earthly fathers and how they sacrifice their own families; to fulfill prohecy.

The wisemen could have been fathers traveling with their earthly treasures. They were sacrificing each family's treasures of the land; Precious Stones. We are reminded that on Father's Day we are thanking our Heavenly Father for earthly fathers and how they sacrifice their own treasures; to show honor to the ruler of Israel.

Prayer: Dear God, we present to You, Precious Stones; precious treasures, to thank you for being an Heavenly Father who not only supplies Your Son Jesus with earthly fathers who sacrifice their time, family, and treasures.

June 21 Precious Stones

Scripture Text: Mark 12: 10

"And have ye not read this scripture; The stone which the builders have rejected is become the head of the corner"

Saint Mark recalls the ministry and prophecy of Jesus Christ at the temple where his listeners were chief priests, scribes and elders. (11:27) Jesus was answering their question: "By what authority and who gave you the authority to do these things..."? (11:28). Jesus asks His listeners a question in return to theirs:

Jesus asks His listeners if they have read the scripture. He quotes Psalm 118:22-23. The Psalmist David starts his song of praise by giving thanks to the Lord who is good and whose mercy endureth forever (118:1). We are reminded to read the scriptures as Jesus speaks to us in parables.

Jesus asks His listeners if they have read about the stone rejected by the builders. Jesus starts His parables of His very own prophecy by clearing the temple. His authority was questioned and He compares Himself to the rejected stone. We are reminded to not question the authority of the Lord even when we recognize He has been rejected by some of His listeners.

Jesus asks His listeners if they have read that the rejected stone becomes the corner. Jesus includes in His parable the final part of His own prophecy while emphasizing the authority of the Lord to fulfill salvation. We are reminded to seek out the entire scripture to grasp the full knowledge of the authority of the Lord.

Prayer: Dear God, we present to You a precious corner stone to thank You for Your Son, Jesus Christ's obedience to Your authority so that salvation for the world would be fulfilled.

June 22 Precious Stones

Scripture Text: Luke 24:2

"And they found the stone rolled away from the sepulchre."

Jesus had prophesized about His own death and resurrection . The same women and group who had followed Jesus to the sepulchre with their spices and witnessed His burial, now faced an empty tomb. They found the stone rolled away.

God prepared a place for Jesus' burial including the stone to cover the opening of the sepulchre. Jesus had prophesized that His followers would find the stone rolled away. We are reminded that our sins because of His death have been rolled away.

God performed a miracle for Jesus' resurrection including the stone rolling away from the sepulchre. Jesus had prophesized that His followers would not find Him in the sepulchre. We are reminded that our own sins because of His resurrection will be forgotten.

God produces a plan for Jesus' ascension including the rolled away stone becoming a reminder. Jesus had prophesized that His followers would recall His ascension to Heaven. We are reminded that no stone will block the sepulchre of the believers.

Prayer: Dear God, we present to You a precious stone to thank Your Son, Jesus Christ for giving us, His followers a visual memory to allow for the forgiveness of sins.

June 23 Precious Stones

Scripture Text: John 1: 42

"And he brought him to Jesus. And when Jesus beheld him, He said, 'Thou art Simon the son of Jona; thou shall be called Cephas', which is by interpretation, A stone."

Saint John the Baptist recalls the scene where Jesus is found by him and two disciples (1:37). They follow the "Lamb of God" and brought others to Him. One of the followers, Andrew. brings his own brother, Simon. Jesus gives Simon a name which is interpreted; A stone. He would be able to perform miracles of healing and purifying with the use of stones (2:6).

Jesus beheld Simon. This follower of the Lamb of would be given the name Cephas; "A Stone". Jesus beheld me; Patricia Lee Appelt, on June 23, 1952. I lived my childhood years on Stone Road, on a small dairy farm, just outside of Prattsburg, New York. Stone Road was for our family appropriately named. The stones on that road were often gathered by myself and my siblings for "valuable collections" in our eyes. Mother and Dad with their teasing eyes would say that the stony road would eventually disappear!

Jesus beheld Cephas; as one of His disciples, to walk the narrow, stony path; to preach the good news. Jesus beheld me; Cadet Patricia Lee Appelt, in September of 1976. I lived two years with other "Disciples of Jesus" at The Salvation Army School For Officers' Training College in Suffern, New York. The stony paths were often traveled by us Disciples of Jesus, to preach the good news. We joined "Companions of Christ", and were joined by "Joyful Evangelists". Our teachers with their teasing eyes would say that the stony road would eventually become crowded!

Prayer: Dear God, we present to You Precious Stones to thank Your Son, Jesus for beholding and walking with us on the stony paths of life.

June 24 Precious Stones

Scripture Text: Revelation 21: 14

"And the wall of the city had twelve foundations, and in them the names of the twelve apostles of the Lamb."

Saint John The Divine; a servant of Jesus Christ presents to the reader of the book of Revelation a vivid picture of heaven. We read of the wall of the city having twelve foundations.

In the Old Testament, the twelve foundations have the names of the twelve tribes of Israel. We know our christian calendar contains twelve months and have been given unique names. We each have a birthday month; mine being named; June.

In the New Testament, the twelve foundations have the names of the twelve apostles of Earth. We know our christian calendar contains twelve months and have been given Precious Stones. We each have a birthday gem; mine being; the pearl.

What is your birthday month?

Which precious gem is given for your birthday month? In our calendar, December is Jesus' birthday month. The precious gem for December is the Turquoise.

Prayer: Dear God, we present to You the precious gems of our birthday months, to thank You for sending Your only begotten Son, Jesus and allowing us to celebrate His birth every year!

June 25 Precious Stones

Scripture Text: Revelation 21:19

"And the foundations of the wall of the city were garnished with all manner of Precious Stones. The first foundation was jasper; the second sapphire; the third a chalcedony; the fourth an emerald."

Saint John the Divine continues his vivid description of the first four foundations of the beautiful city of heaven.

Jasper is the precious stone for the first foundation. It's yellowish brown color shows beauty and it's formation from quartz shows strength for the walls of heaven. January is the first month of the calendar year. It's precious stone is the garnet. It's array of colors: red, brown, black, green, or yellow show beauty and it's formation from silcate minerals shows strength for the start of the new calendar year.

Sapphire is the precious stone for the second foundation. It's blue color shows beauty and it's formation from corundum shows strength for the walls of heaven. February is the second month of the calendar year. It's precious stone is the amethyst. It's purple or violet color shows beauty and it's formation from quartz shows strength for the love month.

Chalcedony is the precious stone for the third foundation. It's array of colors shows beauty and it's formation from an array of other precious stone shows strength for the walls of heaven. March is the third month of the year. It's precious stone is the aquamarine. It's blue and green color shows beauty and it's formation of beryl shows strength for the month for Spring.

Emerald is the precious stone for the fourth foundation. It's green color shows beauty and it's formation from beryl shows strength for the walls of heaven. April is the fourth month of the year. It's precious stone is the diamond. It's colorless hue shows beauty and it's formation of carbon shows strength for rain showers.

Prayer: Dear God, we present to you Precious Stones tothank You for sending Your Son, Jesus to receive us; Your precious jewels and take us to Your Heaven of precious gems.

June 26 Precious Stones

Scripture Text: Revelation 21: 20

"The fifth saronyx; the sixth sardius, the seventh chrysolite..."

St. John the Divine continues his description of the heavenly kingdom. He names the Precious Stones for the fifth, sixth and seventh foundation of Heaven. We will continue comparing these Precious Stones with the gems for the fifth, sixth and seventh month of the year.

Saronyx is a banded form of chalcedony (multi colored and mixture of Precious Stones shows it's beauty and strength for the fifth foundation of Heaven. Emerald is green and formed from beryl. This gem represents May; the month of planting and Mother's Day.

Sardius is a form of chalcedony; red in color and shows it's beauty and strength for the sixth foundation of Heaven. Pearl is white or pink and formed from mollusk. This gem represents June; the month of picnics, graduations, and many weddings.

Chrysolite is a greenish yellow formation of silicate(compared to our topaz), and shows it's beauty and strength for the seventh foundation of Heaven. Ruby is deep red and formed of corundum. This gem represents July, the month of picnics, parades and Independence day.

Prayer: Dear God, we present to You Precious Stones of bold colors to thank You for sending Your Son, Jesus Christ to be our Saviour and face boldly His death for our salvation.

June 27 Precious Stones

Scripture Text: Revelation 21: 20

"...the eighth, beryl, the ninth, a topaz, and the tenth, a chrysoprasus..."

Saint John the Divine writes of the eight, ninth, and tenth Precious Stones used in the foundations close to the top of the walls of Heaven.

Beryl is usually green and is a silicate of beryllium and aluminum. It is in the eigth foundation of Heaven. August is the eighth month and is represented by the precious stone; peridot. The green or yellow formation of quartz represents the beginning of the harvest on earth.

Topaz can come in an array of blues, browns, and yellows. It is a formation of mineral, and granite. We see the ninth foundation of Heaven. September is the ninth month and is represented by the precious stone; sapphire. The blue shade formation of corundum represents the beginning of a new school year, and the starting with a clean slate.

Chrysoprasus is an apple green variety of the formation of chalcedony. We admire the tenth foundation of Heaven. October is the tenth month and is represented by the precious stone; opal. The milky colored formation of silicon represents the harvesting of orchards and fields.

Prayer: Dear God, we present to You Precious Stones to thank You for sending Your Son, Jesus to assist us with the earthly harvesting of souls for Your heavenly kingdom.

June 28 Precious Stones

Scripture Text: Revelation 21: 20

"... the eleventh, a jacinth; the twelfth, an amethyst."

Saint John the Divine's vivid description of the foundations of Heaven is coming to a climax; the top two of the twelve foundations mentioned.

Jacinth is reddish-orange variety of zircon. The eleventh foundation is made with beauty and strength such as a sunset. Topaz is the precious stone of November. The array of colors in shades of blue, yellow, or brown and the formation of minerals, granite, and rocks represent the gathering in of people and the harvest of the earth on Thanksgiving.

Amethyst is purple or violet formed of quartz. The twelfth foundation of Heaven is made with beauty and strength such as a cold starry evening sky. Turquoise is blue-green formed of aluminum and copper. The color of Spruce and other pines and the stands of aluminum and copper is the earthly sight we partake as we celebrate the birth of Jesus Christ in December.

Prayer: Dear God, we present to You Precious Stones to thank You for sending Your Son, Jesus and to celebrate His birth.

June 29 Precious Stones

Scripture Text: Revelation 21: 21

"And the twelve gates were twelve pearls; every several gate was of one pearl; and the street of the city was pure gold."

Saint John the Divine finalizes his description of heaven by describing the white or pink colors of pearls for the twelve gates of heaven. The street is paved with pure gold.

Since June is my birthday month, I would like to expound on my birthstone; the pearl. This precious stone; gem has three important lessons to prepare us for the gates of Heaven.

The first lesson is where the pearl was first found. We read in one bible dictionary that pearls were found in the Red Sea. We are reminded that Moses; a prophet of God parted the Red Sea, set up altars to represent the safe crossing over by the Twelve Tribes of Israel. The altar was formed by the pearls mysteriously created by the mollusk; sea creature.

The second lesson is how the pearl was created by the mollusk. We read in one reference dictionary that pearls were smooth, often rounded, lustrous deposits formed in the shell of certain oysters and other mollusks. We are reminded that the builders of earthly temples included this valuable; hard to find precious stone from the sea.

The third lesson is the value of this precious stone; precious gem; the pearl. We see necklaces of pearl, we read the name Pearl in the list of suggested names for girls, and we read in the Holy Bible of the precious value of pearls in earthly temples and the building of the Heavenly Kingdom. We are reminded that our individual, personal lives are as precious and valuable as the pearl of the sea.

Prayer: Dear God, we present to You Precious Stones to thank You for sending Your Son, Jesus for a valuable price such as we find in the precious gem; the pearl.

June 30 Precious Stones

Scripture Text: Ephesians 4: 7

"But unto every one of us is given grace according to the measure of the gift of Christ."

The Apostle Paul writes another of his encouraging letters to the churches; this one being of Ephesus. We are reminded of how precious the gift of Christ for the whole world has become. This is possible through given grace.

My sister Sue has given me presents of precious stone and often made by her own hands. Today is her day to illustrate June's theme: Precious Stones.

Prayer: Thank You, Lord for family and how You shared Your Son, Jesus to be our precious cornerstone!

July 1 Wise Creatures

Scripture Text: Genesis 1: 20

"And God said, Let the waters bring forth abudantly the moving creature that hath life, and fowl that May fly above the earth in the open firnament of heavens."

In the first book of Moses we read of God's creation of Wise Creatures on earth. We read of moving creatures of the water and flying fowl of the skies. God's perfect plan of creation prepared these Wise Creatures.

The abundance of moving creatures of the water included the great whales (1:21). They were respected as Wise Creatures of the waters due to their size and strength! God created enough water for abundant seas prior to creating abundant moving creatures of the sea!

The abundance of flying fowl of the skies included the winged fowl. They were respected as Wise Creatures of the air due to the wing-span and strength!. God created enough firnaments for vast skies prior to creating abundant flying creatures of the air!

Prayer: Dear God, we respect Your Wise Creatures, and for the creation of Adam and Eve Your first respectors of these Wise Creatures.

July 2 Wise Creatures

Scripture Text: Genesis 1: 24

"And God said, Let the earth bring forth the living creature after his kind, cattle, and creeping thing, and beast of the earth after his kind, and it was so."

Moses, the prophet continues to give an account of God's creation of Wise Creatures. In today's text we read of cattle and creeping things.

Man; starting with Adam and Eve would have dominion over the wise cattle. They were free to roam and were wise when it came to feeding themselves from the earth's fields. We are reminded that the wise cattle were part of the heavenly scene at God's dear son, Jesus' birth.

Man, including Adam and Eve would have dominion over the wise creeping creature. The first would be the serpent (snake); 3:1.

We are reminded that the wise serpent was part of the sorrow and curse put upon the earth due to human error that God allowed to exist.

Prayer: Dear God, we respect the wise cattle and wise creeping snake of the field and respect other humans created by God to have dominion over these Wise Creatures.

July 3 Wise Creatures

Scripture Text: Genesis 1: 28

"And God blessed them, and God said unto them, "Be fruitful, and multiply, and replenish the earth, and subdue it: and have dominion over the fish of the sea, and over the fowl of the air, and over every living thing that moveth upon the earth."

Moses included in his account to God's creation the blessings upon every living thing including Adam and Eve. God gave a blessing to replenish and subdue the earth.

Each blessed wise creature within God's creation of earth would be replenished by Adam and Eve caring and tending of the grass and green herb for meat. They would care and tend the gardens; orchards while replenishing the abundant supply of Wise Creatures.

Each blessed wise creature within God's creation of earth would be subdued by Adam and Eve caring and tending of the waters and the land for sustenance. They would care and tend the gardens, fields while subduing the variety of Wise Creatures.

Prayer: Dear God, we respect Your wise fish of the sea, and Your wise fowl of the air. We show respect to Your past generations who cared and tended the land and the waters by replenishing and subduing Your Wise Creatures.

July 4 Wise Creatures

Scripture Text: Genesis 6: 19

"And of every living thing of all flesh, two of every sort shall thou shall bring into the ark, to keep them alive with thee; they shall be male and female."

Moses, the prophet continues in the first book of the Holy Bible of the replenishing and subduing of the Wise Creatures made by God for His people on earth. He writes about the well-known flood; of Noah's ark, and the gathering of a a female and male of a variety of Wise Creatures. Included were fowls of the air. One such wise fowl May have been the eagle. We remember the wise American Bald Eagle today:

Independence Day. The eagle represents freedom in a land dominated by humans who replenish and subdue these wise fowls of the air.

The eagle is majestic in flight, displaying their wisdom above the earth's land. Unfortunately they have become extinct due to the dominion of human beings. May we be reminded that the surviving eagle continues to soar towards the heavens.

The eagle is powerful in landing, displaying their wisdom amongst other creatures of the land. Unfortunately they have been an endangered species due to the dominion of human beings. May we be reminded that the surviving eagle continues to carry food to replenish its own.

Prayer: Dear God, we respect Your wise creature; wise fowl of the air; the eagle. May we respect it's wisdom and ability to survive the human domination and subduing of this creature of the air.

July 5 Wise Creatures

Scripture Text: Genesis 13: 2, & 5

"And Abram was very rich in cattle, in silver, and in gold. And Lot also, which went with Abram, had flocks, and herds, and tents."

Moses gives an account of Abram and his brother's son; Lot going out of Egypt due to their being sent away by Pharaoh. They left with the flocks and herds of God's Wise Creatures. Today we will recognize the rich flocks and the rich herds.

Abram was rich in herds of cattle. Moses mentions a strife between Abram and Lot over the land. Abram encouraged Lot to separate; to expand within the vast plain of Jordan. He chose to dwell with his cattle in the land of Canaan. He would become richer in cattle;

to receive all the land he could see from northward, southward, eastward, and westward (3:14).

Lot was rich in flocks of sheep. Moses mentions that Lot choses to dwell with his sheep in the plain of Jordan. He chose to dwell in Jordan which was well watered . He would become richer in sheep as his land was compared to the garden of the Lord (13: 10).

Prayer: Dear God, we respect Your abundant herds and flocks. May we respect the abundance and valuable use as meat; provisions for other Wise Creatures and wise human beings.

July 6 Wise Creatures

Scripture Text: Genesis 22: 7

"And Isaac spake unto Abraham his father, and said, My Father: and he said, Here am I, my son. And he said, behold the fire and the wood: but where is the lamb for a burnt offering."

Moses recalls the touching story of Abraham obeying His God and willing to present his son as a burnt offering. We know that the wise sheep of the flock follow their shepherd. Unfortunately, one particular ram spied by Abraham was caught in a thicket by his horns. Abraham's son Issac had his life spared that day.

Moses continues to write of the sacrificial burnt offering of the ram.and the blessings from God because of Abraham's obedience. Abraham's seed would be multiplied and we can surmise that his herds of cattle and flocks of sheep would be in abundance.

There would be enough sheep to provide daily burnt offerings on the altars prepared for God. We are reminded that even Jesus was given the name; Lamb of God and sacrificed His life for our sins.

Prayer: Dear God, we respect Your choice of one of Your Wise Creatures to serve as a sacrifice for our sins. We respect, Jesus; Lamb of God and how He did present Himself as a sacrifice for the world, and He rose from the grave so our lives can be spared.

July 7 Wise Creatures

Scripture Text: Genesis 37: 31, 32

"And they took Joseph's coat, and killed a kid of goats, and dipped the coat in the blood; and they sent the coat of many colours, and they brought it to their father; and said, This have we found: know now whether it be thy son's coat or no."

Moses recalls the story of Joseph, one of Jacob's sons; at the age of seventeen, tending the flock of goats and envied by his brothers due to his dreams and their father's obvious favor toward him (37: 8). We are reminded of how Jesus called Himself the Great Shepherd; envied for His prophecies and miracles. May we follow as his Wise Creatures of His flock.

Moses relates to the reader that Joseph's brothers did not tear the colorful coat but dipped it in the blood of a kid goat; another one of God's Wise Creatures whose blood would be mistaken for an evil beast that supposedly killed Joseph (37:20). We are reminded of how Jesus called Himself the Lamb of God; envied for His parables and authority. May we recognize Him as did the Wise Creatures of His flock.

Prayer: Dear God, we respect Your wise herds of goats as they know and recognize their shepherd's voice as leader and guide. We respect Your Great Shepherd and Your Lamb of God; our Lord Jesus Christ.

July 8 Wise Creatures

Scripture Text: Exodus 8: 8

"Then Pharoah called for Moses and Aaron, and said, Intreat Lord, that he May take away the frogs from me, and from my people; and I will let the people go, that they May do sacrifice unto the Lord."

This text found in the second book written by Moses is in the form of a personal diary or journal. Moses writes about the many plagues upon the land that involve creatures of the water and land. We read about the plague of lice, flies, and locusts and the frogs. The plague would involve these Wise Creatures staying in huge swarms, and large groups. They would be able to feast off the fields, forests and homes in Egypt. It took the plague of all the firstborn of Egypt to be slain before Pharoah would cry out to Moses and his people to go; serve their Lord, and bless him.

This text found in Exodus is in the form of an ordinance or law. Moses writes about the redemption of each firstborn human and creature. There was deliverance for humans and their flocks and herds of Wise Creatures. They would once again feast off the fields and forests, and homes of the land flowing with milk and honey (13: 5).

God's creatures in their wisdom stay in groups, herds, swarms, and flocks. He allows these groups of Wise Creatures to feast off the land tended by human beings.

Prayer: Dear God, we respect the frogs, lice, and locust that show wisdom and strength in groups; swarms. We respect the care-takers of these groups of Wise Creatures.

July 9 Wise Creatures

Scripture Text: Deuteronomy 32: 11, 12

"As an eagle stirreth up her nest, fluttereth over her young, spreadeth abroad her wings, taketh them, beareth them on her wings: So the Lord alone did lead him, and there was no strange god with him. "

Moses recalls in his fifth book of prophecy the inheritance Jacob found in a desert land and how the Lord led him, instructed him, and kept him as the "apple of his eye" (32:10). Moses compares God to one of His wise fowls; the eagle.

First, the wise eagle stirs up her nest. So God stirs up His people including His Son. The preparations are made for the motherly care by the eagle and the preparations are made for the fatherly care by God, our Heavenly Father.

Secondly, the wise eagle fluttereth over her young; spreads her wings to protect them. The continual care by the wise mother eagle and by the continual care by God, our all-knowing Heavenly Father is beyond our comprehension of His protection.

Finally, the wise eagle takes her young and bears them on their wings. The patient guidance and direction by the wise mother eagle is a lesson taught by God, our all powerful Heavenly Father are there for us to receive.

Prayer: Dear God, we respect the preparations, care and guidance of Your wise fowl of the air; the eagle. We respect the same loving preparations, care, and guidance for Your Son, Jesus.

July 10 Wise Creatures

Scripture Text: Joshua 6: 2,3, 4

"And the Lord said unto Joshua, See, I have given into thine hand, Jericho, and the king thereof, and the mighty men of valour. And ye shall compass the city, all ye men of war, and go around about the city once. Thus shalt thou do six days. And seven priests shall bear before the ark seven trumpets of rams' horns: and the seventh day ye shall compass the city seven times, and the priests shall blow with the trumpets."

Joshua: Moses' minister would become God's leader for the children of Israel and go over Jordan to all the land given to him. The city of Jericho was shut up and Joshua was directed how to get into claim the city ofJericho.

Joshua and his men of war would go around Jericho once for six days. We are reminded that Jesus and His followers would go around the city of Jersusalem and directed how to spread the news of an heavenly city prepared for them.

Joshua would instruct seven priests to blow the trumpets of rams' horns. We are reminded that Jesus and His followers come into the city of Jerusalem and be directed to ride an humble creature; the donkey as instrumental in providing Jesus to enter as the earthly King of God's world.

Prayer: Dear God, we respect Your Wise Creatures; the rams who supplied the horns to be blasted by priests; to cause the walls of Jericho to fall. We respect the trumpets from the ram's horns sounding the call of victory for Your Son,Jesus Christ, and His triumphant entry into Your heavenly kingdom.

July 11 Wise Creatures

Scripture Text: I Kings 4: 22, 23

"And Solomon's provision for one day was thirty measures of fine flour, and three score measures of meal, ten fat oxen, and twenty oxen out of the pastures, and an hundred sheep, beside harts, and roebucks, and fallowdeer, and fatted fowl."

King Solomon was recognized for his wisdom. His wisdom supported his kingdom with enough provisions for one day. This passage would be interesting to an avid hunter of today! Let us base our devotional today on the following three Wise Creatures: hart, roebuck, and fallowdeer.

The hart was common in ancient times and were depicted on the monuments of Egypt. The hart was the adult male deer. Thus the hart as a wise creature was the protector and provider for its family.

The roebuck was also common in the Old World and they were recognized for their short antlers. Thus the roebuck as a wise creature was not easily entangled in the thickets of the desert.

The fallowdeer was common in the Near and Middle East. They were recognized for their white spotted summer coat and broad flat antlers. Thus the fallowdeer as a wise creature was able to survive with its own defensive antlers!

Prayer: Dear God, we respect Your Wise Creatures; the deer who supplied their skins and flat antlers for King Solomon's provisions.

July 12 Wise Creatures

Scripture Text: II Chronicles 9: 23, 24

"And all the kings of the earth sought the presence of Solomon, to hear his wisdom that God had put in his heart. And they brought every man his present, vessels of silver, vessels of gold, and rainment, harness, and spices, and horses, and mules, a rate year by year."

We continue to read of the wide spreading of King Solomon's wisdom and how other kings brought their treasures; including horses and mules.

King Solomon had four thousand stalls for horses (9:25). These Wise Creatures of God presented by other kings of the earth would pull chariots for the horsemen. The horses would provide the speedy transportation needed by the wise King Solomon to reign over all the kings (9:26).

King Solomon had enough vessels of silver and vessels of gold to load up mules brought by other kings, a rate year by year. These Wise Creatures of God presented by other kings of the earth would carry the wealth of the land needed by the wise King Solomon to build up to and all around the other kingdoms; even the land of the Phillistines, and to the border of Egypt (9: 26).

Prayer: Dear God, we respect Your Wise Creatures; the horse and the mule. They pulled the chariots and carried the supplies for the expanding kingdom of wise King Solomon.

July 13 Wise Creatures

Scripture Text: Job 40: 15, 19

"Behold now behemoth, which I made with thee; he eateth grass as an ox...he is the chief of the ways of God..."

Job was recognized as the greatest of all the men of the east as he had seven thousand sheep, and three thousand camels, five hundred yoke of oxen, and five hundred she asses (1: 3). We are familiar with his affliction and patience (Chapters 2-12) and his repentance (Chapters 13-36). We read from Chapters 37-40 the words spoken by God to Job. The question we read that Job asked of God in Chapter 40 was: "What shall I answer thee?" (40: 4)

God reminds Job to depend on His strength and compares that strength to one of His Wise Creatures; the behemoth. This creature is compared to the hippopotamus. This wise creature eats of the grass as an ox; therefore preparing the body to be of great strength. The behemoth's loins, sinews are massive, and even the bones are as strong as brass and iron (40: 18)

God reminds Job to depend on His power and compares that power over one of His wise, strong behemoths. This beast compared to the hippo is the "chief ot the ways of God" but is not exempt from the approach of God's powerful sword (40:19).

Prayer: Dear God, we respect Your wise creature, the behemoth, known for its strength and power as chief of the ways of God. but not exempt from God's omnipotence.

July 14 Wise Creatures

Scripture Text: Psalm 8: 6-8

"Thou madest him to have dominion over the works of thy hands; thou hast put all things under his feet: All sheep and oxen, yea, and the beasts of the field; The fowl of the air, and the fish of the sea, and whatsoever passeth throught the paths of the sea."

The Psalmist and King David wrote many praises to God and thanked Him for giving man dominion over creatures such as the fowl of the air and the fish of the sea.

The fowl of the air are Wise Creatures of God even though man has been given dominion over them. We are reminded of their intricate nests and they can sing!

The fish of the sea are Wise Creatures of God even though man has been given dominion over them. We are reminded of their wide area and they can swim!

Prayer: Dear God, we respect Your Wise Creatures of the air and sea.

They have their territory and share their wisdom in recoginzing provisions and protection from You.

PEARLS OF WISDOM

July 15 Wise Creatures 207

Scripture Text: Psalm 19: 9, 10

"The fear of the Lord is clean, enduring for ever: the judgments of the Lord are true and righteous altogether. More to be desired are they than gold, yea, than much fine gold: sweeter than honey and the honeycomb."

The Psalmist David is recognizing the omnipotence of the Lord. He compares the fear of the Lord to be desired; sweeter than honey and sweeter than the honeycomb.

Honey was part of John the Baptist's daily diet and it was known for its' sweetness. We are reminded that we collect honey from bees. Bees are wise as they collect the pollen.

Honecombs were part of John The Baptist's daily storage and it was known for its' thickness and being sweet. We are reminded that we find the storage from bees. Bees are wise as the store the honey.

Prayer: Dear God, we respect the wise creature; one of Your bees and how they are able to produce and provide honey.

July 16 Wise Creatures

Scripture Text: Psalm 23: 1, 2

The Lord is my shepherd, I shall not want. He maketh me to lie down in green pastures: He leads me by the still waters.

King David, a shepherd praises His Lord for there is nothing he wants . He knows His sheep just as the Lord knows His flock.

Sheep lie down in green pastures. In their wisdom they stay close to where they will be nourished. We are reminded that each one of us are as one of His sheep waiting to be found and to receive the best from our Lord and Shepherd.

Sheep are lead by the still waters. In their wisdom they follow closely to where they will be quenched of thiirst. We are reminded that each one of us are as one of His sheep waiting to join the flock and receive the best from our Lord and Shepherd.

Prayer: Dear God, we respect Your wise creature; sheep who give us the best example of how to follow their leader and stay with the flock.

July 17 Wise Creatures

Scripture Text: Psalm 50: 9-11

"I will take no bullock out of thy house, nor he goats out of the folds. For every beast of the forest is mine, and the cattle upon a thousand hills. "

King David writes of God's power, possession and preservation of the entire world. David's Kingdom of Israel is powerful and He owns bullock and goats that the Lord needs not possess. David is reminded that His Lord has an abundance of Wise Creatures of the forest and of the hills.

The beast of the forest could be the many species of deer. The forest is their choice of habitation due to rivers, trees, and grass. We are reminded that God has created deer in abundance and allows man to either possess or preserve these Wise Creatures of the forest.

The cattle of the hills could be the many species of bullocks. The hills is their choice of habitation due to open ranges with creeks, trees, and grass. We are reminded that God has created bullocks in abundance and allows man to either possess or preserve these Wise Creatures of the hills.

Prayer: Dear God, we respect the Wise Creatures of the forest and the hills; such as the deer and the bullock for their powerful size, and strength.

July 18 Wise Creatures

Scripture Text: Psalm 100: 1-3

"Make a joyful noise unto the Lord, all ye lands. Serve the Lord with gladness: come into His presence with singing. Know ye that the Lord, He is God: it is He that has made us, and not we ourselves; we are His people, and the sheep of His pasture. "

King David was a shepherd as a boy. Once a shepherd, always a shepherd. No doubt King David used many of his skills as a shepherd leading his flock to lead the people of his Kingdom of Israel. He served his sheep while constantly remembering the creator of these wise sheep who knew their master.

The Lord is King David's shepherd. The Great Shepherd daily calls out to His angels to come into His presence with singing. We are reminded that as His sheep we are a flock that is surrounded by the Lord's heavenly hosts singing 'alleluia". The Lord's pasture is full of joyful noise; including the praises of His shepherds and the audible sounds of responses from His flock.

The Lord is King David's leader. The Great Shepherd daily calls out to His Musicians to come into His presence with singing. We are reminded that as His sheep, we are a flock that is herded together by the shepherd singing praises to their creator. The Lord's pasture is full of joyful noise, in thanksgiving for the flock in the shepherd's care.

Prayer: Dear God, we respect Your Wise Creatures; the sheep who hear and follow Your voice and the voices of Your shepherds chosen to tend to the flock.

July 19 Wise Creatures

Scripture Text: Psalm 104: 24-27

"O Lord, how manifold are Thy works: in wisdom has Thou made them all: the earth is full of Thy riches. So is this great and wide sea, wherein are things creeping innumerable, both small and great beasts. There go the ships: there is that leviathan, whom Thou has made to play therein. These all wait upon Thee; that Thou Mayest give them their meat in due season."

King and Psalmist David writes about the wise creature of the sea. Of all the innumerable creatures of the sea; both small and great, David writes about the playful great Leviathan. In the Hebrew language this great creature was called the 'coiled one'. We read that this wise beast could be our primeval dragon, or a sea monster, or a crocodile. We are also referred to the whale.

The Lord in His wisdom allowed the great creatures of the sea to be feared but also observed as playful among man's creation of ships. We are reminded that the Lord in His wisdom created the great creatures of the sea to grow and be provided meat.

The Lord in His wisdom allowed the great creatures of the sea to wait upon Him, and within the numerous man made ships. We are reminded that the Lord in His wisdom created the great creatures of the sea to roam and even rule the sea.

Prayer: Dear God, we respect the Wise Creatures of the sea as they show us how to depend on Your provisions and wait for Your power within the world of the sea.

July 20 Wise Creatures

Scripture Text: Proverbs 6: 5

"Deliver thyself as a roe from the hand of the hunter, and as a bird from the hand of the fowler."

Proverbs was written by Solomon, the son of David, the King of Israel. These wise sayings serve as instructions, knowledge, and understanding the word of our Lord God. Within these proverbs we are commanded to deliver or save ourselves from the hand of the hunter or the fowler.

The Lord created the wise creature; the roe to possess the speed, agility, and the determination to survive from the hand of the hunter. The Lord created the wise human to possess the ability to create hunting tools to provide themselves by feasting off the land. We are reminded that the roe often times out runs the hunter.

The Lord created the wise creature, the bird to possess the speed, agility, and the determination to survive from the hand of the fowler. The Lord created the wise human to possess the ability to create hunting tools to provide themselves by feasting off the land and air. We are reminded that the bird often times flies far enough away from the fowler.

Prayer: Dear God, we respect Your Wise Creatures; the roe and the bird because You provided them survival skills and provided enough meat for Your other creatures and Your humans.

July 21 Wise Creatures

Scripture Text: Proverbs 28: 15

"As a roaring lion, and a ranging bear; so is a wicked ruler over the poor people."

King Solomon wrote with the great wisdom he was noted for within his kingdom by surrounding rulers. He warns against wicked rulers and compares them to these Wise Creatures; a roaring lion and a ranging bear.

God made the lion strong, often called the ruler of the jungle. It's mighty roar can bring upon fear among the other creatures. It's mighty roar can bring respect among other lions. We are reminded of how Satan as a roaring lion; roams around, tempts to lead the sinner away from the Lord.

God made the bear to be able to stand tall , often called the giant of the forest. It's mighty stance can bring upon fear among other creatures. It's mighty growl can bring respect among other bears. We are reminded of how Satan as a ranging bear; lumbers around, and imposes on lives of those trying to follow the Lord.

Prayer: Dear God, we respect Your Wise Creatures, the lion and the bear. We know You created them to protect their own but they also choose to look out for theselves. They have the power to rule the jungle or forest.

July 22 Wise Creatures

Scripture Text: Proverbs 30: 24- 28

"There be four things which are little upon the earth, but they are exceeding wise: The ants are a people not strong, yet they prepare their meat in the summer. The conies are but a feeble folk, yet they make their houses in the rocks. Thelocusts have no kings, yet go they forth all of them by bands. The spider taketh hold with her hands, and is in kings' palaces."

God's servant, King Solomon shared his wisdom to all his people; whether great of small. The four little exceeding Wise Creatures are examples for us to follow.

The ant with its thin legs and narrow body is able to carry food to a shallow nest. Their days of summer are busy in preparation for they work in the heat. We witness an army of ants working together.

The conies with their short legs good for hopping are able to climb out of danger and make their houses in the rocks. We witness a hutch of conies finding shelter in crevices close together.

The locusts have wings to fly in swarms with no obvious leader. We witness them staying close together not inhibited by man who fear for their crops and land.

The spiders have hands to weave webs and have no specific home. We witness them producing intricate webs even in palaces.

Prayer: Dear God, we respect your little Wise Creatures, ants, conies, locusts, and spiders. They protect themselves with work, determination, team effort, and production.

July 23 Wise Creatures

Scripture Text: Isaiah 11: 6

"The wolf also shall dwell with the lamb, and the leopard shall lie down with the kid; and the calf and the young lion and the fatling together; and a little child shall lead them. "

The Prophet Isaiah writes a parable about the kingdom of Christ. The Wise Creatures featured in this parable are examples of how to live in harmony and be lead by a little child who has no prejudices.

Picture the strong and quick wolf living with the gentle and casual lamb without creating fear to the flock of sheep. We are reminded of infant Jesus, who would some day be the Great Shepherd, being born to dwell here on earth with the strong and gentle of God's kingdom.

Picture the strong and quick leopard lying down with the helpless kid without any worries by the heifer or the bull. We are reminded of the child Jesus, who would some day be the Great Teacher, being found at the temple with the strong and powerful builders of God's kingdom.

Picture the young, hungry, self-efficient lion being found together with the care-free fatling without any worries of it's life. We are reminded of the youth Jesus, who would someday be the Great Ruler, being found in the wilderness with the weapon carrying warriors of God's kingdom.

Prayer: Dear God, we respect the Wise Creatures of Your world. The dwelling together of the wolf and the lamb, the groups of leopards mixed with the kid, and the lion found with the fatling is a picture of harmony, peace on God's earth.

July 24 Wise Creatures

Scripture Text: Ezekiel 17: 3

"...A great eagle with great wings, longwinged, full of feathers, which had divers colours, came unto Lebanon, and took the highest branch of the cedar."

The Prophet Ezekiel wrote many descriptive visions; parables. This particular one of a majestic, wise creature of God; the eagle is a valuable lessons in the provisions for the Kingdom of God. We are familiar with Jesus, the Great Teacher teaching from the prophets such as Ezekiel; providing lessons in preparation for the coming of the Kingdom of God.

The great eagle was provided with great, longwinged wings. Their strength and endurance during flight were visible even high above Lebanon's forests cedar. We can follow the example of the eagle and allow the Trinity to provide us with strength and endurance to be a part of the team of providers for the Kingdom of God.

The great eagle was equipped with feathers of divers color. Their beauty and majesty during ascension; landing were visible even amidst the relocation of the highest branch of the cedar. We can learn from the eagle how the land of God's people can work together for the Kingdom of God.

Prayer: Dear God, we respect the power and majest of Your wise creature; the eagle who teaches us to be provided, equipped and sent to prepare the way for Your Kingdom.

July 25 Wise Creatures

Scripture Text: Daniel 6: 16

"Then the king commanded , and they brought Daniel, and cast him into the den of lions. Now the king spake and said unto Daniel, Thy God whom thou servest continually, he will deliver thee."

The Prophet Daniel was very familiar with King Darius' creed that he joined others in signing; a command that no one would for thirty days ask a petition of God of any man besides the King Darius; lest they be cast into the lion's den. We learn from Daniel's miraculous protection and deliverance by God even when he chose to disobey another human.

God allowed His servant Daniel to disobey King Darius and his creed. We are reminded that we have the freedom to choose. We either obey or disobey man"s creeds or laws. Are we willing to be cast into prison (often compared to the lion's den) because of our disobedience toward another human who is not preparing us for the Kingdom of God?

God allowed His servant Daniel to share his faith with King Darius. We are reminded that we have the freedom to choose We either follow or ignore man's creeds or laws. Are we willing to be surrounded by other prisoners (often labeled has lions) because of our punishment by humans who are not preparing for the Kingdom of God?

Prayer: Dear God, we are reminded of your wise, strong, and often dangerous creature; the lion. We learn from Daniel's encounter with the lion's and their den, that God protects us from human selfishness and punishments that could easily heed us from preparing for the Kingdom of God.

July 26 Wise Creatures

Scripture Text: Joel 2: 22

"Be not afraid, ye beasts of the field: for the pastures of the wilderness do spring, for the tree beareth fruit, the fig tree and the vine do yield their strength."

The Prophet Joel writes of the coming of God's kingdom and pleads to the followers of earthly kings, joining the sinful ways of men. One such sinful way was the worshipping of earthly kings and recognizing that only serving and worshipping God prepares the way for a ripe and fruitful field (God's Kingdom).

God's beasts of the field will feed from pastures of the wilderness. These wise beasts of the pastures that spring, drink freely from the rivers, ponds, and puddles. We are reminded that we are to drink freely from God's bountiful water of the wilderness.

God's beasts of the field will feed from trees and vines that bearfruit and yield their strength. These wise beasts of the pastures depend on the fruit and the vine of the trees, bushes, and plants. We are reminded that we are to take in freely from God's bountiful supply of food.

Prayer: Dear God we respect Your beasts of the field and their dependence on the pastures being bountiful.

July 27 Wise Creatures

Scripture Text: Isaiah 13: 9, 10

"Behold, the day of the Lord cometh, cruel both with wrath and fierce anger, to lay the land desolate: and he shall destroy the sinners thereof out of it. For the stars of heaven and the constellations thereof shall not give their light: the sun shall be darkened in his going forth, and the moon shall not cause her light to shine."

The Prophet Isaiah wrote about the desolation and burden of the powerful kingdom of Babylon and how the Lord gave him a vision of what was to come: destruction for the sinful nation. The stars and the constellations would not give light. How devastating that must have been for the people who depended on the light to travel. How important these constellations were to the point they were named by the Greek and included names of Wise Creatures.

Our christian calendar depicts in the zodiac sign for December

22nd to January 19th: Capricorn. This constellation gives us a picture of an horned goat. We recognize the significance of the sacrifical role of goats; Wise Creatures that learned to follow their shepherd. My prayer for those born under this zodiac sign would be that they follow their Great Shepherd who leads us into His fold.

Our christian calendar depicts in the zodiac sign for January 20th to February 18th: Aquarius. This constellation is located in the equalatorial region of the Southern Hemisphere. We recognize the location of this zodiac sign close to the sun. My prayer for those born under this zodiac sign would be that they stay close to their Lord; the only Son of God.

Our christian calendar depicts in the zodiac sign for February 19th to March 20th: Pisces. This constellation gives us a picture of a fish. We recognize the significance of the provisional role of fish; Wise Creatures of the sea that travel in schools. My prayer for those under this zodiac sign would be that they become fishermen for Jesus, the Man of Galilee.

Prayer: Dear God, we respect the Wise Creatures, the goat, other humans, and the fish as they are reminders shown in the heavenly constellations of Your omnipotent power.

July 28 Wise Creatures

Scripture Text: Isaiah 13: 10

"For the stars of heaven and the constellations thereof shall not give their light...."

We continue to ponder Isaiah's prophecy and the devastation created when there are no heavenly lights to guide travelers.

Our christian calendar year depicts in the zodiac sign for March 21st to April 19th: Ram. This constellation gives us a picture of a male sheep. We recognize the significance of the sacrificial role of the male sheep. My prayer for those under this zodiac sign would be that they would be willing to sacrifice their time, talents, and whole being for the coming of the Greatest Sacrifice; our Lord, Jesus Christ.

Our christian calendar year dpicts in the zodiac sign for April 20th to May 20th: Taurus. This constellation gives us a picture of a bull. We recognize the significance of the strong provisional role of the bull. My prayer for those under this zodiac sign would be that they become strong providers through the omnipotent power of the Trinity.

Our christian calendar year depicts in the zodiac sign for May 21st to June 20th: Gemini. This constellation gives us a picture of twins. We recognize the significance of witnessing and working in twos of humans. My prayer for those under this zodiac sign would be that they become witnessing and working partners for the Kingdom of the Trinity.

Prayer: Dear God, we respect the wise sheep, bull, and twins as they are all found staying and working together within Your Kingdom.

July 29 Wise Creatures

Scripture Text: Isaiah 13: 10

"For the stars of heaven and the constellations thereof shall not give their light..."

The people of the Prophet Isaiah's time depended on the lights of heaven as they followed their leaders; earthly kings. Isaiah's prophecy included news of a greater kingdom and the destruction of those who followed other gods. Let us continue to ponder the constellations that provide light to guide us.

Our christian calendar year depicts in the zodiac sign for June 21st to July 22nd: Crab. This constellation gives us a picture of a clawed sea creature. We recognize the significance of being properly equipped for survival. My prayer for those under this zodiac sign to be properly equipped for the coming of God's KIngdom.

Our christian calendar year depicts in the zodiac sign for July 23rd to August 22nd: Leo. This constellation gives us a picture of the king of the jungle. We recognize the significance of strong rulers, kings within the earthly kingdom. My prayer for those under this zodiac sign to be strong rulers with one motive: bring all those under their leadership to the strongest ruler, leader; our Heavenly Father, God.

Our christian calendar year depicts in the zodiac sign for August 23rd to September 22nd: Virgin. This constellation gives us a picture of an adult female. We recognize the significance of Jesus' mother; Mary and how she gave birth to the saviour of the world. My prayer for those under this zodiac sign to mother the children under their care to prepare them to follow their Heavenly Father.

Prayer: Dear God, we respect the wise crab, lion, and virgin as they strive to be equipped, provide leadership and motherly roles for the salvation of the whole world.

July 30 Wise Creatures

Scripture: Isaiah 13: 10

"For the stars of heaven and the constellations thereof shall not give their light..."

The Prophet Isaiah depended on the light of the constellations As we conclude the pondering of the zodiac signs May we let our lights shine.

Our christian calendar year depicts in the zodiac sign for September 23rd to October 22nd: Libra. This constellations gives us a picture of a balance; weighing scales. We recognize the significance of measurement in the time before Christ (B.C). My prayer for those under this zodiac sign to be that they measure their time, talents, treasures according to God's Kingdom.

Our christian calendar year depicts in the zodiac sign for October 23rd to November 21st: Scorpio. This constellation gives us a picture of a scorpion. We recognize the significance of the protective sting of the scorpion against the enemies of the sea. My prayer for those under this zodiac sign to be u der the protection against Satan's sting.

Our christian calendar year depicts in the zodiac sign for November 22nd to December 21st: Sagitarius. This constellation gives us a picture of an archer. We recognize the significance of the equipped hunter. My prayer for those under this zodiac sign to be equipped hunters for God's Kingdom.

Prayer: Dear God, we respect the wise measurers, scorpions, and archers with the same motive; to prepare the world for Your just, protective, and provisional Heavenly kingdom

July 31 Wise Creatures

Scripture Text: Matthew 19: 4

"And he answered and said unto them, 'Have ye not read, that he which made them at the beginning made them male and female?"Jesus was in the midst of the multitudes of followers; those being healed by Him. There were those who followed and attempted to tempt Him! They were challenging Jesus and twisting the law. Jesus answers with a question that proves that we can become Wise Creatures.

Have I had a chance to read many messages(including holiday cards) from my sister, Sue! Her wisdom shows in her illustration for the July theme: Wise Creatures.

Prayer: Thank You, Wise God, for allowing Your Son to lead us; Your children to follow the wisdom of Your creatures.

August 1 Wise Words

Scripture Text: Genesis 1:1

"In the beginning God created the heaven and the earth."

The Prophet Moses is the first wise author of the Holy Bible and starts out with words often used today by wise authors: "In the beginning". We recognize the significance of this introduction to what is often called the Holy Scriptures, the history book, and even the christian manual.

Other names for this introduction are: the Pentateuch (five books), The Torah Law, and five distinctive titles (Genesis, Exodus, Leviticus ,Numbers, and Deuternonomy). For the next few devotionals we will share Moses' wisdom in each of these first five books.

Our Holy Bible starts ... in the beginning ....in the first book: Genesis; or translated by the Greeks as "origin of the world and man" . The reader of Genesis shares in Moses' wisdom to record history and law to begin the Holy Bible we use as a manual. There are fifty chapters in Genesis with the familiar historical accounts of the creation of Adam and Eve to Jacob's blessings and Joseph's comfort. We are reminded that in the beginnning of each day on God's earth we are to bless and comfort others in preparation for His created Heaven.

The second book is Exodus; or translated "departure". Moses recalls how the Israelites departed from Egypt. The reader of Exodus shares in Moses' wisdom to record a census, history, and law. There are forty chapters in Exodus with the familiar historical accounts of the flight of the Israelites to the building of the temple. We are reminded that in the traveling through each day on God's earth we are to build and gather others in preparation for His created Kingdom.

The third book is Leviticus; or translated "law of the priest". Moses lists the rules, regulations for the tribe of Israel. The reader of Leviticus shares in Moses' wisdom to organize the rules and laws.

There are twenty seven chapters in Leviticus with the familiar listings of rules for the builders and inhabitants of the holy tabernacle. We are reminded that in the starting of each day on God's earth we are to build and prepare to live upon His created earth.

Prayer: Dear God, we learn from the wisdom of Moses and the first three books of his introduction, recording, and organizing the beginning of the Holy Bible; our manual in preparation for God's Heavenly KIngdom.

August 2 Wise Words

Scripture Text: Numbers 1: 1

"And the Lord spake unto Moses in the wilderness of Sinai, in the tabernacle of the congregation, on the first day of the second month, in the second year after they were come out of land of Egypt..."

Moses continues to be God's prophet and recalls the formation of what we could call the first census! In his wisdom, Moses lists names of males by their "polls" (1:2) and adds up the number of children and their families. Numbers has thirty six chapters with the familiar rituals and rites important to the tribe of Israel. We are reminded that each day of each month we are to come out of the sinful nature of our earthly bodies.

The fifth book of the Pentateuch is Deuteronomy; translated "second law" . Moses recalls the rules and regulations for a new; second law inspired by God's omnipotent power over His people. Deuteronomy has thirty three chapters with the familiar parable of the eagle (32: 11) to pass on to their generations. We are reminded that each day of each month we are to listen, share, pass down the familiar parables; lessons of life to prepare us for the beginning of God's Heavenly Kingdom.

Prayer: Dear God, we learn from the wisdom of Moses that where there is a congregation; group of followers, there needs to be a census, a compilation of rules and regulations and the passing down of parables (lessons) to prepare us for God Kingdom.

August 3 Wise Words

Scripture Text: Joshua 1: 1

"Now after the death of Moses the servant of the Lord it came to pass, that the Lord spoke unto Joshua, Moses' minister...."

We begin the next several books of the Holy Bible with Joshua. He writes as a minister...perhaps in the form of sermons, tabernacle talks, and counselling sessions. His wisdom is familiar to us as he records within twenty four chapters the promises and instructions he receives from God. We are reminded to daily become familiar to God's promises and instructions.

The next book of the Old Testament is: Judges. Judah becomes the leader upon Joshua's death. He and his brother Simeon fought against the Canaanites; attempting to drive them out of their kingdom. God had other plans....as recorded in Judges' twenty one chapters. Judah's wisdom is familiar as he records the familiar fate of Gideon's army (7:20), and the desolation of the tribe of Benjamin. We are daily reminded to remember the fate and desolation of the unsaved.

Judges is followed by the book of : Ruth. The judges ruled and there was a famine in the land. Ruth would be recognized as a wise follower of God and spoke some inspiring words out of desperation to save her family from famine. Within the four chapters of Ruth we find recorded Ruth's familiar words of wisdom; displaying her faith and loyalty to Her God the provider. We are daily reminded to show our faith and loyalty to One Heavenly, Holy God.

Prayer: Dear God, we learn from the wisdom of Judah, Judges, and Ruth to daily take in the promises and instructions of God and to be loyal and faithful to Him.

August 4 Wise Words

Scripture Text: I Samuel 2: 1

"And Hannah prayed, and said, My heart rejoiceth in the Lord, mine horn is exalted in the Lord: my mouth is enlarged over mine enemies; because I rejoice in thy salvation."

Hannah's prayer to God follows the birth of Samuel. I Samuel and II Samuel are also called the First and Second Book of The Kings. Their thirty one and twenty four chapters contain familiar words of wisdom such as Hannah's; displaying her faith in conceiving a son and naming him Samuel; (asked of the Lord) (1:20). We are reminded of how we daily seek God's guidance in our prayers.

I Kings and II Kings follow with twenty three and twenty five chapters. I Kings contains familiar words of wisdom from prominent kings and prophets such as David, Solomon, Queen Sheba (chapter 10), and Elijah (chapter 17).

They stress their worshipping no other gods such as Baalim but the One Lord, God (chapter 18). We are reminded of how we daiy seek the One and Only Lord, God as we pray.

I Chronicles and II Chronicles continue the theme of serving Our God with familiar words of wisdom tucked between the twenty nine and thirty thirty six chapters that remind us of those men (starting with Adam) of the first family tree. They stress their allegiance to no other gods but the One Father, God. Within their words of wisdom the nations and their kings recognized their prosperity coming from their Holy God.

(I Chronicles 4: 10, 11:1, 16:4, and II Chronicles 3:1, 17:3).

Their words of wisdom also include the dedication of rulers and tabernacles to the Holy God.

(I Chronicles 6: 31, 32, 29: 23, and II Chronicles 29: 15, 34: 13, 14).

We are reminded of how we daily proclaim our allegiance to our Heavenly Father and dedicate daily our tabernacles to our One, Holy God.

Prayer: Dear God, we learn words of wisdom from Hannah, Adam, David, Solomon, and King Hezekiah as they stress their allegiance and dedicate their tabernacles to You, Holy God.

August 5 Wise Words

Scripture Text: Ezra 7: 6

"This Ezra went up from Babylon; and he was a ready scribe in the law of Moses, which the Lord of Israel had given; and the king granted him all his request, according to the hand of the Lord his God upon him."

Ezra the Priest was commissioned by King Artaxerxes and sent to Jerusalem. He was ready; prepared in the law of Moses. His request involved using his wisdom to delegate companions to assist in the traveling to Jerusalem and encouraging the people to reform ie. strange marriages (chapter 10). We are reminded to keep the Law of the Lord and be ready to reform.

Jerusalem remains important in the book of Nehemiah. King Artaxerxes sent Nehemiah to build the wall of Jeruasalem. Nehemiah was the king's cupbearer and encouraged the people to follow the covenant. His covenant included a dedication of the wall (Chapter 12). We are reminded to keep a covenant and dedicate all in the name of God.

Jerusalem remains important in the book of Esther. Esther is made queen because she was found in King Ahasuerus' favor. In her wisdom Esther was able to set Mordecai over the house of Haman; who would save the Jews (Chapter 8).

Prayer: Dear God we learn wisdom from Ezra, Nehemiah, and Esther. as they encouraged others to follow only the Holy God and to dedicate their lives.

August 6 Wise Words

Scripture Text: Job 1:1

"There was a man in the land of Uz, whose name was Job; and that man was perfect and upright, and one that feared God and eschewed evil."

Job, a servant of God is "plagued" by Satan who tempts those who fear God and hate evil. In his debates with prophets and priests, Job finally shows his wisdom by testifying that he is only perfect and upright because of God's power (chapter 29). We are reminded that we need to seek daily God's preservation.

God's preservation and His followers delight in following His law is the theme of the book of Psalms written and inspired by the Wise Words of David. David as a shepherd, a king, and a writer of Psalm shows wisdom throughout the entire 150 chapters. David writes Wise Words in the form of prayers, songs, such as the familiar Psalms: 23:1-6, 27: 1, 46:1, 66:1, 75: 1, 119:169, 121:1, and 139: 23,24. We are reminded that we need to pray daily for God is praise worthy!

God's power and His followers need to follow His law is the theme of the book of Proverbs which contains the wisdom of Solomon. Solomon as a man of God, full of wisdom, proverbs, lessons to learn from God. Solomon expresses promises, prayers, and songs such as the familiar Proverbs: 3:5,6, 8: 11, 11:30. 17:1 , and 22:6. We are reminded of the instructions given by God to His servants to share with others.

Prayer: Dear God, we learn wisdom from Job, David and Solomon who are Your servants in preserving Your Kingdom.

August 7 Wise Words

Scripture Text: Ecclesiastes 1: 1,2

"The words of the Preacher, the son of David, king in Jerusalem, Vanity of vanities", saith the Preacher, "vanity of vanities, all is vanity."

Ecclesiastes is the Preacher for God and recognizes that all is vanity. We are familiar with the Wise Words of Ecclesiastes in 3: 5,6, 7: 13, 9: 16-18, 11:1, and 12: 13,14. We are reminded all is in vain without daily encounters with God.

King Solomon who shares Wise Words in Proverbs now shares his wisdom in Song of Solomon. We are familiar with the Wise Words within this song of love in 1: 9, 2: 1-4, 3: 9,10, 4:16, and 8: 11-14. We are reminded all is in love as we daily encounter God.

The Prophet Isaiah shares Wise Words of prophecy; of the birth, life, death, resurrection and coming again of our Lord, Jesus Christ. We are familiar with his Wise Words in 1:1, 9: 6,7, 11: 1-4, 26: 1-4, 28: 16, 35, 6-8, 55:1, and 66: 1, 2. We are reminded all is for our Holy God as we encounter Him daily.

Prayer: Dear God, we learn wisdom from Ecclesiastes, Solomon, and Isaiah about Your omnipotent power and how we can serve You, and Your Trinity Team.

August 8 Wise Words

Scripture Text: Jeremiah 1: 7

"But the Lord said unto me, Say not I am a child: for thou shall go to all that I shall send thee, and whatever I command thee thou shall speak."

The Prophet Jeremiah was commanded to prophecy to the nations and speak of the carrying the captive of Jerusalem. We are familiar with his Wise Words in 2:5, 12:1, 18: 1-8, 26:2, 36: 16, 50: 33,34, and 52: 31,32. We are reminded our daily estate is in the hands of our One and Holy God.

The Prophet Jeremiah continues his prophecy in the book of Lamentions. We are familiar with his Wise Words in 3: 22. 23, and 5: 19. We are reminded our daily fate is in the hands of our One and Holy God.

The Priest Ezekiel recalls vivid visions and includes Wise Words in 1: 4, 3:1, 8:2, 12: 1,2, 20: 15, 34: 23-26, 40: 2-5, and 48: 29. We are reminded our daily portion i from the only One and Holy God.

Prayer: Dear God, we learn wisdom from Jeremiah and Ezekiel the prophets of our daily estate, fate, and portions from You, our One and Holy God.

August 9 Wise Words

Scripture Text: Daniel 1: 5-7

"And the king appointed them a daily provision of the king's meat, and of the wine which he drank: so nourishing them three years, that at the end thereof they might stand before the king. Now among these were of the children of Judah, Daniel, Hananiah, Mishael, and Azariah: Unto whom the prince of the eunuchs gave names: for he gave Daniel the name of Belteshazar, and to Hananiah of Shadrach; and to Mishael of eshach, and to Azariah of Abednego."

We are familiar with the wisdom of Daniel and his friends. They were given knowledge and skill in all learning and wisdom. (1:17). Included was the interpretation of the king's dreams. We are familiar with the wisdom of Daniel even when he was cast into the lion's den. (6:16). Daniel sees glorious visions (10: 10-12) and (12:5-7). We are reminded our daily dreams or visions include our Heavenly and Holy God.

Prophet Hosea expresses words of wisdom concerning there being no truth, nor mercy, nor knowledge of God in the land (4:1). He pleas for his followers to return to the Lord (6:1) and to sow in righteousness, reap in mercy..(10:12). We are reminded our daily knowlege or truth include our Heavenly and Holy God.

Prophet Joel expresses words of wisdom concerning there being fields wasted, wine dried, trees withered and the importance of priests, ministers of the altar to repent. (1:14). We are reminded our daily repentance should inlcude our Heavenly and Holy God.

Prayer: Dear God, we learn wisdom from Daniel, Hosea, and Joel, and to be recipients of daily visions, truths and repentance are most important to You, our Holy Lord, God.

August 10 Wise Words

Scripture Text: Amos 1:1

"The words of Amos, who was among the herdmen of Tekoa, which he saw concerning Israel in the days of Ozziah king of Judah, and in the days of Jerobaom, the son of Joash king of Israel, two years before the earthquake."

The herdsman and a prophet, Amos shares his Wise Words and how the Lord mentions such a great number of transgressions of His nations. We are familiar with Amos' Wise Words; 3:3&4, 4:5, and 9:6. We are reminded how we are to allow daily our Lord, God to correct us from our great number of transgressions.

Obadiah joins the group of Minor Prophets; ambassador being sent among the heathen; 1:1, and 1: 15. The kingdom shall be the Lord's (1:21). We are reminded how we are to allow daily our Lord, God to correct us from our great number of failures.

Jonah was sent to cry against the wickedness of Nineveh. We are familiar with how he ended up in the belly of a great fish (1: 17), and when he was released was displeased with the Lord because of his grief towards the city (4:5). We are reminded how we are to allow daily our Lord, God to prepare us for greater number of successes.

Prayer: Dear God, we learn wisdom from Amos, Obadiah, and Jonah as we allow You to correct and prepare us for His kingdom.

August 11 Wise Words

Scripture Text: Micah 1: 1

"The word of the Lord that came to Micah the Morasthite in the days of Jotham, Ahaz, and Hezekiah, kings of Judah, which he saw concerning Samaria and Jerusalem."

Micah joins the minor prophets in sharing wisdom concerning the expression against evil and the vision that all people are to walk in the name of the Lord (4:5). and to follow the Lord's requirements (6:8). We are reminded that God intends to allow each one of us to build strong cities amidst the Lord's requirements.

Nahum, the Elkoshite recalls in his words of wisdom write about a jealous God especially of His adversaries. We are familiar with such expressions of God's power nce (1:7, and 3:14). We are thusreminded that God is the Lord of strength.

The Prophet Habakkuk continues the use of Wise Words to share what has been seen and heard among the heathen. We are familiar his words in Chapter 2:1, 2:18, and 3: 18 & 19.

Prayer: Dear God we learn wisdom from Micah, Nahum, and Habakkuk as they share the power of their God, Lord .

August 12 Wise Words

Scripture Text: Zephaniah 1: 7

"Hold thy peace at the presence of the Lord God: for the day of the Lord is at hand; for the Lord hath prepared a sacrifice, he hath bid his guests."

The Prophet Zephaniah continues the cry to repent. His Wise Words include familiar promises of God: 1: 14, 2: 7, 3: 9 and 3: 15. We are reminded that only our Holy God prepared a sacrifice (His Son) to bid us (His guests).

The Prophet Haggai echoes the cry to repent. His Wise Words include familiar performances of God: 1: 8, 2: 7, and 2: 19. We are reminded that only our Holy God prepared the way (His Son) to come into His presence.

The Prophet Zechariah proclaims the cry to repent. His Wise Words include familiar plans of God: 1: 8-10, 4: 1-6, 9: 9 and 14: 20, 21. We are reminded that only our Holy God prepared truth (His Son) to remain within His favour.

Prayer: Dear God, we learn from the Wise Words of Zephaniah, Haggai and Zechariah who cry for repentenance through You, Your Son; Jesus, and Your Holy Spirit.

August 13 Wise Words

Scripture Text: Malachi 1: 1, 2

"The burden of the word of the Lord to Israel by Malachi. I have loved you, saith the Lord, Yet ye say, Wherein hast thou loved us? ..."

The Prophet Malachi's Wise Words are the last to be recorded in the Old Testament. We are familiar with the burden Malachi writes about since the Wise Words echo a familiar paradox: The Lord has shown His love; yet we ask where He has loved us.

Malachi reminds us that God's love is visible as we take in the sights of His love even when His people despise and ask whereis that love. We are reminded that God's love is gracious; 1: 9.

Malachi reminds us that God's love is audible as we take in the sounds of His love even when His people despise and ask where is that love. We are reminded that God's love is gracious; 2: 5,6.

Malachi reminds us that God's love is reachable as we take in the promises of His love even when His people despise and ask where is that love. We are reminded that God's love is gracious; 3: 1.

Malachi reminds us that God's love is established as we take in the promises of His love even when His people despise and ask where is that love. We are reminded that God's love is gracious; 4: 1, 2.

Prayer: Dear God, we learn from the Wise Words of Malachi that remind us of Your visible, audible, reachable and established; gracious love.

August 14 Wise Words

Scripture Text: Introduction to the New Testament

"The New Testament of Our Lord and Saviour Jesus Christ...with the words of our Lord while upon earth..."

King James authorized the translation of the Wise Words of our Lord while upon earth. For the remainder of the month of August we will ponder the words of our Lord.

Matthew, the first gospel of four begins with familiar Wise Words of our Lord; 3: 15.

Jesus' baptism is the fulfillment of all righteousness. We are reminded that we must allow God's love, grace and power to enter our lives daily to fulfill all His righteousness.

Mark, the second gospel of four begins with familiar Wise Words; 1;15. Jesus' ministry is the fulfillment of all repentance. We are reminded that we must allow God's love, grace and power to enter our lives daily to fulfill all His gospel.

Luke, the third gospel of four begins with familiar Wise Words; 2: 49 . Jesus' mission is the fulfillment of His Father's business! We are reminded that we must allow God's love, grace and power to enter our lives daily to fulfill all His plans.

John, the fourth and final gospel begins with familiar Wise Words; 1: 38 Jesus' lessons are the fulfillment of His searching. We are reminded that we must allow God's love, grace and power to enter our lives daily to fulfill all His Word.

Prayer: Dear God, we learn from Your Son, Jesus through His Wise Words spoken during His baptism, ministry, mission, and lessons to fulfill the coming of Your Kingdom.

August 15 Wise Words

Scripture Text: Acts 1: 4

"...But wait for the promise of the Father which...ye have learned of me."

Acts is also known as the Acts of the Apostles. Jesus has risen, and appears to His apostles; through the Holy Ghost. He gives commandments to the apostles He has chosen (1: 2). The first commandment and Wise Words of Jesus in Acts include waiting for the promise of God. We are reminded that daily we must wait for the promise of God.

Romans is the the first epistle of Paul the Apostle. Paul waits for the promise and commands the people of Rome to continue being saints. Paul writes to the Romans that he is not ashamed of the gospel of Christ (1:16). He concludes his letter to them with these words:

"To God only wise, be glory through Jesus Christ for ever.Amen." (16:27)

I and II Corinthians are epistles also written by the Apostle Paul. Paul waits for the will of God and commands the people of Corinth to continue to be sanctified. Paul writes to the Corinthians that he does not want to hear of any contentions among them (1:10). He concludes these two letters to them with these words: "The grace of the Lord Jesus Christ, and the love of God, and the commandments of the Holy Ghost be with you all. Amen."

(II Corinthians 13: 14)

Prayer: Dear God, we learn from Your Son, Jesus Christ when He appeared to His apostles. Thank you for their Wise Words learned from Jesus and written for us to receive.

August 16 Wise Words

Scripture Text: Galations 1: 6

"I marvel that ye are so soon removed from him that called you into the grace of Christ unto another gospel."

This epistle or letter written by Paul to the people of Galatia contains Wise Words. The Apostle Paul wonders how these people can be learning from another gospel which does not call them into the grace of Christ. We are familiar with the churches having the gospel of Christ being perverted (1: 7). Paul writes from Rome to the Galations and concludes this letter with these Wise Words: "Brethren, the grace of our Lord Jesus Christ be with your spirit. Amen." (6:18)

The epistle from the Apostle Paul to the Church of Ephesus contains Wise Words. Paul heard of their faith in the Lord Jesus, and love unto all the saints (1:15). He gives thanks and prayers including these Wise Words:

"That the God of our Lord Jesus Christ, the Father of glory, May give unto you the spirit of wisdom and revelation in the knowledge of him...(1: 17).

Paul concludes this letter to the Ephesians with these Wise Words: "Grace be with all them that love our LordJesus Christ in sincerity. Amen." (6:24)

The epistle from the Apostle Paul to the Church of Philippi contains Wise Words. Paul thanks God for their fellowship in the gospel from the first day until now (1: 5). He thanks the Philippians and includes these Wise Words: "And having this confidence, I know that I shall abide and continue with you all for your furtherance and joy of faith (1: 25). Paul concludes this letter to the Philippians with these Wise Words: "The grace of our Lord Jesus Christ be with you all. Amen." (4: 23)

Dear God, We learn Wise Words from Your Son, Christ who left commandments for His apostles. Thank you for the grace You give to all to continue following the gospel of our Lord Jesus Christ.

August 17 Wise Words

Scripture Text: Colossians 1: 3, 4

"We give thanks to God and the Father of our Lord Jesus Christ, praying always for you, Since we heard of your faith in Christ Jesus, and of the love which ye have to all the saints."

The Apostle Paul's letters (epistles) to yet another church; of the Colossians contain Wise Words: "For the hope which is laid up for you in heaven, whereof ye heard before in the word of the truth of the gospel; "(1: 5). We are reminded to be steadfast as Paulconcludes this letter: "The salutation by the hand of me Paul. Remember my bonds. Grace be with you. Amen. (4:18)"

The two epistles to the churches of Thessalonians written by Paul while yet in Rome contain Wise Words: "Remembering without ceasing your work of faith and labour of love, and patience of hope in our Lord Jesus Christ, in the sight of God and our Father (1: 3)." We agree with the conclusion of I and II Thessalonians: "The grace of our Lord Jesus Christ be with you all. Amen. (3: 18)"

Yet another two epistles; to the youthful minister Timothy by Paul contain Wise Words (written while away from Rome for the first and upon returning before Nero in Rome for the second letter). Paul writes: "Neither give to fables and endless genealogies, which minister questions, rather than godly edifying which is in faith; so do." (1: 4) We are reminded to study and preach the word; learning in our youth the words of the concluding words of I and II Timothy: "The Lord Jesus Christ be with thy spirit." Amen. (4: 22)"

Prayer: Dear God, we learn from Your Son, Lord Jesus Christ the Wise Words of reminders that we are to remember each other in prayer; whether in bonds or learning in our yourth the grace and spirit of You and Your Son.

August 18 Wise Words

Scripture Text: Titus 1: 5

"For this cause left I thee to Crete, that thou shouldest set in order the things that are wanting, and ordain elders in every city, as I had appointed thee; "

The Apostle Paul writes to another youthful leader of the church. Titus was to set things in order and ordain elders. He also held the title of bishop. Titus receives these Wise Words: "But, speak thou the things which become sound doctrine." Titus 2: 1 We are reminded as leaders to set things in order and ordain elders. We continue to be reminded to speak with sound doctrine.

The Apostle Paul writes to Philemon; another individual very close to him; with love and grace. He was a servant. He also was a fellowlabourer. Philemon receives these Wise Words: "Hearing of thy love and faith, which thou hast toward the Lord Jesus, and toward all saints; That the communication of thy faith May become effectual by the acknowledging of every good thing which is in you in Christ Jesus." (5, 6) We are reminded to receive beloved brothers.

The Apostle Paul writes to the Hebrews encouraging them to consider and profess Christ Jesus as Apostle and High Priest (3: 1). Paul also states that Christ is the mediator of the new testament (9: 14,15). The Hebrews receive these Wise Words: "Now faith is the substance of things hoped for, the evidence of things hoped for, the evidence of things not seen (10:1)." We are reminded to receive Christ as our High Priest.

Prayer: Dear God we learn from the Wise Words of Your Son Jesus through Apostle Paul's Wise Words to follow You Son, Priest, Brother, and Mediator.

August 19 Wise Words

Scripture Text: James 1: 5

"If any of you lack wisdom, let him ask of God, that giveth to all men liberally, and upbraideth not; and it shall be given him. "

The Apostle James, a servant of God and of Christ writes to the twelve tribes of Israel. They are scattered and are encouraged by James to be patient amidst temptations and trying of their faith. The tribes receive these Wise Words in the conclusion of James' letter to them:

"Let him know, that he which converteth the sinner from the error of his way shall save a soul from death, and shall hide a multitude of sins (5: 20)."

We are reminded that we are to receive others patiently and by the trying of our faith as servants of God and Christ.

The Apostle Peter, an apostle of Jesus Christ writes two letters to "strangers scattered throughout"

(First book; 1:1). and to "them that have obtained like precious faith" (Second book; 2:1).

These listeners receive Wise Words from Peter:

"But the God of all grace, who hath called us unto his eternal glory by Christ Jesus, after ye have suffered a while, make you perfect, stablish, strengthen, settle you." (First book; 5: 10.) and:

"But grow in grace, and in the knowledge of our Lord and Saviour Jesus Christ. To Him be glory both now and for ever. Amen." (Second book 3: 18.)

The Apostle John an apostle of Jesus Christ writes three letters to "my little children "(First book 2:1), to "the elder unto the elect lady and her children (Second book 1:1), and to "the elder (Third book 1:1). These listeners receive Wise Words from John: "If we confess our sins, he is faithful and just to forgive us our sins, and to cleanse us from all unrighteousness (First book; 1:9)."

"And this is love, that we walk after his commandments. This is the commandment, That as he have heard from the beginning, ye should walk in it (Second book 2: 6)."

"I have no greater joy than to hear that my children walk in truth (Third book; verse 4)."

Prayer: Dear God, we learn from Your Son, Jesus Christ and the other apostles, James, Peter and John how to follow as we walk and grow in truth and knowledge.

August 20 Wise Words

Scripture Text: Jude - verse 14

"And Enoch also, the seventh from Adam, prophesized of these, saying, Behold the Lord cometh with ten thousand of his saints."

The Apostle Jude and apostle of Jesus Christ writes his letter to the "sanctified by God the Father, and preserved in Jesus Christ,and called..." (verse 1). These listeners receive Wise Words from Jude:

"But ye, beloved, building up yourselves on your most holy faith, praying in the Holy Ghost..." (verse 20).

The Apostle Saint John the Divine and apostle of Jesus Christ writes a letter which is also called Revelation. It is a letter to the seven churches in Asia (1: 4). These churches receive Wise Words from Saint John concerning Christ: "I am Alpha and Omega; the first and the last: "And, What thou seest, write in a book and send it unto the seven churches." (see their names in 1:11)

Saint John's shared wisdom through a vision of a man like unto the Son of man amidst seven candlesticks, seven stars, and a two-edged sword and their mystery explained (1: 12, 13 16 and 20).

Also we learn wisdom from the vision that includes God's throne, with seven lamps, four beasts, seven seals and their mystery explained (4: 2, 5, 9, and 5: 1), a vision that includes the opening of the seven seals, hearing the noise of beasts, horses (6: 1-8), the souls of them slain for the word of God (6:9), an earthquake, four angels called upon by another angel (7: 1, 2), and seven angels with seven trumpets (8: 2).

Saint John's Wise Words continue in vivid visions (chapters 9-22).

He concludes his letter of Revelation with these Wise Words: "He which testifieth these things saith, Surely I come quickly. Amen." 22: 20.

Prayer: Dear God, we learn from Your Son, Jesus Christ an Apostle with Jude and Saint John the Divine Wise Words of faith, warnings, and advise received by The Holy Ghost.

August 21 Wise Words

Scripture Text: Proverbs 1: 7

"The fear of the Lord is the beginning of knowledge: but fools despise wisdom and instruction. "

Solomon, the son of David, king of Israel writes proverbs for wisdom and instruction. He makes mention of the instructions of fathers, and law of mothers; (1: 8). Their wisdom is not to be dispised but to be understood; (2: 5). Solomon commands us to trust in the Lord with all our hearts; (3: 5, 6). Moral virtues are included in the Wise Words of Solomon; (chapters 4-24).

Solomon's, a writer of proverbs includes those from the men of Hezekiah king of Judah that were copied (25: 1). These Wise Words include: "Take away the wicked from before the king, and his throne shall be established in righteousness." 25: 5 Solomon, known as one of the wisest kings spent the first part of his proverbs listing moral virtues and their contrary vices. Now he preaches rightousness preached by maxims and observations of other kings.

For the remainder of August we will learn from these Wise Words as knowledge, wisdom, instruction.

Prayer: Dear God, we learn from Your Son, Jesus Chrit who spoke in parables, proverbs, for our instruction.

August 22 Wise Words

Scripture Text: Proverbs 25: 13

"As the cold of snow in the time of harvest, so is a faithful messenger to them that send him; for he refresheth the soul of his masters. "

Solomon allows the readers to form a vivid picture in their minds:

A snowy day in time of harvest could be in October. The cold of the snow May be a welcome during Indian Summer! We know this can be refreshing to the crop being harvested.

Solomon was a faithful messenger to those who welcomed the cold facts in time of harvesting for the Lord. This was a daily endeavour.

Faithful messengers are refreshers. They refresh the soul of their masters. We are reminded to be messengers with the Trinity for the souls of those we encounter.

We are reminded that Jesus, as a faithful messenger urged us to be His messengers concerning the cold facts of His physical death by human kings, During this season of changes, God refreshed His only son's soul so He could be our master of Wise Words.

Prayer: Dear God, we learn from Solomon's Proverbs; often quoted by Your Son, Jesus Christ; our Messenger.

August 23 Wise Words

Scripture Text: Proverbs 26: 20

"Where no wood is, there the fire goeth out: so where there is no talebearer, the strife ceaseth. "

Solomon allows his readers to envision a place of burning offerings; the flames have slowly gone out due to the lack of wood. We recognize that the fire May have burned the wood, or there was the building of an altar without enough wood. Either way the fire is out.

Solomon allows his readers to hear the words of talebearers; also called liars. They could easily be the leaves or green shrubery if thrown in a huge mass into the flames, the fire is stifled; goes out, and creates thick smoke instead, or the fire will smolder. Either way the fire is out.

The talebearer can be of abundance in number but surrounded by strife (enough to form a forest of wood!). The strife is so massive and just like a huge fire will destroy anything in its' path; gaining fuel along the way woods or wooden houses. Either way the fire is not going out.

The lack of talebearers can leave room for numbers of neighbors surrounded by fairness; standing together as a forest of healthy trees. The wood gathered from the healthy forest creates a fire that will not be consumed by dampness. Our healthy lives create a fire of the Holy Ghost that will not be consumed by unwanted dampness of negative souls.

Prayer: Dear God, we learn from Solomon's Proverbs; often quoted by Your Son, Jesus Christ; our Bearer of Good News.

August 24 Wise Words

Scripture Text: Proverbs 27: 3

"A stone is heavy, and the sand weighty; but a fool's wrath is heavier than them both."

Solomon allows his readers to envision a heavy stone. Perhaps we see a huge boulder that has to be moved from the field, and ready to be plowed. Imagine the pulley system of Solomon's time and what heavy machinery we have invented in our days.

Solomon allows his readers to envision weighty sand. Perhaps we see a sand pit that has to be transported to be used for building. Imagine the donkey or oxen of Solomon's time and what machinery we have invented in our days.

Solomon allows his readers to envision an angry fool. Perhaps we ourselves have "worn those shoes or sandals".

Imagine the enemies of Solomon's time and what enemies we know lurk in our days.

Prayer: Dear God, we learn from Solomon's Proverbs the Wise Words often quoted by Your Son, Jesus Christ the often depised King.

August 25 Wise Words

cripture Text: Proverbs 27: 8

"As a bird that wandereth from her nest, so is a man that wandereth from his place. "

Solomon creates within his proverbs a scenario for us to picture: We May in our walks find a bird that has wandered from the protection provision, and pleasure of living in her own nest. Imagine where the places would be where the bird has wandered; close to danger, or close to another place of safety.

Solomon creates a scenario for us to picture a man wandering from the protection, provision, and pleasure of living in his own home. Imagine where the places would be where the man has wandered; close to danger or close to safety.

Solomon allows his readers to envision a lost wanderer. Perhaps we have been as lost sheep; oblivious that our One Shepherd, Jesus Christ looks for our protection, provision, and pleasure to live for Him.

Prayer: Dear God, we learn from the Wise Words of Your Son,

Jesus Christ to us that wander from the fold; that He will lead us back to safety.

August 26 Wise Words

Scripture Text: Proverbs 28: 15

"As a roaring lion, and a ranging bear; so is a wicked ruler over the poor people. "

Solomon allows the reader to envision the sights and sounds of the roaring lion. No wonder they are called the leaders of the jungle, with their mighty roar and their majestic presence amidst God's created beasts.

Solomon allows the reader to envision the sights and sounds of a ranging bear. No wonder they are called the leaders of the forest with their mighty growl and their towering presence amidst God's created beasts.

Solomon allows the reader to envision the sights and sounds of a wicked ruler. No wonder they are called the leaders of people with their mighty threats and their haughty presence amidst God's created humans.

Prayer: Dear God, we learn from the Wise Words of Your Son, Jesus Christ to us that meet those who have become wicked towards Your children.

August 27 Wise Words

Scripture Text: Proverbs 29: 18

"Where there is no vision, the people perish: but he that keepeth the law, happy is he. "

Solomon reminds us the importance of vision. We know there are humans lacking vision to see the beauty of God's creation. We also know humans lacking vision to protect the beauty of God's creation.

Solomon reminds us the importance of a vision. We know there are humans lacking positive visions for the coming of the Trinity's kingdom. We also know humans lacking vision to protect the coming of the Trinity's kingdom.

So, Solomon reminds us the importance of law. We know there are humans ignoring the law concerning the fulfillment of the Trinity's kingdom. We also know humans lacking the knowlege of the law concerning the fulfilment of the Trinity's Kingdom.

Solomon as a wise king wishes his people not to perish but keep the law so they will make the people will be happy.

Prayer: Dear God, we learn from Solomon's Proverbs often quoted by Your Son Jesus Christ, the King of Kings and Lord of Lords.

August 28 Wise Words

Scripture Text: Proverbs 30: 2, 3

"Surely I am more brutish than any man, and have not the understanding of a man. I neither learned wisdom, nor have the knowledge of the holy. "

Solomon quotes the proverbs; words of Agur. who spoke to Ithiel, who spoke to Ucal (sounds like our modern chain calling without the use of the convenience of a phone) !

Agur's Wise Words involve a sincere confession: His ways were rough, he was ignorant of the mind of men, he was unlearned, and he lacked knowing about following the Holy God.

Solomon reminds the reader that God will accept us the way we are; brutish or gentle. There have been generations of rough and tough servants of God and generations of gentle and mild servants.

Solomon reminds the reader that God will accept us the way we are; understanding or confused. There have been generations of well-versed leaders of God and generations of unsure leaders.

Solomon reminds the reader that god will accept us the way we are; eager to learn and receive holiness or hesitant to learn holiness. There have been generations of "fired up" messengers and generations of "cooled down" messengers.

Prayer: Dear God, we learn from Solomon's Proverbs often quoted by Your Son, Jesus.

August 29 Wise Words

Scripture Text: Proverbs 31: 1

"The words of king Lemuel, the prophecy that his mother taught him."

Solomon shares the Wise Words of king Lemuel taught by his mother. Solomon shares with the reader that we receive motherly wisdom. Mothers are our first teachers. It is our choice whether we want to learn from her wisdom or forget about what we have been taught.

Solomon would have examples of previous generations of mothers: Eve, Adah, Zillah, Naamah (Genesis 1:-6) were the first to be recorded prior to Noah and the flood. The next series of mothers would be in the days of Abraham: Sarai, Milcah, Hagar (Genesis 7-16) were the next to be recorded during the acquisition of more land promised by God.

Solomon mentions that king Lemuel's words were the prophecy that his mother taught him. The prophecy passed down from generation to generation would be that of God's provision, power, and protection to His followers. We are hopefully continuing that prophecy.

Prayer: Dear God, we learn from Solomon and the prophecy of king Lemuel that was passed down, passed on, bby his mother and that Your Son Jesus would preach during His days on earth.

August 30 Wise Words

Scripture Text: Proverbs 31: 10

"Who can find a virtuous woman? for her price is far above rubies."

Solomon continues to refer to the Wise Words that king Leumel learned from his mother. The entire chapter 31 of Proverbs is dedicated to the qualities of a virtuous woman and her valuable price.

A virtuous woman is trusted by her husband as she does him good. (31: 11) Her goal daily is to do good . (31:12) Is there such a ruby that does not glimmer and shine before the buyer's eyes?

A virtuous woman works willing with her hands as she spins, feeds family, and plants a vineyard. (13-16) . Her goal daily is to gain strength in her arms. (31: 17) Is there such a ruby that does not come from the strength of the miner's arms?

A virtuous woman perceives that her merchandise is good as she uses what is provided by her own harvest. (18-24) Her final goal daily is ready to rejoice (31: 25) Is there such a ruby that does not make a miner rejoice?

A virtuous woman opens her mouth with wisdom, kindness, and no idle words come out. (26, 27) Her final goal daily is to be blessed and praised for her strength by her family. (31: 28). Is there such a ruby that does not receive praise from the miner's labour?

Prayer: Dear God, we learn from Solomon's Proverbs quoted by Your Son, Jesus Christ the brightest and strongest gem.

August 31 Wise Words

Scripture Text: Acts 19: 11

"And God wrought special miracles by the hands of Paul."

Saint Luke, within his gospel shares his wisdom of God's miracle of Saul being converted, annointed to prepare him for becoming the Apostle (follower) of God. We are familiar with Paul's letters to numerous churches (fourteen are recorded in the New Testament).

The Apostle Paul's vacation was over. No more pleasures of sitting back and gloating over the hurt and damage he made by using his hands and words unwisely. Today's text reminds us that we have had vacation; now there is work to do.

My sister Sue knows so well the importance of vacations, and now.retirement! But, that does not mean she stops sharing her God-given wisdom. Today she shares another of her illustrations and easily reminds us of how special we are to God !

September 1 ABC's of Wisdom

Scripture Text: Romans 15: 7

"Wherefore, receive ye one another, as Christ also received us to the glory of God."

The Apostle Paul encourages us to receive each other and introduces us to the the ABC's of Wisdom. Christ is our teacher, instructor and we are to follow His example and that of His churches.

Let us begin with the letter A:

Christ has a positive ATTITUDE towards receiving us to the glory of God. Christ is our teacher.

Christ ACCEPTS us and encourages us to share His glory. Christ is our instructor.

Christ inspires Paul to follow Him and put his faith into ACTION. Christ is our example.

Prayer: Thank you God for Your Son, Christ and His example of wisdom shown by attitude, acceptance and action.

September 2 ABC's of Wisdom

Scripture Text: John 15 : 27

"And ye also shall bear witness, because ye have been with me from the beginning."

Saint John wrote in his gospel a conversation between Jesus and His disciples. He was talking and comforting them just previous to His death. Just as He chose the Disciples from the beginning of His ministry, He chooses His followers to follow the beginning of the Christian way.

In our Christian way we are on the letter B::

Jesus chose Andrew. Andrew was BUSY BRINGING others to Him. Andrew witnessed that Christ was there from the BEGINNING.

Jesus chose Peter. Peter was BEING BRAVE for Him. Peter witnessed that Christ was the BEGINNING.

Jesus chose Thomas. Thomas BEGINS BELIEVING in Him. Thomas witnessed that Christ will always be the BEGINNING.

Jesus chose Philip. Right from the beginning of Philip was busy lighting the way. Philip witnessed that Christ was to be followed earnestly.

Prayer: Thank You, God for the example of four of Jesus' chosen disciples who were with Him from the beginning.

September 3 ABC's of Wisdom

Scripture Text: Matthew 5: 15

"Neither do men light a candle, and put it under a bushel, but on a candlestick; and it giveth light unto all that are in the house."

Jesus had just spoken the well-known Sermon on The Mount with wisdom through parables; lessons and commands. He shows by example for He does not hide.

C is the next letter:

Jesus shares His wisdom and becomes known as CHRIST. He is our COMMUNICATOR.

Jesus in His wisdom commands us to be CANDLES. He is our COMMANDER.

Jesus by His wisdom prepares us to be CANDLESTICKS. He is our CHANNEL.

Prayer: Thank You God, for the example found in Your Son, Jesus CHRIST in lighting the world as a candle.

September 4 ABC's of Wisdom

Scripture Text: Proverbs 4: 5

"Get wisdom...get understanding..."

Solomon, a wise king advises us to get wisdom. Christ quoted from Proverbs; Solomon's written wisdom.

We continue our path of wisdom with the letter D:

Jesus had to make some tough DECISIONS. By His example and in His wisdom, we are encouraged to make safe DECISIONS.

Jesus had to show during tough times: DETERMINATION. By His example and in His wisdom, we are allowed to follow Him with sincere DETERMINATION.

Jesus had to express daily to His Father God; DELIGHT. By His example as His only begotten Son, we come to Him with joyful DELIGHT.

Prayer: Thank You, God for the example of Your Son, Jesus Christ in getting wisdom for decisions, with determination, and in delight.

September 5 ABC's of Wisdom

Scripture Text: Hebrews 11: 1

"Now faith is the substance of things hoped for, evidence of things not seen."

The Apostle Paul writes to other apostles concerning the importance of faith in following the way of Christ.

Jesus' death and resurrection present us with EVIDENCE. We follow Him; having the facts about His Salvation for the world. Let us show the EVIDENCE to a world that needs a little more faith.

Jesus' resurrection and promises present us an ENTRANCE. We follow Him; having the door to enter into His salvation.

Let us guide others to ENTER a world that needs a little more hope.

Jesus' promises and recorded words present us with EVENTS. We follow His life; having the faith recorded in the Holy Bible. Let us plan EVENTS to a world that needs a little more substance in their lives.

Prayer: Thank You, God for the example of Your Son Jesus as He provides evidence, entrance and events towards the salvation of the world.

September 6 ABC's of Wisdom

Scripture Text: I Corinthians 4: 1, 2

"Let a man so account of us, as of the ministers of Christ, and as stewards of the mysteries of God. Moreover it is required in stewards, that a man be found faithful."

The Apostle Paul in writting two separate letters to the Church of Corinth. He encourages us on our path.

Jesus is mentioned by Paul as the most FAITHFUL to His FATHER. God has plans for those who are FAITHFUL. Let us encourage others to be FAITHFUL to our Heavenly FATHER by our examples as ministers.

Jesus is mentioned by Paul as giving back to His FATHER FREELY . God has plans for those who give FREELY. Let us give account to others of our FAITHFULNESS to our Heavenly FATHER as stewards.

Jesus is mentioned by Paul as living FOREVER with His FATHER. God has plans for those who want to live with Him FOREVER. Let us FOLLOW the requirement to be FAITHFUL to God in FRONTof others.

Prayer: Thank you, God for the example of Your Son, Jesus Christ as our FRIEND; being FAITHFUL to You, giving FREELY , and preparing us to live with You FOREVER.

September 7 ABC's of Wisdom

Scripture Text: I Chronicles 16:11

"Seek the Lord and His face continually"

I Chronicles is one of the Old Testament Books of The Holy Bible and where we find the records and references to the Kings of powerful kingdoms. Their power in seeking God is evident in our walk today.

Jesus often quoted from the Old Testament of His Father; a GIVING GOD . He created the Earth for us to dwell. We are encouraged to seek Him daily; continually. If the records of kings and past rulers can include the advise to seek the Lord continually, so the epistles of our daily lives should include seeking the King of Kings.

Jesus often quoted prophets for His Father; a GRANTING GOD. He prepared His Son to provide salvation for the earth. We are encouraged to find Him daily; continually. If the records of nations and past followers of God can include the advise to seek the Lord continually, so the epistles of our daily lives should include seeking the Lord of Lords.

Jesus often quoted His heavenly Father: a GRATEFUL GOD. He planned for His Son to prepare the earth for Heaven. We are encouraged to follow Him daily; continually.

If the records of generations and past christians of God can include the advise to seek the Lord continually, so the epistles of our daily lives should include seeking the GIVING and GRANTING GOD.

Prayer: Thank You, God for the example of Your Son Jesus Christ as one who GAVE

and GRANTED GRATEFULLY of Himself so that we May continue to seek Your Son and Saviour.

September 8 ABC's of Wisdom

Scripture Text: Colossians 1: 3 - 5

"We give thanks to God and the Father of our Lord Jesus Christ, praying always for you, since we heard of your faith in Christ Jesus, and of the love which ye have to all the saints, for the hope which is laid up for you in heaven, whereof ye heard before in the word of the truth of the gospel."

Apostle Paul writes to another church; this time to the Colossians. He preaches of salvation through Jesus.

Jesus is our everlasting HOPE. We join the saints in waiting in HOPE for reaching HEAVEN! Faithful Christians will give thanks to the Trinity upon reaching Heaven!

Jesus is our pure HAPPINESS. We join the saints in witnessing the HAPPINESS to be found in HEAVEN! Faithful Christians will give thanks to the Trinity upon arriving at HEAVEN!

Jesus is a son of man and Son of God; of HONOR. We join the saints in giving the HONOR towards the King of HEAVEN ! Faithful Christians will take their places with the Trinity upon walking through HEAVEN!

Prayer: Thank You, God for Your Son Jesus Christ as one who is The Saviour of HOPE, HAPPINESS and HONOR.

September 9 ABC's of Wisdom

Scripture Text: John 1: 1

"In the beginning was the Word, and the Word was with God, and the Word was God."

Saint John was one of the writers of the four gospels within the New Testament. He preaches of the Word (Jesus) being with man and God; following the path with God. Today we are on the letter I:

Jesus was known by man and God for He was IN the beginning. He was the Word created by God. We begin each day by coming to the Word; Jesus who shares His wisdom with the Trinity Team.

Jesus was known as an INFANT of man and God for He was he was from the beginning of life. He was the Word delivered by God. We begin each day by coming as little children to the Trinity Team.

Jesus was known as the Word of God written down with INK from the beginning of time. He is the word passed down by God's generations. We begin each day by writing on our hearts the wisdom of the Trinity Team.

PRAYER:

Thank You, God for Your Son Jesus Christ and the Word that is still with us today, read to infants, read by adults, and written down through the ages from tablets of rock to tablets of ink.

September 10 ABC's of Wisdom

Scripture Text: Nehemiah 8: 9, 10

"And Nehemiah, which is the Tirshatha, and Ezra the priest the scribe, and the Levites that brought the people, said unto all the people, This day is holy unto the Lord your God; mourn not, nor weep, when they heard the words of the law. Then he said unto them, Go your way, eat the fat, and drink the sweet and send portions unto them for whom nothing is prepared: for this day is holy unto the Lord; neither be ye sorry; for the joy of the Lord is your strength."

Nehemiah is one of the prophets of the Old Testament and is known for his title "Cup-Bearer" (for the king) and as thebuilder of the wall of Jerusalem. Today we build on the letter J:

Nehemiah's expression: "the JOY of the Lord is your strength" is relevant today. Nehemiah as a builder recognized the Lord's strength while building for God's kingdom. We are builders of God's kingdom and can experience the same JOY of the Lord.

Nehemiah was building the wall of JERUSALEM and depended on strength which is relevant for builders of today. We are builders of walls of power and can construct experiences in the Lord.

Nehemiah recognized the importance of JUSTICE when building for God; whether the wall of Jerusalem or His kingdom. We are builders of God's kingdom and can create a community with JUSTICE.

Prayer: Dear God, we learn from Your Son, Jesus the importance of

JOY , cities such as JERUSALEM, and the significance of JUSTICE. Each is significant for the building of Your kingdom.

September 11 ABC's of Wisdom

Scripture Text: II Peter 3: 18

"But grow in grace, and in the knowledge of our Lord and Saviour Jesus Christ. To him be glory both now and for ever. Amen. "

Peter writes to encourage other apostles to grow while being led away from the wicked (3: 17). This scripture text expounds on K; today's letter.

Peter encourages the reader to grow in grace and KNOWLEDGE. This is a process that takes time and does not happen all at once. We are reminded to allow daily growth with the Lord.

Peter encourages the reader to grow in KINDNESS.

This is a process acquired and does not happen as a solo experience. We are reminded to allow daily experience with the Lord.

Peter encourages the reader to grow in the KINGDOM. This is a process everlasting and does not happen without the Trinity Team. We are reminded to allow our future with the Lord.

Prayer: Dear God, we learn from Your Son, Jesus Christ as He allows us to grow in grace and KNOWLEDGE for Him.

September 12 ABC's of Wisdom

Scripture Text: John 12: 32

"And, I, if I be lifted up from the earth, will draw all men unto me. "

Saint John records in one of the four gospel Wise Words of Jesus and reminds us of Jesus' goal for man: to lift Him up.

Today we lift up the letter L:

One of the commandments from Jesus is to LIFT Him up from

the earth. Jesus was LIFTED on the cross to die for our sins. We are reminded to daily LIFT Jesus as our only salvation.

One of the commandments from Jesus is to LOVE Him who loved us. Jesus was LOVED from the cross to show His sacrifice. We are reminded to daily LOVE Jesus as our only comfort.

One of the commandments from Jesus is to LEARN of Him who is the only Way. Jesus was LEARNED because of the cross where He died. We are reminded to daily LEARN of Jesus and His plan.

Prayer: Dear God, we LEARN from Your Son, Jesus Christ as He allows the fulfillment of Your plan for Your world.

September 13 ABC's of Wisdom

Scripture Text: I Peter 5: 6, 7

"Humble yourselves under the mighty hand of God, casting you care upon HIm for He careth for you."

The Apostle Peter writes and encourages his followers to heed to Jesus' example of humility under the mighty hand of God. We approach the letter M today:

The apostles walked with Jesus; under the Trinity's MIGHTY hand. They cast their care for the MIGHTY hand of the Trinity to MINISTER to everyone under their care. We are reminded to cast our care upon the MIGHTY Trinity; perhaps as MINISTERS of Their plan.

The apostles walked with Christ; under the Trinity's MAJESTY. They cast their care for the MAJESTIC hand of the Trinity to MOVE towards everyone to cast their care. We are reminded to cast our care upon the MAJESTIC Trinity; perhaps as MOVERS for Their plan.

The apostles and their Lord were under the MARVELLOUS Trinity. They cast their care for the MARVELLOUS hand of the Trinity to MAKE everyone want to cast their care. We are reminded to cast our care upon the MARVELLOUS Trinity; perhaps as MAKERS within Their plan.

Prayer: Dear God, we learn from Your Son, Jesus Christ as He shows how MIGHTY the Trinity Team and Their Plan is to each of Their followers.

September 14 ABC's of Wisdom

Scripture Text: Hebrews 4: 16

"Let us therefore come boldly unto the throne of grace, that we May obtain mercy, and find grace in help in time of need. "

The Apostle Paul writes to the Hebrews who he encourages to be bold in coming to the throne of grace. We have come to the letter N:

The Hebrews were encouraged to come unto the Trinity's throne of grace. They NEEDED to come boldly with their NEEDS. We are reminded to come boldly before the throne of the Trinity with our wish list (some longer than others!) of NEEDS.

The Hebrews were encouraged to tell others of the Trinity's throne of grace. They NEEDED to share boldly with their NEIGHBORS. We are reminded to come boldly before the throne of the Trinity with our guest list (some from way back!) of NEIGHBORS.

The Hebrews were encouraged to take in daily the Trinity's throne of grace. Their NEWS would be NEWS to support the greatest NEWS; the Good NEWS. We are reminded to come boldly before the throne of the Trinity with our route list (some longer than others!) of NEWS.

Prayer: Dear God, we learn from Your Son Jesus Christ as He is with the Trinity the Good NEWS much NEEDED by us and our NEIGHBOR.

September 15 ABC's of Wisdom

Scripture Text: I Samuel 15: 22

"And Samuel said, Hath the Lord as great delight in burnt offerings and acrifices, as in obeying the voice of the Lord? Behold, to obey is better than sacrifice, and to hearken than the fat of rams."

Samuel the King of the Israelites enccouraged them to follow the Lord's voice even more than the presentation of offerings; sacrifices. We follow today with the letter O:

The tribes of Israel under King Samuel's rule were familiar with the OFFERINGS and sacrifices to the Lord. Their OFFERINGS served to delight their God. We are reminded to daily present OFFERINGS to the same delightful God.

The tribes of Israel under King Samuel's law were familiar with his OBEDIENCE and the voice of the Lord. Their OBEDIENCE gave even more delight to their God. We are reminded to daily show OBEDIENCE to the same delightful God.

The tribes of Israel under King Samuel's decrees were familiar with ORATORS of ORACLES of the Lord. These ORATORS spoke of their delight to their God. We are reminded to daily speak; be ORATORS about our delightful God.

Prayer: Dear God, we learn from Your Son, Jesus Christ to be OBEDIENT to the Trinity Team.

September 16 ABC's of Wisdom

Scripture Text: Daniel 3: 14, 15

"Nebuchadnezzor spoke and said,...at that time that ye hear the sound of the horn, pipe, lyre, sackbut, psaltery, dulcimer, fall down and worship the image."

Daniel was a sincere follower of God and also was familiar with the ways of King Nebuchadnezzor. Daniel daily fell down before the Holy God and worshipped Him. The decree from the king involved his followers to fall down before human made images to worship. Daniel's example of wisdom becomes our introduction of today's letter P:

Daniel heard the sound of the PSALTERY in the temple where he worshipped. He also heard the harp like instrument played within the king's PALACE. Daniel would remain God's follower and end up interpreting the king's dreams. We are reminded that we have earthly rulers to follow but still worship our Holy God.

Daniel heard the voices of PRAYER in the temple where he worshipped. He also heard the PRAYERS to the images within the king's palace. Daniel would remain God's servant and end up joining other servants in handling affairs for the king. We are reminded that we have earthly affairs to follow but still PRAY for our Holy God's kingdom.

Daniel heard the decree or PROCLAMATION in the temple where he worshipped. He also heard the PROCLAMATION of the king's PALACE. Daniel would remain God's servant and end up joining other servants in walking right out of a fiery furnace; upon the king's command. We are reminded that we have earthly demands to follow but still PROCLAIM our Holy Trinity Team's POWER.

Prayer: Dear God, we learn from Your Son Jesus Christ how to hear only Your Trinity Team's PROCLAMATION.

September 17 ABC's of Wisdom

Scripture Text: Genesis 3: 9

"And the Lord God called unto Adam, and said unto him, where art thou? "

God was perfectly aware of Adam's whereabouts! Yet, He was seeking more than a 'yes' or 'no' reply! This is God's way of wisdom and in the ABC's of Wisdom we are on the letter Q:

Our Holy God asked His first created man a QUESTION:

"Where art thou? "We are familiar with Adam's reply (3:10). Adam had disobeyed God's commands not to eat from the forbidden fruit of the tree of knowledge. Now Adam and Eve would have QUESTIONS about their future in the Garden of Eden. We are reminded that God can pop the same QUESTION to us...asking where we are. What will be our answer?

Our Saviour Jesus asked Mary Magdalene a question: "Whom seek ye?" (John 17:4) We are familiar with her reply. She had searched for her beloved Christ, and here appears a 'stranger'; asking her who she was seeking. (John 20: 15). Now Mary would have QUESTIONS about her QUEST in the Garden of the Lord. We are reminded that God can pop the same QUESTION to us...asking of whom we seek. What will be our answer?

Our Saint Paul's (in a letter) asks the Romans a question: "If God is for us, who can be against us? "(Romans 8: 31) We are familiar with their reply. They were called to be saints who would seek wisdom. Now the Romans would have QUESTIONS about her own QUIETNESS in front of God...asking who is against us. We are reminded that God can pop the same question to us...asking who is for us.

What will be our answer?

Prayer: Dear God, we learn from Your Son Jesus Christ what will be our answers to QUESTIONS regarding Your QUEST.

September 18 ABC's of Wisdom

Scripture Text: Ephesians 3: 17

"That Christ May dwell in your hearts by faith; that ye, being rooted and grounded in love..."

The Apostle Paul writes to the Church of Ephesus to encourage them to receive the "spirit of wisdom and revelation in the knowledge" of Him (Christ Jesus) (1: 17). Today we ponder the letter R:

The Ephesians RECEIVED Paul's letter encouraging them to RECEIVE the same Lord Jesus Christ as they became His saints and followers. We are REMINDED that Jesus Christ Himself asks us to RECEIVE Him and allow Him to dwell in our hearts.

The Ephesian were encouraged by the Apostle Paul to REVEAL by faith to other saints the REVELATION of their Lord Jesus Christ. This could only be done because they allowed their Lord to REIGNin their hearts. We are REMINDED that Jesus Christ with the REST of the Trinity wants us to RECEIVE their love.

The Ephesians RECEIVED from the Apostle Paul a REMINDER of the REVELATION of their King who has to be invited to REIGN in the hearts of each saint that is ROOTED and grounded in the love of the Trinity. We are REMINDED to RECEIVE the command to have ROOTED and grounded within our hearts, the love of our one and only REDEEMER.

Prayer: Dear God, we learn from Your Lord Jesus Christ the daily REMINDER of His REDEMPTION, how He must REIGN. His love must be securely ROOTED.

September 19 ABC's of Wisdom

Scripture Text: Mark 1: 17

"And Jesus said unto them, come ye after me and I will make you fishers of men."

The book of Mark is one of the four Gospels of the ministry of Jesus. One common thread in each good news is the calling by Jesus for His followers to be fishers of men; disciples. I was called to be a member of the "Disciples of Jesus "session at The Salvation Army School For Officer's Training College (SFOT) located near Nyack, New York. Allow me to tell you more by introducing the letter S:

The SALVATION Army Church's founder; William Booth was a fisher of men as he ministered with SOUP, SOAP, and SALVATION. General Booth led his new uniformed followers to wear the letter S to follow Jesus' motto: "To SAVE and to SERVE". One pre-requisite to entering the college (SFOT), is to to be a SENIOR SOLDIER; a member of The SALVATION Army. In 1975, I became a SAVED, SENIOR SOLDIER of the Wellsville, New York SALVATION Army Citadel and enrolled by Captain Barbara Torbitt. My SESSION was given the name from 1976 to1978: Disciple of Jesus".

The first SALVATION Army training SESSION with a name was the: "Commander's Own"-1914-1915. Notice they only received one year of training! The first two year SESSION was named "SOLDIERS of Christ; 1960-1962. In that session there was a Cadet Barbara

Torbitt! The SESSION following hers was "SERVANTS of Christ; 1961-1963.

Finally in 1976-1978 I STUDIED as Cadet Patricia Appelt; "Disciple of Jesus" SESSION along side "Companions of Christ" (1976) and "Joyful Evangelists" (1978). Today: September 19, 2010 s I continue to SAVE and to SERVE as a Disciple of Jesus, remaining an adherent for the Canandaigua, New York SALVATION Army Corps. Perhaps you are a SOLDIER of one of the SALVATION Army Citadels as you STUDY Mark's testimony of his Lord, Jesus Christ's wisdom.

Prayer: Dear God, we learn from Your Son, Jesus Christ to be his SERVANTS willing to SAVE and SERVE within churches such as The SALVATION Army.

September 20 ABC's of Wisdom

Scripture Text: Psalm 69: 13

"But as for me, my prayer is unto thee, O Lord , in an acceptable time: O God, in the multitude of thy mercy hear me, in the truth of thy salvation."

The Psalmist, Shepherd, King David prays to his Lord, God. He had just complained about the fact he was a "stranger"; an "alien" to his own "brethren" (69: 8). He made sure that he was not a stranger to God. We can follow his wisdom while ponder- ing the letter T:

When we recite David's prayer to You (THEE), Oh God, we join in becoming familiar to Your Kingdom. We are reminded that Jesus quoted from the book of Psalms as the Great Shepherd of Your world . We pray daily to THEE and Your TRINITY TEAM.

When we recite David's prayer with others, Oh God, we join in an acceptable TIME for Your Kingdom. We are reminded that Jesus sought God's multitude of mercy as the TEACHER, Rabbi of Your world. We spend TIME giving THANKS to THEE and Your TRINITY TEAM.

When we recite David's prayer TIME after TIME to THEE, Oh God, we join in TELLING others of the TRUTH of THY salvation. for Your Kingdom. We are reminded that Jesus fulfilled the plan of salvation as the Saviour, Redeemer of Your world. We spend TIME spreading the TRUTH about Your TRINITY TEAM.

Prayer: Dear God, we learn from Your Son, Jesus Christ because He is THINE.

In Your TIME he became the TRUTH for You (Thee) and the entire world.

September 21 ABC's of Wisdom

Scripture Text: Psalm 133: 1

"Behold, how good and how pleasant it is for brethren to dwell together in unity."

David continues encouraging in his Psalms (songs) to His God. He continues to struggle with the fact that he remains a stranger to his own brothers. Our Lord Jesus testified to this also as He taught salvation; redemption for His brothers. He brought brothers together; often calling them to meet together. In His wisdom He spoke words that began with today's letter U:

Our Lord, Jesus would quote from David's psalms to multitudes of UPSET brothers. We are reminded of the devasting UPSET when Jesus had to calm the seas for His fishermen. The calming of the seas was an example of how to handle the future.

Our Lord, Jesus would quote from David's psalms to multitudes of UNDERSTANDING brothers. We are reminded of the deep UNDERSTANDING when Jesus had to calm the crowds for His disciples. The calming of the crowds was an example of how to preach so others could handle the future.

Our Lord, Jesus would quote from David's psalms to multitudes of UNITED brothers. We are reminded of the UNITY when Jesus had to calm His own family at His crucifixion. The calming of His own family was an example of how to strive for handling the future.

Prayer: Dear God, we learn from Your Son, Jesus Christ as He showed us His calming example during times of UNIVERSAL UPSET.

September 22 ABC's of Wisdom

Scripture Text: I Corinithians 15: 57

"But Thanks Be To God, which giveth us the victory through our Lord Jesus Christ."

The Apostle Paul when writing two letters to the Church of Corinth made sure to include thanks to His God. We are familiar with Jesus including thanks in His prayers to God; even when it was not His will. We ponder God's will for His world with today's letter V:

Jesus would pray to His Heavenly Father and would include His concern for the VIOLENCE overtaking His world. We are reminded that our Lord Jesus Christ with His Trinity Team the world would find peace.

Jesus would pray with a VOICE of concern, compassion and confidence to His Heavenly Father and knew His words would not come back VOID! We are reminded that our Lord Jesus Christ with His Trinity Team the world would find answers.

Jesus would pray in a garden, and on a mountain that have become for us the landscape for portrayal of our Heavenly Father's VICTORY for His world. We are reminded that our Lord Jesus Christ with His Trinity Team; the world would win over sin!

Prayer: Dear God, we learn from Your Son, Jesus Christ as He taught against VIOLENCE as the Trinity Team listened to the VOICES of concern.

September 23 ABC's of Wisdom

Scripture Text: Colossians 1: 9, 10

"For this cause we also, since the day we heard it, do not cease to pray for you, and to desire that ye might be filled with the knowlege of his will in all wisdom and spiritual understanding."

The Apostle Paul is writing to yet another one of the churches; this particular one at the city of Colosse. He writes the letter with the use of today's letter W:

The Apostle Paul writes to the Colossians with Timotheus; thus explaining the use of 'WE' in praying and desiring for the Colossians to be filled from the knowledge of God and the Father of our Lord Jesus Christ. WE are reminded that WE pray to the same God and Father of our Lord Jesus Christ.

The Apostle Paul and Timotheus pray and desire the Colossians to be filled from the knowlege of God's WILL; His plan, goal, strategy as Father of our Lord Jesus Christ. WE are reminded that God's WILL is from the same God and Father of our Lord.

Let's join other readers of the Apostle Paul and Timotheus letter to the Colossians to be filled from the knowledge of God's WILL and WISDOM; spiritual understanding. Christ. WE are reminded that God's WILL and WISDOM is from the same God and Father of our Lord JesusChrist.

Prayer: Dear God, we learn from Your Son, Jesus Christ to pray anddesire for others to join in being filled with Your WILL and WISDOM.

September 24 ABC's of Wisdom

Scripture Text: Revelation 22 : 19

"And if any man shall take away from the words of the book of this prophecy , God shall take away his part out of the book of life, and out of the holy city, and from the things which are in this book."

St. John The Divine wrote of the revelation of the Lord Jesus

Christ. He concludes the letter by warning no man to take away from the book. We cannot take away from any part of The Holy Bible. We ponder this thought with today's letter X

Thousands of years later from the writing of Revelation by St. John The Divine, there are servants of his God reading of the Lord Jesus Christ. What His reader does is to allow the words of The Holy Word to be studied thoroughly just as our X-RAY. We are reminded that God through His Son, Jesus Christ has a clear picture of us with His 'X-RAY eyes' !

Thousands of years later from the writing of Revelation by John, there are servants of his God sharing the Lord Jesus Christ. What His servant does is to allow the words of the Holy Book to be translated and copied thoroughly with the X-EROX machine! We are reminded that God through His Son, Jesus Christ has a clear copy of us with His Book of Life!

Thousands of years later from the writing of Revelation by St. John The Divine, there are messengers allowing the words of the Holy Book to be shared through Music with the use of the psaltery, cymbal, trumpet and even the XLOPHONE!

We are reminded that God through His Son, Jesus Christ has a clear sight and hearing of His words sung and played because of the inspired word.

Prayer: Dear God, we learn from Your Lord, Jesus Christ how to be ready as servants to present our spiritual bodies to be studied daily.

September 25 ABC's of Wisdom

Scripture Text: John 14: 1

"Let not your heart be troubled: ye believe in God, believe also in me."

St. John wrote words of wisdom in one of the four books of the New Testament called the Gospels or Good News. We read many quotes of Jesus that contain words of wisdom that start with today's letter; Y.

John quotes comforting words of God's Son, Jesus Christ. John allows the reader to take these words personally. He does not quote the Lord saying; 'our hearts', instead: 'YOUR hearts'. Each of us are reminded how these comforting words have become personal.

John quotes commanding words of God's Son, Jesus Christ. John allows YOU to take the commands of Jesus personally. YOU are reminded how these comforting words have become powerful.

John quotes words of wisdom of God's Son, Jesus Christ. John allows the reader to YIELD and take these words even when troubled. Each of us are reminded how these comforting words have become helpful forever!

Prayer: Dear God, we learn from Your Son, Jesus Christ how you personally presented words of Your family for us so that we yield not unto temptation from evil.

September 26 ABC's of Wisdom

Scripture Text: Romans 10: 2, 3

"For I bear them record that they have a zeal of God, but not according to knowledge. For they being ignorant of God's righteousness, and going about to establish their own righteousness, have not submitted themselves unto the righteousness of God."

The Apostle Paul writes to the Romans and states that salvation is open to all believers. His words of wisdom help us to ponder today's letter Z.

Time after time since God's creation of man there has been ZEALOUS people. We read in Romans, Chapter 10 Paul's reminder that the nation has misplaced God's righteousness. We are reminded to place our submissive faith in our righteous God.

Time after time since God's creation of man there have been preachers, rulers, and prophets such as ZECHARIAH. We read in 1: 7,8 ZECHARIAH'S reminder that those under the rule of King Darius to learn of the righteousness of God. Perhaps there were those

PONDERING PEARLS OF WISDOM

who were more prone to place their submissive faith in kings rather than our righteous God.

Time after time since God's creation of man there have been builders of God's kingdom such as the Israelites. They built the fortified hill of ZION (Sion). We read in chapter 1; verse 17 under the rule of King Darius there were extra measures set to build God's kingdom rather than man's

Prayer: Dear God, we learn from Your Son, Jesus Christ; a zealot for You!

September 27 ABC's of Wisdom

Scripture Text: Proverbs 3: 13

"Happy is the man that findeth wisdom, and the man that getteth understanding."

Since the beginning of September we have been pondering wisdom. We have pondered with the help of the twenty-six letters of the ABC's. King Solomon of Israel has his readers find wisdom. Let us look at letters A to H for helping us to find wisdom daily.

Wise King Solomon of Israel reminds his readers that wisdom can be ACQUIRED from reading the Holy Bible and learning the lessons. BELIEVE happily what you can read and learn of wisdom daily.

Wise King Solomon of Israel reminds his reader that wisdom can be COLLECTED because of the all knowing Holy Trinity. DELVE joyfully into what you can read and learn of wisdom daily.

Wise King Solomon of Israel reminds his reader that wisdom can be EFFECTIVE because of the easy access of the Bible. FORM FRIENDSHIPS with others who read and learn of wisdom daily.

Wise King Solomon of Israel reminds his reader that wisdom can be GRANTED because of answered prayer. HELP others to rely on the wisdom of the Trinity,

Prayer: Dear God, we learn from Your Son, Jesus Christ who daily sought your wisdom.

September 28 ABC's of Wisdom

Scripture Text: II Corinthains 3: 3

"For asmuch as ye are manifestly declared to be the epistle of Christ minstered by us, written not with ink, but with the Spirit of the living God; not in tables of stone, but in fleshy tables of the heart."

Today we review the ABC's of God's wisdom by reciting the letters from I to Q.

Apostle Paul has his readers continue in God's wisdom that is INTERESTING. There is no doubt that we are epistles of our IMPRESSIVE Christ.

Apostle Paul has his readers dig into God's wisdom that is JUST. There is no doubt that we are epistles of our JUDICIAL Christ.

Apostle Paul has his readers study God's wisdom that is KNOWLEDGE. there is no doubt that we are epistles of our KING and Christ.

Apostle Paul has his readers share God's wisdom by LIFTING. There is no doubt that we are epistles of our LOVING Christ.

Apostle Paul has his readers share God's wisdom that is MARVELLOUS! There is no doubt we are epistles of our MAGNIFICENT Christ.

Apostle Paul has his readers share God's wisdom that is only good NEWS. There is no doubt that we are epistles of our NOBLE Christ.

Apostle Paul has his readers share God's wisdom that is OPEN-MINDED. There is no doubt that we are epistles of our OMNIPOTENT Christ.

Apostle Paul has his readers share God's wisdom that is PERFECT. There is no doubt that we are epistles of our PRAYING Christ.

Apostle Paul has his readers share God's wisdom that is His QUEST. There is no doubt that we are epistles of our Christ without any QUESTION!

Prayer: Dear God, we learn from Your Son, Jesus Christ who is our daily wisdom without question!

September 29 ABC's of Wisdom

Scripture Text: Revelation 3:20

"Behold, I stand at the door and knock: if any man hear my voice, and open the door, I will come in to him, and will sup with him, and he with me."

St. John the Divine writes about the ending of Christ's life here on earth as a human. Today's devotional features the remainder of the ABC's of Wisdom with letters R to Z.

Jesus Christ states that He is at our heart's door and is knocking. How RECEPTIVE of a RECEIVER am I ?

Jesus Christ states that He is knocking at our heart's door and talking. How SOUND of a SERVANT am I ?

Jesus Christ states that He is at our heart's door and is asking. How THOUGHTFUL of a TEACHER am I ?

Jesus Christ states that He is at our heart's door and is inviting. How UNDERSTANDING of an UNDER-STUDY am I ?

Jesus Christ states that He is at our heart's door and is coming. How VERBAL of a VICTORIOUS Christian am I ?

Jesus Christ states that He is at our heart's door and wants to sup. How much of a WISE Christian WOMAN am I?

Jesus Christ states that He is at our heart's door and wants to give. How much of my Christian life is an X-RAY with positive results?

Jesus Christ states that He is at our heart's door and wants to stay. How YIELDING of a YOUTH in Christ am I ?

Jesus Christ states that He is at our heart's door and wants me to stay. How ZEALOUS of a Christian heading for Heaven's ZION am I ?

Prayer: Dear God, we learn from Your Jesus Christ that He is the Alpha and the Omega; the Beginning and the End.

September 30 ABC's of Wisdom

Scripture Text: Daniel 4: 37

"Now I Nebuchadnezzar praise and extol and honour the King of heaven, all whose works are truth, and his ways judgment: and those that walk in pride he is able to abase."

Thanks to Daniel's interpretation of King Nebuchanadnezzar's dreams, God's kingdom is recognized as having dominion over any earthly kingdom. The interpretation would not have been made without a common understanding. This would involve a common language to understand. And, there would have to be a common alphabet. Thanks to God for allowing His scholars to translate, using a common alphabet.

Today, Sue's monthly drawing is presented so that we May recognize the infinite wisdom of God and His Trinity Team.

Prayer: Thank You, God for sending Your Son, Jesus to be the Alpha (beginning) and the Omega (end) for our ordered lives.

October 1 Wit and Wisdom

Scripture Text: Genesis 1: 3

"And God said, Let there be light; and there was light."

God the Creator of heaven and earth said; "Let there be" . These words Moses wrote in his first book; Genesis. He quoted his God the Creator of earth. There is Wit and Wisdom in God's first command:

"Let there be light" !

Can you picture the wit of God as He saw the light He created.? He even gave it a name; day! He even divided the light; allowing for sunrises and sunsets! He even divided it?

God knew how to fill the void. He created light out of darkness!

Do you picture the wisdom of God as He created man to sharelight? From Adam to the Apostles of His Son we witness how each individual was allowed to depend on God's light and eventually His Son, Lord and Light of the World. We are reminded to let our little lights shine!

Do you understand the wisdom of God as He created man to share the light and even separate light from darkness? God knew how to lead His people with the light of the moon, and stars! We are reminded to be beams of light that shine just like a flashlight or candle that only lights temporarily and then needs to be re-lit. Oh how dependent we are on the light of the world!

Prayer: Thank You God for creating, sending and saving light for Your earth.

October 2 Wit and Wisdom

Scripture Text: Genesis 1: 9

"And God said, Let the waters under the heavens be gathered together unto one place, and let the dry land appear; and it was so."

Our Creator, our God said once again; "Let there be". His business of creating was not finished! There is Wit and Wisdom found in these words of God!

Can you picture the wit of God as He watched the gathering of the waters?. He gave them names; the first water being seas. God even divided them. He knew once again how to fill the void. God allowed for puddles, creeks, rivers, ponds, lakes, and oceans!

Can you understand the wit of God as He separated the water from the land? He allowed for banks, gullies, inlets, and shores to surround the water. Of course, God knew how to provide for Man and allowed creatures of the land, air and seas!

Do you picture the wit of God as He shared water with Adam to the Apostles of His Son who stated He was the Living Water? We are reminded to be refreshing witnesses as His pure water!

Do you understand the wisdom of God as He provides water that will never make us thirst (we know that is not the water of the sea)! We know in His wisdom, God's Son; Jesus Christ who shared His wisdom as the Living Water.

Prayer: Thank You God, for creating, saving and sharing Your water!

October 3 Wit and Wisdom

Scripture Text: Matthew 5: 13 & 14

"Ye are the salt of the earth: but if the salt have lost his savour, wherewith shall it be salted? It is thenceforth good for nothing, but to be cast out, and to be trodden under foot of men. Ye are the light of the world. A city that is set on a hill cannot be hid."

We continue to picture and understand the Wit and Wisdom of God as Creator of light and water (Genesis 1: 3, 9). Jesus passes this Wit and Wisdom to His followers. I share with you today a new poem as my way of passing along God's Wit and Wisdom:

STEADY FLOW AND GLOW

You are the salt of the earth Just a little pinch will do !

Put a bit of flavor on earth Share a little pinch of salt with others Share with a steady flow!

You are the light of the world Just a little flicker will do!

Put a bit of glimmer in our world Share a little flicker of light with others share with a steady glow!

Prayer: Thank You God, for sharing Your Wit and Wisdom in every light and water.

October 4 Wit and Wisdom

Scripture Text: Psalm 23 : 1

"The Lord is my shepherd; I shall not want."

The Psalmist David we know was a young shepherd and loved God. He reminds us that a good shepherd tends to his sheep so they are not wanting anything because all is provided! We are reminded of how our Lord is the Great Shepherd.

Can you picture the wit of God as He inspires a King to relate to sheep? God knew to relate to King David as he ruled a people who wandered around aimlessly without their shepherd! God would watch as David used his shepherding skills to find the lost and keep the flock (his kingdom) together. I am reminded that as we become lost in the hustle and bustle of the day that as we May get tangled up in the sins of the world, our Lord; our Shepherd frees us!

Can you understand the wisdom of God as He teaches a King to relate to his people by using his talent (profession); a shepherd. David leads his people into a safe and secure environment and it is their choice to wander or stay in the 'fold'. I am reminded that as we May wander away from the flock, our Lord; our Shepherd finds usl

We recall that God helped prepare His Son, Jesus Christ to be the Good Shepherd here on earth and that His followers would not need anything. Jesus Christ Himself gives praises to His Heavenly Father who He trusted to meet His need; to minister to His earthly followers.

Prayer: Thank You God, Your Wit and Wisdom as my Good Shepherd.

October 5 Wit and Wisdom

Scripture Text: Psalm 23: 2

"He maketh me to lie down in green pastures: He leadeth me beside the still waters."

The Psalmist and King David continues to praise God's ways of providing the needs of His people.

Can you picture the wit of God as He watches His people in the green pastures? He makes us lie down and can you picture how He smiles as He sees us trying to wander about on our own? I am reminded that God allowed His Son to be the Great Shepherd and He probably smiled as Jesus tended to His people (sheep) and how some tried to wander around independently.

Can you understand the wisdom of God as He guides His people to green pastures?

He knew that Jesus would be the Great Shepherd; caring for every one of the fold. I am reminded that God allowed Jesus to shepherd His people through the inspiration of His wisdom.

Can you picture the wit of God as He watches His people in the still waters? He allows us to drink; become refreshed and can you picture how He smiles as He sees us trying to drink from the still waters? He watches the shoving and the playful antics of a lamb hesitant to enter deep enough to be refreshed. I am reminded of how we follow God to be refreshed but May be offensive to others.

Can you understand the wisdom of God as He leads us to water? He knows our thirst and the thirst of our Great Shepherd; Jesus Christ. The still cool, refreshing water is tempting to anyone who is thirsty. The fold of our Great Shepherd is tempting to anyone who is thirsty!

Prayer: Thank You God, Your Wit and Wisdom as my Shepherd when I am thirsty.

October 6 Wit and Wisdom

Scripture Text: Psalm 23: 3

"He restoreth my soul: He leadeth me in the paths of righteousness for His name's sake."

David reminds us that even the shepherds need restoration and leadership to continue as herders of the flock. God in His Wit and Wisdom restores, leads His people.

Can you picture the wit of God as He allows His people to have leaders for His kingdom that have to rule by example? He would smile as He watches the tired shepherd and King trying to sneak away to be restored, and after a few futile attempts is led by Christ in the correct path to follow God. I am reminded that God is a daily restorer and leader down His paths of righteousness.

Can you understand the wisdom of God as He restores and leads one of His shepherds? God's path is one of righteousness. He allowed David to rule but to recognize the human need to be restored and after a few futile attempts is aided in preparation to follow the paths of righteousness. I am reminded that God's Son, Jesus was restored and led by God in preparation to lead us down the paths of His Heavenly Father's righteousness.

Prayer: Thank You God, for Wit and Wisdom as You lead us with the help of Your Son.

October 7 Wit and Wisdom

Scripture Text: Psalm 23: 4

"Yea, though I walk through the valley of the shadow of death, I will fear no evil: for thou art with me; thy rod and thy staff they comfort me."

King David continues His psalm to God; his shepherd. He recalls the valleys of the green pasture and still waters. He mentions the rod and staff used by shepherds such as he was familiar using.

Can you picture the wit of God; as He allows the herd of sheep to literally bump into each other as they enter into a darkened valley? I am reminded how as groups following our Lord; the Great Shepherd, we stumble as we go.

Can you understand the wisdom of God; as He has taught His shepherds to position a confident leader within the fold of sheep? I am reminded how a confident leader is easier to follow who walks with God.

Can you picture the wit of God; as He allows the use of the rod and staff to comfort the herd? I am reminded of how most people do not accept graciously the correction of their leaders by visible ways (especially in front of peers).

Can you understand the wisdom of God; as He provides the use of the rod and staff to His Son, the Great Shepherd? I am reminded of how Jesus' followers did not do so very graciously...the very rod and staff of comfort was used by those who followed for evil motives.

Prayer: Thank You God, Your Wit and Wisdom for us wanderers.

October 8 Wit and Wisdom

Scripture Text: Psalm 23: 5

"Thou preparest a table before me in the presence of mine enemies: thou anointest my head with oil; my cup runneth over."

Banquets and feasts planned by King David would be hosted and prepared in order to give thanks to God for His provision and protection.

Can you picture the wit of God as He allowed King David to eat in front of his enemies? He smiles at how we eat hurriedly the fruits and meat of our fields and even in front of the enemy. I am reminded of how God sent His Son Jesus to have His disciples to partake of the prepared Lord's Supper; amidst doubters and betrayers.

Can you understand the wisdom of God as He allows enough food for the table; even for the enemy? He leads us to save and to serve. I am reminded of how God sent His Son Jesus to have each of us to partake of His prepared table; not leaving out the enemy.

Can you picture the wit of God as He allowed King David to be annointed in front of his people and his enemies? He smiles as he watches and listens to His people who with various backgrounds converse at the table. I am reminded of how God sent His Son Jesus to have communion with all of His Heavenly Father's children.

Can you understand the wisdom of God as he allows us to mingle; feast at the same table; receive His annointing; blessed by His Great Shepherd and His Holy Spirit? I am reminded of how God sent His Son Jesus to annointment for all of His Heavenly Father's children.

Prayer: Thank You God, Your Wit and Wisdom includes annointing and blessing.

October 9 Wit and Wisdom

Scripture Text: Psalm 23: 6

"Surely goodness and mercy shall follow me all the days of my life; and I will dwell in the house of the Lord for ever."

King David knows he has earthly goods and blessings and lives in a palace known by other kings. He thanks His Lord for being his Shepherd and within the conclusion of this psalm he acknowledges God's goodness, mercy and provision as his Shepherd.

Can you picture the wit of God as He allowed David to be an earthly King? He smiles at the earthly wealth and the riches within David's palace and knows He has the power to give everlasting riches and provide a heavenly home. We are reminded that goodness and mercy follow us daily when we allow our Lord Jesus Christ to be our Great Shepherd.

Can you understand the wisdom of God as He allowed David to depend on Him as the Shepherd. God allowed His Son, Christ Jesus to quote from King David's psalms and become the Great Shepherd of goodness, mercy and provisions for a heavenly home. We are reminded that we are able to live with our Lord Jesus Christ; our

Great Shepherd.

Prayer: Thank You God, Your Wit and Wisdom evident in our daily lives.

October 10 Wit and Wisdom

Scripture Text: I Corinthians 3: 18

"Let no man deceive himself. If any man among you seemeth to be wise in this world, let him become a fool, that he May be wise."

We continue to picture and understand the Wit and Wisdom of God. The Apostle Paul writes to the Church of Corinth about earthly wisdom. We know we have palaces and kingdoms just like King David. However,just as King David and Apostle Paul wrote: We are deceived if our earthly wisdom prevents us from following our Great Shepherd. (Psalm 23: 1-6). I wrote a new poem to profess my faith in the Great Shepherd:

Nature's Mirrors

The gentle rains of a spring or summer day form God's tiniest mirror for us to see ourselves and perhaps a tiny sparrow sipping away in the puddle that reflects the flight of the bumble-bee Am I reflecting God's love in some tiny way?

The steady rains of an autumn day form God's larger mirror for us to see ourselves and the flight of an hawk soaring away in the pool that reflects the clouds, trees, and me. Am I reflecting God's love in some larger way?

The gentle, steady snow of a winter day form one of God's largest mirrors for us to see ourselves and fields of grain and hay in the pond that reflects the flock of geese forming the letter 'V' Am I reflecting God's love in a majestic way?

Prayer: Thank You God, Your Wit and Wisdom are beyond my comprehension as I become one of your sheep.

October 11 Wit and Wisdom

Scripture Text: Acts 9: 26

"And when Saul was come to Jerusalem, he assayed to join himself to the disciples; but they were all afraid of him, and believed not that he was a disciple."

The Acts Of The Apostles was written (some say by Luke) as a ' treatise to Theophilus' (Acts 1: 1). Acts records all that Jesus did and taught. Today's scripture reveals Jesus' Wit and Wisdom in the conversion of Saul.

Can you picture the wit of Jesus as He allows Saul to be going about his business of persecuting the Jews and allows him to go on his own mission? Jesus shows His own mission for Saul on the road to Damascus; Saul is converted and named Paul. I am reminded of my own personal conversion and how God's mission for me is to be a "Disciple of Jesus".

Can you understand the wisdom of Jesus as He allows Saul to continue on the same road but with a different mission? Jesus allows the newly converted Paul to join other disciples in carrying the good news. I am reminded of my own decision to join other disciples of Jesus; daily following God's mission.

Prayer: Thank You God, Your Wit and Wisdom are beyond my comprehension as a Disciple of Jesus.

October 12 Wit and Wisdom

Scripture Text: II Corinthians 9:6

"For this I say, He which soweth sparingly shall reap also sparingly; and he which soweth bountifully shall reap also bountifully."

The Apostle Paul learned from his conversion on that road to join the disciples of Jesus. God's Wit and Wisdom would be Paul's tools to preach to the churches such as Corinth of God's mission through His Son, Jesus Christ. This poem is my reaction to God's Wit and Wisdom as He allows me to daily be His 'Disciple of Jesus' :

Tote to Tow

The green flower tote is 'chic' as I carry it to work in 2008 at Clifton Springs Hospital & Clinic "Bloom where you grow is my daily fate!

My sister Sue tucked a poem inside: Whatever you May reap whatever you May sow throughout the season this tote will help you keep you in tow! You'll find it to be of use from seeds to produce.

Sister Sue's gift is at my side as I carry what I May reap or sow working within the Activities Team; side by side Yes, residents, families, and staff keep me in tow!

I open and share what words are printed: "Bloom where you grow". I carry the title 'Plant Lady' I should note as I learn from what others know!

I carry my sister Sue's gift in Spring & Summer the seasons when we watch plants grow I tuck away the tote in Autumn and Winter the seasons when I carry a tote with a rainbow!

Prayer: Thank You God for Your Wit and Wisdom by gifts we receive.

October 13 Wit and Wisdom

Scripture Text: I John 4: 19

"We love him because he first loved us. "

The Apostle John wrote three letters (epistles) to little children, the elder, and the fellow helpers. In each of these three epistles is woven the theme of God's love.

Can you picture the wit of God as He allows us to love Him as little children?. He smiles as the child loves unconditionally the parents who loved first. I am reminded that God as our Creator loved us first is to be loved by us.

Can you understand the wisdom of God as He loved His world that He sent His only Son, Jesus, Now that is unconditional love! I am reminded that God as our Heavenly Father loved His Son first and is to be loved by us.

We do not have to play the game (even as adults) with God: "He loves me; He loves me not! We seek God's love because He seeks us in His love.

We are to love God beyond the earthly love; looking beyond the show of love here on earth.

Prayer: Thank You God, Your Wit and Wisdom emulates love.

October 14 Wit and Wisdom

Scripture Text: Psalm 105: 1, 2

"O give thanks unto the Lord; call upon HIs name: make known his deeds among the people. Sing unto him, sing psalms unto him: talk ye of all his wondrous works."

The Psalmist David shows His love for His Lord, God by singing to Him . Can you picture the wit of God as He allowed David to sing to Him? I am reminded that God allowed even a shepherd to be loved and smiles down on those who show their praise for His love.

Can you understand the wisdom of God as He inspires David to create in writing a show of love toward the God who first loved Him? Jesus followed the passages of the Holy Scriptures and talked of loving our neighbor as ourself. I am reminded that God allowed His only Son to love and to put on the greatest show of love! The following poem expresses my love to God:

Music Memories

Music memories....how they linger stirred up once again from the past as we try to sing along as if we were professional singers... those lyrics and tunes that last and last!

Music memories...tease my mind stirring up my inner emotions as we try to be to those songs so kind those lyrics and tunes keeping my body in motion!

Music memories by Joe Trionfero; "A Show of Love" lifting my spirit high stirring my heart as a piercing arrow lifting my voice...

perhaps a sigh othr lyrics and tunes momentarily I borrow!

Prayer: Thank You God, Your Wit and Wisdom is a huge part of Your love.

October 15 Wit and Wisdom

Scripture Text: John 3: 16

"For God so loved the world that he gave his only begotten son , that whosoever believeth in him shall not perish but have everlasting life. "

The Apostle John writes of God's love for His only Son; Jesus Christ. We are familiar with today's text and perhaps be able to recite from memory. God's word can be inspiring and reflects His Wit and Wisdom:

Can you picture God's wit since He allows us to believe in His Son's mission here on earth. He smiles down on the ones who choose to believe and continues to love the entire world. I am reminded that God's love is just so!

Can you understand God's wisdom as He surrounds His loving arms around His world and gave us a Saviour through His Son. He inspires the writers of each book of the Holy Bible to become believers of everlasting life.

Prayer: Thank You God, Your Wit and Wisdom make us recipients of salvation.

October 16 Wit and Wisdom

Scripture Text: Matthew 2 (Christmas Story)

Jesus was a symbol of love even as a baby. Can you picture the wit of God as He allowed the rulers of His earthly kingdom to worship an infant? I am reminded that God sends His children to be loved.

Jesus' birth as we are told in the Christmas story is a miracle. Can you picture the wisdom of God as He continues to create daily? I am reminded that God sent His only son to be loved.

Today I share a poem that keeps me focused on the Christmas story all year:

Little Things Mean Alot

Oh, little town of Bethlehem, you mean alot Our savious Jesus was born here; a very safe, secure spot!

Oh, little baby Jesus, our King You mean alot; Your eye will be on the littlest sparrow one of your caring 'lot'!

Oh, little sparrow perched in a tree you mean alot; reminding of us our Lord's care not a one of us will He forget!

Oh, little present under the tree you mean alot; the one wrapped with love from the family whose lives together Jesus brought!

Prayer: Thank You God, Your Wit and Wisdom show us the influence of little things. all through the year.

October 17 Wit and Wisdom

Scripture Text: I Peter 5: 7

"Casting all your care upon him for he careth for you."

The Apostle Peter was also a fisherman. He speaks of man's need to cast for fish and all their cares. God, in His Wit and Wisdom allowed for an ample supply of nets to cast for fish and an ample supply of cares to cast for Jesus.

Can you picture the wit of God as He allows His fishermen to cast their nets? He smiles down upon us who cast our cares upon Him. I I am reminded that God smiled down upon His people and their Saviour with the goal of salvation for the whole world.

Can you understand the wisdom of God as He allows the nets to be full and running over. He has the same offer of salvation through His Son for our world today. I am reminded that God inspired the writers of the Old and New Testament to proclaim salvation through our Saviour, Jesus Christ.

Prayer: Thank You God, Your wit and widom as recipients of Your care.

October 18 Wit and Wisdom

Scripture Text: John 18: 37

"Pilate therefore said unto him, Art thou a king then? Jesus answered, 'Thou sayest that I am a king. To this end was I born, and for this cause come I unto this world, that I should bear witness unto the truth. Every one that is of the truth heareth my voice' ".

The Apostle and one of the fishermen; John writes of the apprehension, the denial, and arraignment of Jesus Christ. God in His Wit and Wisdom prepares His Son to be the way, the truth, and the life (John 14: 6); the King of Kings:

Can you picture the wit of God as He allows a great ruler such as Pilate to sit on his royal throne and question the authority of Jesus? God smiled approvingly at Jesus' answer. I am reminded that we can sit at the Saviour's feet and try to grasp His truth.

Can you understand the wisdom of God as He allows His earthly rulers to sit and question Jesus' followers and grasp His truth? IGod wisely allows His Son to be the Truth. I am reminded that we May be alone at the Saviour's feet and try to share His truth.

I share with you a new poem about sitting:

Sitting Alone

Sitting along in an hand-me-down high chair along side three older and one younger sibling watching each action and facial expression cooing and enjoying all this special attention!

Sitting alone in a first and used car Chevy...Vega...Hatch-back purchased from a special Oswego family traveling and enjoying new adventures!

Sitting alone in a rickety, old rocking chair an heirloom with fancy rungs and high back passed down by precious ancestors reading and enjoying this simple past-time!

Prayer: Thank You God, Your Wit and Wisdom are for me to follow.

October 19 Wit and Wisdom

Scripture Text: Luke 23: 42

"And he said unto Jesus, Lord remember me when thou comest unto thy kingdom. "

Luke the writer of the third gospel (good news) records how one of the other malefactors along side Jesus had just rebuked the other who wanted Jesus to save him from the terrible death at the cross. Jesus' malefactor who remembered that Jesus would set him free puts forth a request:

Can you picture the wit of God as He allows the malefactors along each side of Jesus to be pleading for their salvation. God must have been delighted to hear the request asked of His Son, Jesus. We are reminded to seek grace from God's Son, His Saviour.

Can you understand the wisdom of God as He allows the other malefactors being hung with Jesus to be overheard discussing the power and authority of His Son? We are reminded to daily be overheard discussing the grace of our Lord and Saviour, Jesus Christ.

Prayer: Thank You God, Your Wit and Wisdom are for us to seek.

October 20 Wit and Wisdom

Scripture Text: Philippians 4: 4

"Rejoice in the Lord alway: and again I say, Rejoice."

The Apostle Paul writes to the Church of Philippi and encourages them to rejoice (even in trials). We are reminded of these words when we lose dear ones here on earth. We go forward; remembering the special times and now the loved ones rejoice always! God in His Wit and Wisdom inspired me to rejoice in my separation from my earthly parents; Herbert and Virginia Appelt:

We Will Remember December

Dear Mother, and Dad We will remember December a month that made your parents glad! the 15th of 1926 for you, dear Mother the

21st of 1924 for you, dear Dad

a month that makes your five children glad! two of us having birthdays each of us sharing Christmas with precious memories, dear Mother & Dad

a month that makes our family glad relatives having birthdays loved ones sharing holiday greetings from a long....line...of love

a month that makes our families glad Dear Mother and Dad, you are together! Your parting from earth May make us sad... You would want us to hold on...be happy rejoice in our Lord!

Prayer: Thank You God, Your Wit and Wisdom You provide our parents.

October 21 Wit and Wisdom

Scripture Text: Mark 16: 15

"And he said unto them, 'Go ye into all the world, and preach the gospel to every creature.' "

Mark joins the other three gospel (good news) writers in sharing an account of Jesus appearing to the disciples after His death. God in His Wit and Wisdom allows Jesus to continue to command His people.

Can you picture the wit of God as He allows Jesus to appear to the disciples. He had to be smiling when they were so flaber- gasted and some did not even recognize Him. I am reminded that when God is smiling down on us, it is because of our faith; our belief that we can go and preach the gospel.

Can you understand the wisdom of God as He allows the followers of Jesus to go and preach the gospel. He had the power to prepare His Son who would then prepare the way for His disiples. We go in belief and in faith in what we preach.

Prayer: Thank You God, Your Wit and Wisdom instill faith and belief.

October 22 Wit and Wisdom

Scripture Text: Acts 1: 8

"But ye shall receive power, after that the Holy Ghost is come upon you: and ye shall be witnesses unto me both in Jerusalem, and in all Judea, and in Samaria, and unto the uttermost parts of the earth."

The disciples are communing with their risen Lord Jesus Christ. They are given instructions; a prophecy from their Great Shepherd; their King of Kings; Lord of Lords. I am reminded how that power is for me also:

Are You A Missionary?

Are you a missionary? I was asked one day as I waited at the drive-thru of a local pharmacy.

My reply was positive as I stated that I believe so and that I belong to a local church; The Salvation Army.

Are you a missionary? Someone May ask you one day as you wait on family or friend.

Will your reply be positive? Will you state you believe so? and that you belong to a local church; a church family?

Prayer: Thank You God, Your Wit and Wisdom are prophecy fulfilled.

October 23 Wit and Wisdom

Scripture Text: Luke 6: 20

"And he lifted up his eyes on his disciples , and said, 'Blessed be ye poor; for yours is the kingdom of God'."

Today's scripture text is the introduction to Jesus' Beatitudes or what we know as His 'Sermon On The Mount'. His Wit and Wisdom are heard in every choice of words:

Can you picture the wit of Jesus as He looks straight into the eyes of His disciples and saying; 'Blessed be ye poor' ? In His wit, our Lord is watching the reaction of His disciples who are human; and desire to be rich! I am reminded that God allowed His Son to be poor; seeking food, shelter, provisions.

Can you understand the wisdom of Jesus; God's Son and Saviour of the world; kingdom? In His wisdom; received only from His own Heavenly Father, Jesus is named King of Kings; claiming authority and power to bless the poor. I am reminded that God allowed His Son to preach to the rich and the poor.

Prayer: Thank You God, Your Wit and Wisdom bring on the blessings.

October 24 Wit and Wisdom

Scripture Text: Luke 6: 21

"Blessed are ye that hunger now: for ye shall be filled. Blessed are ye that weep now: for ye shall laugh."

We continue the study of the Beatitudes and picture the Wit and Wisdom of Jesus as He somes to preaching His second point in His Sermon On The Mount. His disciples listen just as eagerly as usual as they seek to be one of the blessed by their Lord Jesus Christ.

Can you picture the wit of Jesus as He watches His disciples as they react to being blessed if they hunger or weep? I am reminded that God sent His Son to preach salvation for all; even the hungry and sorrowful.

Can you understand the wisdom of Jesus as He speaks of the hungry being filled and the sorrowful laughing? I am re- minded that God sent His Son to preach salvation for all; even the filled and the happy.

Prayer: Thank You God, Your Wit and Wisdom includes Your beloved Son of peace.

October 25 Wit and Wisdom

Scripture Text: Luke 6:22

"Blessed are ye, when men shall hate you, and when they shall separate you from their company, and shall reproach you, and cast out your name as evil, for the Son of man's sake. "

Today's scripture text is the conclusion of Jesus' Beatitudes from The Sermon On The Mount. Jesus talks about blessings when there is hate and grumbling. I was inspired by God in His Wit and Wisdom to write the following poem:

Grumbling

Did you hear that low grumble? I believe the grumble came from underground. Oh, how buildings crumble Oh, help and hope can be found!

Did you hear that low grumble? I believe the grumble came from the throat. Oh, how words jumble Oh, May they each turn into a thankful note!

Did you hear that low grumble? I bellieve the grumble came from the stomach! Oh, how someone May mumble "I better eat so I won't get sick" !

Did you hear that low grumble? I believe the grumble came from the grave Oh, how the Saviour] helps when we fumble Oh, Jesus... You are mighty to save!

Prayer: Thank You God, Your Wit and Wisdom continue even when we are grumbling.

October 26 Wit and Wisdom

Scripture Text: Matthew 6: 9

"After this manner therefore pray ye: Our Father which art in heaven, Hallowed be thy name."

Today's text should be familiar to the reader! Perhaps you have heard a child recite the well-known introduction to the Lord's prayer:

"Our Father which art in heaven, How did you know my name?"

Wise parents, siblings, or mentors would have the opportunity to explain that God knows each name and He wants us to know and respect His name!

When Jesus was teaching His disciples how to pray, He allowed His God; His Heavenly Father to be approached with reverance. He allowed God's Wit and Wisdom to teach Him daily how to come to the place of prayer.

Can you picture God allowing Jesus to teach to His disciples how to pray just after He preached against adultery, encouraged loving their enemies, and praying to their God in privacy? I am reminded of how we are all sinners; seeking salvation and need to only confess to God and His Trinity Team! Hallowed be God, Christ, and Holy Spirit!

Can you understand God allowing Jesus to expound on the repect and reverance of introductions for our daily prayers? I am reminded of how we are all students; seeking wisdom and need to only gain wisdom from God and His Trinity Team! God, Christ, and The Holy Spirit knows my name!

Prayer: Thank You God, Your Wit and Wisdom shared with Your Trinity Team.

October 27 Wit and Wisdom

Scripture Text: Matthew 6 : 10

"Thy kingdom come. Thy will be done in earth, as it is in heaven. "

Now that the proper introductions to our Heavenly Father have been made, we continue reciting the prayer He allowed Jesus to first teach His disciples. We continue showing our respect to the Trinity Team:

Can you picture the disciples echoing the words 'Thy kingdom come'? They had just been taught by Jesus to not to swear oathes but to let their communication be 'yea' or 'nay' (5: 33-37). I am reminded that God in His wit allows us to make oathes and often don't keep them!

Can you understand the disciples praying for God's heavenly will be prominent here on earth? They had just been taught by Jesus to not use vain repetitions but to follow Jesus' prayer (6: 7-9). I am reminded that God in His wisdom allows us to pray for His will to be done. This oath is not being said in vain!

Prayer: Thank You God, Your Wit and Wisdom are not vain repetition!

October 28 Wit and Wisdom

Scripture Text: Matthew 6: 11

"Give us this day our daily bread."

Now that the introductions and oath of respect and honor have been made to God, we can continue in the Lord's prayer:

Can you picture the miracles that God allowed Jesus to perform here on earth to provide daily bread? We are reminded of God's wit as He allowed the disciples to find a young lad to an important part of the miracle that we find recorded as "The Feeding of the Five Thousand". I am reminded that my spiritual hunger can only be satisfied by daily receiving God and His Trinity Team's bread!

Can you understand the miracles that God allowed Jesus to perform here on earth to provide daily bread? We are reminded of God's wisdom as He allowed the disciples to break bread with Jesus as an important part of a major miracle that we find recorded as "The Last Supper". I am reminded that my daily asking of bread from God and His Trinity Team is an appropriate request!

Prayer: Thank You God, Your Wit and Wisdom help us meet our needs.

October 29 Wit and Wisdom

Scripture Text: Matthew 6: 12

"And forgive us our debts, as we forgive our debtors."

Now that our introductions, oath and needs are being presented to our Heavenly Father we have a specific request within the Lord's prayer:

Can you picture the parables God allowed Jesus to tell His disciples? God would be nodding in agreement when the lesson was about forgiveness. He would be smiling with approval at those followers who were able to follow a simple commandment (our text today). I am reminded that Jesus had every reason to ask this request of His Heavenly Father!

Can you understand the wisdom of Jesus allowed by God to be an example of one who forgave His debtors? God allowed Jesus to learn of His Scriptures and Commandments so He would know how to forgive. I am reminded that Jesus became the reason (answer) for the world of debts and debtors!

Prayer: Thank You God, Your Wit and Wisdom exist even though I owe Him.

October 30 Wit and Wisdom

Scripture Text: Matthew 6: 13

"And lead us not into temptation, but deliver us from evil: For thine is the kingdom, and the power, and the glory, for ever. Amen. "

Only after introductions, an oath, and specific requests we find ourselves in the conclusion of the Lord's prayer taught by Jesus:

Can you picture the wit of God as He allowed Jesus to preach to His disciples regarding being not led unto temptation? Just prior to Jesus preaching the "Sermon On The Mount", Satan tempted HIm in the wilderness (4: 6,7). I am reminded that God led His Son to learn how to handle temptation as long as He did not tempt His Heavenly Father.

Can you understand the wisdom of God as He allowed Jesus be delivered from evil ? God owns the kingdom (world) with its power and glory. Jesus' disiples would be reminded that just as they began their prayer to God with honor and respect they would conclude with sincerity. I am reminded how I will end my daily prayers to God with a thankful and hearty: AMEN!

Prayer: Thank You God, Your Wit and Wisdom reminds us to believe.

October 31 Wit and Wsdom

Scripture Text: Psalms 101: 2

"I will behave myself wisely in a perfect way. O when wilt thou come unto me? I will walk within my house with a perfect heart."

King David continues to express his God given wisdom What does he mean by behaving wisely? David seeks God daily. On this last day of October, Sue shares one of her drawing for October.

Prayer: Thank You for the bright picture of October with its Autumn slowly creeping along wiith the colorful costumes of Halloween.

November 1 Thanks Be To God

Scripture Text: Genesis 1: 28

"And God blessed them, and God said unto them, Be fruitful, and multiply, and replenish the earth, and subdue it: and have dominion over the fish of the sea, and the fowl of the air, and over every living thing that moveth upon the earth. "

Thanks Be To God for His blessing to His family of humans. He began by blessing Adam and Eve. Are you thankful to God as a member of His family? I am reminded daily to show my gratitude for being allowed to be fruitful, mulltiply and replenish the great creation by God; our earth.

Thanks Be To God for His commandment to His family of humans. He instructed Adam and Eve. Are you thankful to God's instructions? I am reminded daily to show my gratitude for the instructions that come with the blessings. My God allows me to have dominion (power) over every creature and human that moves throughout His creation; our earth.

Thanks Be To God for His first humans; Adam and Eve and the generations that followed; right up to this day! Are you thankful for the lessons learned from our first ancestors? Along side the God given dominion over everything that moved on earth, Adam and Eve had lessons of good and evil to learn. I am reminded daily the lesson of good and evil as I live each day amidst God's daily creation of His earth.

Prayer: Thanks be to You, God the Creator of our ancestors who You gave dominion over your creation; earth.

November 2 Thanks Be To God

Scripture Text: Zechariah 2: 8

"For thus saith the Lord of hosts; After the glory hath He sent me unto the nations which spoiled you; for he that toucheth you toucheth the apple of his eye."

The Prophet Zechariah of the Old Testament showed gratitude toward his God; thanks to his ancestors. He preached of redemption of the city of Zion.

Thanks be to You God, for touching me; an "apple of Your eye" and inspiring me to write:

We Are Apples!

Lord, you gave my family a last name: Appelt; German for 'apple garden. We had an apple orchard on our Prattsburg, New York dairy farm! You touched our family as one by one we became apples of Your eye!

Lord, you gave us our orchard apples; tart Macintosh to sweet Cortlands. We tasted from our apple orchard and from our family gardens! You fed our family as one by one we learned to be apples of Your eye!

Lord, you gave us each a special touch; each extended family member. We showed our gratitude by being able to be thankfully sharing with others! You we always let our families be apples....of your eye; Lord!

Prayer: Thanks be to You, God the Creator of our families, and as the apple of Your eye.

November 3 Thanks Be To God

Scripture Text: Genesis 4: 3, 4

"And in process of time it came to pass, that Cain brought of the fruit of the ground an offering unto the Lord. And Abel, he also brought of the firstlings of his flock and of the fat thereof. And the

Lord had respect unto Abel and his offering:"

Thanks Be To God for the creation of the first siblings. They inherited either the tending of the fruit of the ground or the tending of the creatures of the land. Daily thanks would be given to God through an offering. We learn in today's text that God gave respect to Adam and Eve's children.

Why did God not show the same respect to both Cain and Abel? Perhaps the individual offerings were presented to God with the wrong motive. We are reminded of the land being cursed by God because of these twin's parents disobedience. I believe that there was a lack of thanksgiving due to unhealthy competition between the siblings.

Thanks Be To God for His creation of a conscience within His humans. Oh, May we be respected by You God; thanks to those parents who showed respect to You!

Why didn't each sibling; Cain and Abel do well with what they received? Perhaps the individual tasks assigned by parents was to hard to handle. We are reminded of the land being hard to handle because of the twin's parents disobedience to God. I believe that there was a lack of thanksgiving due to ugly jealousy from one sibling over the other.

Thanks Be To God for His creation of work ethics within His humans. Oh, May we be respected by You God; thanks to those parents who worked upon Your earth!

Prayer: Thanks be to You God, the Creator of the fruit and flock of the land and accept our daily offerings.

November 4 Thanks Be To God

Scripture Text: Mark 14: 18

"And as they sat and did eat, Jesus said, 'Verily I say unto you, One of you which eateth with me shall betray me.'"

Saint Mark gave thanks to God as one of the four Gospel writers of the New Testament. Just as he was inspired to quote Jesus' words at a special meal: the Last Supper, I became inspired by God when I was part of one of the re-enactments of this crucial event in Jesus' time here on earth:

Sorry, I Stepped On Your Feet !

Dear Jesus,

This Good Friday, we were reminded of how Your feet were washed by Mary's expensive perfume while others stepped on Your feet; scrambling to get closer to You!

So very sorry!

This Easter Week, we were reminded of how Your feet were bathed by holy water while others stepped on Your clean feet; scrambling to get closer to You!

So very sorry!

This re-enactment of the Lord's Supper we were being reminded of how Your feet were unsandled and nailed to the cross, and I can't believe I stepped on Your representative; scrambling to get the microphone closer to Your representative in 2010! So, very sorry!

Prayer: Thanks be to You, God, for listening to confessions!

November 5 Thanks Be To God

Scripture Text: Genesis 31: 3

"And the Lord said unto Jacob, 'Return unto the land of thy fathers, and to thy kindred: and I will be with thee. "

Thanks Be To God for kindred. Today's text contains the news that Jacob is to leave the land of his Uncle Laban and return to his father's land of sheep and rams.

Thanks Be To God for family . Jacob had to return with immediate family to Mount Gilead (31: 21) Unfortunately family members can turn against each other; in this case, Jacob and Laban had some disagreement over possession of cattle and rams. I am reminded of how God allows family feuds and disagreements (usually over possessions)! I am reminded that God has given us the Ten Commandments to guide us through feuds and disagreements.

Thanks Be To God for reunions. Laban and Jacob are reunited. What started out as a journey to pursue Jacob for taking from his Uncle's flock, ended up with God's plan to reunite! Unfortunately family members will not always see eye to eye; especially over God given possessions. I am reminded of how God allows the family members to present and even ammend wills. I am re- minded that God's Son; our Lord Jesus Christ has given us the Beatitudes to guide us through vows and wills.

Prayer: Thanks be to You, God for caring enough for each of us.

November 6 Thanks Be To God

Scripture Text: Isaiah 58: 11

"And the Lord shall guide thee continually, and satisfy thy soul in drought, and make fat thy bones; and thou shall be like a watered garden, and like a spring of water, whose waters fail not. "

The Prophet Isaiah states that the Lord is our guide and will satisy us daily. The Lord is my guide and inspired the writing of the following poem which I will have the reader start today and finish up tomorrow:

Guide Us In

Guide us in continually, Lord...satisfy our souls in dryness allow your doctors and nurses to teach and nourish like a watered garden allow your caregivers and therapists to learn and serve like a spring of water Thank you Lord for guiding those who study medicine offering treatment and therapy making fat our bones Walk us through the power of nature's healing touch Guide us in the quality and dignity of life that will fail not!

Guide us in continually, Lord...satisfy our souls in dryness allow your leaders and teachers to teach and nourish like a watered garden allow your Musicians and poets to read and share like a spring of water Thank you Lord for guiding those who study the beat offering rhythm and inner connection making fat our bones March us through the power of nature's Musical creation Guide us in the quality and dignity of life that will fail not!

Prayer: Thanks be to You God for guiding us.

November 7 Thanks Be To God

Scripture Text: Isaiah 58: 11 (see yesterday)

Guide Us In (continued)

Guide us in continually, Lord...satisfy our souls of dryness allow your coordinators and presenters to furnish like a watered garden allow your mentors and colleagues to learn and serve like a spring of water Thank You Lord for guiding those who study the mind offering meaningful activities making fat our bones Talk us through the power of life's basic pleasures Guide us in the quality and dignity of life that will fail not!

Guide us in continually, Lord...satisfy our souls of dryness allow your directors and therapists to enhance care like a watered garden allow your professionals and customers to give and take like a spring of water Thank You Lord for guiding those who study movement offering improvement of bodily systems) making fat our bone Work us through the power of life's basic practices Guide us in the quality and dignity of life that will fail not!

Prayer: Thanks be to You, God for daily encounters with You.

November 8 Thanks Be To God

Scripture Text: Psalm 100: 4 ,5

"Enter into his gates with thanksgiving, and into his courts with praise: be thankful unto him, and bless his holy name. For the Lord is good; his mercy is everlasting; and his truth endureth to all generations."

The Psalmist David encouraged others to give God thanks and

praise. His Lord of goodness, mercy and truth is the same God from generation to generation!

God's goodness, mercy and truth is passed down from my parents and I thank God by praising Him through out this poem inspired by Him:

We Will Remember May

Dear Mother and Dad,

We will remember May; a month that made your parents glad! the 31st of 1947 was your wedding day and happiness for another couple in New York State!

We will remember May, a month that made you; parents glad! each anniversary would come your way and happiness for another family in New York State!

We will remember May; a month that made your children glad! the 31st of 1997 was your golden anniversary and happiness for building a new home in Arizona!

We will remember May; a month that made your children glad! 2001 started out as a sad moment but, we remember, Dad all the memories and what we must do for you across the whole U.S.A. !

Prayer: Thanks be to You God, Creator of united lives!

November 9 Thanks Be To God

Scripture Text: Habakkuk 3: 18

"Yet, I will rejoice in the Lord, I will joy in the God of my salvation."

Thanks Be To God for writers. The Old Testament Prophet Habakkuk was inspired by God to write down the vision; to make it plain (2: 2).

Thanks Be To God for poets that inspired me to write down the vision and make it plain:

Helen Steiner Rice is my favorite inspirational poet whose words are plain. Her poems are full of joy and thanks to God. Her poetry has

November 12 Thanks Be To God

Scripture Text: Colossians 3: 15

"And let the peace of God rule in your hearts, to the which you are called in one body; and be ye thankful."

Thanks Be To God for His peace and how it can and should rule in our hearts! Thanks to our Lord Jesus Christ, our Master; who continues with His Heavenly Father; God and The Holy Ghost; Spirit (Trinity Team) to touch the hearts of humans from generation to generation.

I am inspired by one of God's messengers of peace: Myra Brooks Welch and her often quoted poem: "The Touch Of The Master's Hand ". What peace and thanks come from the hearts of those who witness the violin placed in the right hands!

We have all been called in one body; one church. We have each witnessed tired, worn out bodies seeking for peace and rest. God's peace and rest can be found; thank goodness!

We have all been called in one body; one church. We have witnessed unhappy, disgruntled groups seeking for peace and tranquility. God's peace and tranquility can be found; thank goodness!

We have all been called in one body; one church. We have witnessed refreshed, renewed individual seeking for peace and unity. God's peace and unity can be found; thank goodness!

Prayer: Thanks be to You God, creator of salvation and holiness.

November 13 Thanks Be To God

Scripture Text: Matthew 26: 27

"And he took the cup, and gave thanks, and gave it to them saying, ' Drink ye all of it'. "

Today's text is taken from the day of the passover as Jesus' twelve disciples sat down to eat. The meal would be eaten by sorrowful men, yet Jesus continued on with giving thanks to God. The breaking of bread and the taking of the cup of wine would take place even with a bretrayer in their presence. Oh, if we could give thanks to our God!

Since the 1970's I've been inspired by a mentor who gave herself the pen name:

"Sunshine". Her daily inspirational thoughts were kindly introduced to me when I began working at The Salvation Army; Long Point Camp in Penn Yan, New York. "Sunshine" is actually Major Guldenschuh and inspires me yet with her daily prayers to God. She illustrate her poems such as "God Came To Us".

Thanks Be To God for coming to us through His Sonshine! Jesus is the Light of the World. May we give thanks as "Sunbeams" (name given to The Salvation Army young girls group that are the age of girls within a Brownie Troop). May we give thanks to "Torchbearers" (name given to The Salvation Army teen-agers). Let your lights shine!

Prayer: Thanks be to You God, creator of "Sunshine" and her poetry!

PEARLS OF WISDOM

November 14 Thanks Be To God

Scripture Text: Ephesians 5: 20

"Giving thanks always for all things unto God and the Father in the name of our Lord Jesus Christ."

The Apostle Paul writes a letter to the people of Ephesus and includes duties and Christian warfare. We do good to give thanks daily unto God for His good works. He gives each of us the great opportunity to work for Him and His Son Jesus Christ.

Thanks Be To God for those who work with us; fellow employees. I am inspired by the director of the Activities Department at Clifton Springs Hospital and Clinic: Beth Whitbeck. She is recognized by staff and residents for her guitar playing, banjo picking and writing songs. I have been blessed and thank God for her reminders to us as we listen to "Lord You Are My Shepherd and "Fly LIke A Butterfly". She has even written a song where she gives thanks for laundry!

Another acquaintance from Clifton Springs (city and hospital) inspired me to keep writing and our paths cross when he comes to the Rotary Meetings: Ralph Adams. He is recognized for his collection of poems printed up and a copy kept at the local library. He and his wife are important members of the Clifton Springs community and the collection is called "Home-spun Poems". I especially found inspiration by reading: "I Read Within a Poet's Book" and "Swinging".

Prayer: Thanks be to You God, creator of families, homes, and paths to follow while giving thanks to You and Your Trinity Team.

November 15 Thanks Be To God

Scripture Text: John 6: 11

"And Jesus took the loaves; and when he had given thanks, he distributed to the disciples, and the disciples to them that were set down; and likewise of the fishes as much as they would. "

We give thanks to Jesus' disciples as they allowed their Lord to give them the job of distributing the bread and fish to the crowds. God allows us to be fed by others; whether physically, emotionally, or socially.

We know of social workers who take this job seriously. I have been inspired by another poet friend, mentor as he has shared his published books. Oh, to be able to write with social conscience as my friend; Ken Bremer. He has written "Dream scapes" and "9th Ward" with emphasis on distributing the goods to the poor, suffering, and less fortunate due to illness, calamity or ignorance.

One of my favorite poems is "Sunday Morning". I can visualize Ken strolling along the halls of Clifton Springs Hospital and Clinic or the streets of Clifton Springs Village. He continues sharing from the heart and his social conscience. Even his knowlege and "expertise" on raising hamsters is unique! He would give them a home; tending to them daily without really knowing where they are at all times!

He would accompany a group of residents on a ride and allowing them to give him a visual tour because of his impaired eyes.

His philosophy of life includes giving thanks to God that he is able to help distribute as much as he can.

Prayer: Thanks be to You God, for helping us create a philosophy of life.

November 16 Thanks Be To God

Scripture Text: I Peter 2: 19

"For this is thankworthy, If a man for conscience toward God endure grief, suffering wrongfully."

Thanks Be To God for He does not allow us to be alone during grief and suffering. He sends His Son to be our Physician and His Spirit to be our comforter. I believe that Peter is writing of this grace and the well-doing on our part.

A writer of God's grace and promises is Anne Johnson Flint. She is especially remembered for her poem entitled: "What God Hath Promised ". She includes the changes in nature ie. clear sunny day to clouds appearing. Will we ever have to endure grief? Do we ever suffer wrongfully? Of course...but not alone!

Another writer of God's grace and promises is Norman Vincent Peale. He is notably remembered as a Prominent Preacher in New York City and his ungoing message of God's grace and promises: "Tapestries of Life". He includes the work that has to be done and with endurance and changes not in the "cards". Will we ever have to endure hardships? Do we ever suffer deeply? Of course... but never alone!

Prayer: Thanks be to You Lord, Creator of purpose and promises.

November 17 Thanks Be To God

Scripture Text: Colossians 3: 25

"And let the peace of God rule in your hearts, to the which also ye are called in one body, and be ye thankful."

279

Apostle Paul was thankful for acquaintances who gave healthy advise and showed by example. The Colossians were ready to unite and showed their thankfulness daily.

Thanks Be To God for one such acqaintance in my life that shows by example. God's peace rules in her heart. She is ready to unite and is thankful daily. This special acquaintance has a birthday today. You have already learned about her in January devotional !

Happy 80th birthday...2010...to a very special friend... Happy Birthday, Phyllis Culkin! Thanks Be To God for your example; letting His peace rule in your heart and daily being thankful. I am inspired by your love for your country and your humor everytime I read your story that you have so graciously allowed me to quote:

The Fly That Went To Washington

It was a beautiful sunny morning. There was a crowd gathered waiting for an express bus to go from Long Island into New York City.

I am a fly and this is my story... I know there are not many flies around today who write, but I am an exception. My mother bit a writer, while she was pregnant with me. So, I guess some of his ability rubbed off on me! Well, anyway...on with the story...

7:00 A.M. ...wait for New York bus... I'll buzz around...walk across this guy's newspaper... oops...he almost got me! Try buzzing some ears! Look: bus has arrived...we're off...people dozing off... I'll sit up on the rail and rest!

(TO BE CONTINUED TOMORROW)

Prayer: Thanks be to You God, creator of adventures!

November 18 Thanks Be To God

The Fly That Went To Washington (continued)...

Traffic is busy...We're going fast... 1st stop...34th & 3rd...not interesting...2nd stop...42nd & 3rd...interesting! Lots of bustle...so many people...rush!...Whew...close call...tried to hitch a ride on guy's cheek...almost swatted...That's okay...I gave him a good bite to bother him for the day!

Hey! What's this? Grand Central Station...so many trains and people... Let's see...where should I go???...I got it...Washington D.C.... do a little sight-seeing...better rest up...busy day...

11 a.m. ... What a beautiful place...D.C. ! So many white buildings! I show up nice! don't land too low...don't want to miss D.C. ...watch swatters!

Let me read...oh...."Lincoln Memorial" ...really beautiful... Now... Capitol...really exciting ! Finally...The White House Do I dare??? Don't think they can detect flies... Phew... I made it... Wow! place of history! all the pictures of presidents...all the beautiful china from all around!

Wow !..."Oval Office" Should I dare??? Sure...I got this far!... Wait... For the door to open...somebody coming...I'm in! ...sure bright ! all these people...What's going on??? President...giving State of Union Speech...going to be televised!...I've been given an opportunity of a life-time! ...President given signal...on T.V....Here goes nothing... I'll just buzz around...wait...for the right moment...this is it !... President is confident...at the moment...one quick dive... right on his nose!... Hi! Mom! ....I'm on T.V. !!! Nobody would dare...swat me...would they ??!

Well...thank you...Mr. President... you have made my day....quite an adventure! ...think I'll go home now!

Prayer: Thanks be to You God creator of our President and a fly!

November 19 Thanks Be To God

Scripture Text: Leviticus 6: 13

"Besides the cakes, he shall offer for his offering leavened bread with the sacrifice of thanksgiving of his peace offerings."

The Prophet Moses states the laws of sacrifice. He expounds on the offerings of meat, trespass, peace, and thanksgiving. I am reminded of our celebration of Thanksgiving where we give thanks to God.

We offer each other cakes; pies, bread, and there is the sharing of recipes of the food that is to be blessed by God. Thanks Be To God for His bountiful provisions beyond any Thanksgiving Feast!

We offer the sacrifice of thanksgiving; often a turkey that is shared for days after as left-overs that are enjoyed by families. Thanks Be To God for His healthy creatures becoming part of our Feast!

We bring peace offerings; often families take the time to finally get together after a year of missing their loved onesl Thanks Be To God for giving us traveling mercies to join at Thanksgiving time!

Prayer: Thanks to You God, our Creator of thankfulness!

November 20 Thanks Be To God

Scripture Text: Psalms 50: 14

"Offer unto God thanksgiving; and pay thy vows unto the most High."

The Psalmist David ruled the land of Israel and included in his kingdom, rules of offering:

Rule # 1: Offer unto God thanksgiving Even though David was the ruler of the great kingdom of Israel, God was his ruler. Daily offerings were presented to David's Mighty God.

Is it too hard for us to offer unto our Mighty God daily thanksgiving? I am reminded that David's Mighty God offered His Son; Jesus who showed us how to daily offer thanksgiving. He knew His fate. I offer thanksgiving to Mighty God and His Trinity Team. They rule!

Rule # 2: Pay thy vows unto the most High. Even though David was a shepherd of a large flock within the land of Israel, God was his shepherd. Daily vows were offered to David's High,and Mighty God.

Is it too hard for us to pay vows unto our High and Mighty God ? I am reminded that David's Mighty God offered His Son; Jesus who showed us how to daily pay vows. He knew His mission. I pay vows to High and Mighty God and His Trinity Team. They act!

Prayer: Thanks be to You, God; Creator; High and Mighty!

November 21 Thanks Be To God

Scripture Text: Psalm 100: 4

"Enter into his gates with thanksgiving, and unto his courts with praise; be thankful unto him, and bless his name."

Once again King David is sharing with his people of Israel how to express their gratitude toward God:

Enter into God's gates and courts.

King David knew all about gates and courts! God allowed for the building of sanctuaries, palaces, and courtrooms. I am reminded of how God sent His Son, Jesus to minister with the gates and courts; entering them with thanksgiving.

Be thankful unto God.

King David knew all about thankfulness. God allowed for thankful, grateful, and appreciative people. I am reminded of how God sent His Son, Christ to move among His people; sharing His thankfulness.

Bless God's name.

King David knew how to bless God's name. God allowed His people to call out, bless, and pray in God's name. I am reminded of how God sent His Son, Messiah to be the Light, the Shepherd, The Word, and Saviour.

Prayer: Thanks be to You God for sending blessing.

November 22 Thanks Be To God

Scripture Text: II Corinthians 9: 11

"Being enriched in everything to all bountifulness, which causeth through us thanksgiving to God.

The Apostle Paul begins by writing to the Church of Corinth about being enriched. He mentions their zeal toward preaching Christ. I am reminded of the zeal of our Teacher; Rabbi, in all places.

The Apostle Paul continues to write about bountifulness. He mentions their need to be ready for the coming of Christ. I am reminded of the worshipping of our Lord, Shepherd, at all times.

The Apostle Paul included how enrichment and bountifulness cause us to express our gratitude. He mentions how important it is to give thanks to God, His Son Jesus, and His Holy Ghost. I am reminded of the expressing of our love, faith, and gratitude towards our Jesus, Master until eternity.

Prayer: Thanks be to You God for Your Trinity Team!

November 23 Thanks Be To God

Scripture Text: Philippians 4: 6

"Be careful for nothing; but in everything in prayer and supplication with thanksgiving let your requests be known unto God."

The Apostle Paul writes to yet another church; this time the church of Philippi. He advises them on how to stay happy, content, and carefree.

The Philippians are to be careful for nothing. How were they able to stay happpy? Perhaps they were the first to use a familiar phrase of our day: "Don't worry....be happy ! "How many times we have heard God's Son Jesus plead for us not to worry ! Thanks be to the Trinity Team for their extra-ordinary care for each of us!

The Philippians are to pray with gratitude. How were they able to be content? Perhaps they were the first to use a familiar phrase of our day: "I found real contentment...living in accord ! "How many times we hear Jesus bless those who are contented ! Thanks be to the Trinity Team that we can pray to them daily!

The Philippians are to let God know everything. How did they pray in such a carefree way? Perhaps they were the first to use a familiar phrase of our day: "I'm on the top of the world ! "How many times we find that our Lord hears everything ! Thanks be to the Trinity Team that they see, hear, know everything!

Prayer: Thanks be to You God listening and knowing everything!

November 24 Thanks Be To God

Scripture Text: Colossians 2: 6, 7

"As ye have therefore received Christ Jesus the Lord, so walk ye in him: rooted and built up in him, and stablished in the faith, as ye have been taught, abounding therein with thanksgiving. "

Apostle Paul's epistles (letters) to the churches continues with Colosse. They were reminded of how they received Jesus, walked with Him, became rooted and built up in Him, established their learned faith, and abounded with gratitude.

How did the saints and brethren of Colosse receive Jesus? The grace and peace of our same Trinity Team was received. Grace and peace should daily be taken internally by all saints. Don't run ! Don't leap ! Just walk right up and receive grace and peace.

How did the Church of Colosse keep on walking and become rooted and built up in Christ? The strength and firmness of our same Trinity Team was given. Strength and firmness should daily be evident from all saints. Don't run away ! Don't leap way ahead ! Just walk steadily with strength.

How did the readers of Apostle Paul' letter establish their faith and abound with thanksgiving? The establishment and bountifulness of our same Trinity Team existed. Thanksgiving should be daily established and bountiful by all . Don't run on the path of discontentment! Don't leap around the fires of sin! Just walk with gratitude for receiving faith.

Prayer: Thanks be to You God, for keeping us rooted and established.

November 25 Thanks Be To God

Scripture Text: Psalm 95: 1, 2

"O come, let us sing unto the Lord: let us make a joyful noise to the rock of our salvation. Let us come before his presence with thanksgiving and make a joyful noise unto him with psalms. "

King David has been singing to his Lord God since he was a shepherd boy! He reminds the reader of this psalm that God is the rock of our salvation. Remember the rock used to kill Giant Goliath? Shepherds carried rocks for protection. David continues to sing praises to his God of protection.

We are invited to sing unto our Lord. What kinds of songs and psalms will we sing to You, Lord? Songs of praises we sing because of Your protection! God bless our songs even when others do not! Thanks be to You, God that many songs have been sung about You!

We are invited to make a joyful noise unto our Lord. What kind of joyful noise will You hear, Lord? Joyful noises we make because of Your provision! God accept our noises even when others do not! Thanks be to You, God that all kinds of noises You have received!

We are invited to come into the presence of our Lord. What appearance will you notice, Lord? Our presence we make because of Your promises! God, we accept Your invitation even when others do not! Thanks be to You, God that we all have been invited into Your presence!

Prayer: Thanks be to You God for your inspiration to every writer.

November 26 Thanks Be To God

Scripture Text: I Timothy 4: 4. 5

"For every creature of God is good, and nothing to be refused, if it be received with thanksgiving: For it is sanctified by the word of God and prayer."

The Apostle Paul writes two letters to a young leader; Timothy. In this first epistle of Timothy's letters we read how important it is to receive with thanksgiving and to find sanctification by word of God and prayer.

Receiving others with thanksgiving is not always easy! We May struggle with finding the good when we are surrounded by hypocrisy. Our duties March on without us if we allow the bad and ugly to cloud our mission. Thanks Be To God for priests, bishops, disciples, apostles, ministers officers, teachers, and mentors who receive us with thanksgiving.

Receiving ourselves with thanksgiving is not always easy! You May strugggle with reading the scriptures and praying when you are surrounded by hypocrisy. God's Word and The Lord's prayer are uttered or read without you if you allow the numerous dogmas of today to confuse your wisdom. Thanks Be To God for congregations, laymen, tribes, parishioners, soldiers, adherents, and students who individually give thanks.

Prayer: Thanks be to You God for receiving us individually.

November 27 Thanks Be To God

Scripture Text: Isaiah 38: 19

"The living, the living, he shall praise thee, as I do this day: the father to the children shall make known thy truth. "

The Prophet Isaiah records the proclamation of King Hezekiah. Within King Hezekiah's proclamation are the words contained in today's scripture text. He was able to praise, give thanks to a God who allowed him to be sick. He faces the truth; prays as his forefathers did and was able to praise; give gratitude to his Heavenly Father.

We continue to have kings, presidents, leaders, priests, pastors, and mentors to proclaim God's protection and provision for our lives. Today I give thanks to God for the poet whose words and wisdom inspire me to share my wisdom as a poet and writer of God's vision. The poet is Langston Hughes:

"Dreams" is a poem about the living. It contains praises to God. The wisdom of Langson Hughes as a poet is for this day. I am reminded upon reading this poem that God is allowing us to dream; go on with life; with hope. Each day is a new day with God, our Heavenly Father as He welcomes us into His family.

"Dreams" is a poem written by a man who lived with other 19th century fathers (or fatherly figures). The fatherly wisdom of Langston Hughes is for this day. I am reminded upon re-reading this poem that God is allowing dreams to come alive with gratitude. Each day is a new day with God, our Heavenly Father as He welcomes each of us into His family.

Prayer: Thanks be to You God for the vision from dreams.

November 28 Thanks Be To God

Scripture Text: Psalm 16: 11

"Thou wilt shew me the path of life; in thy presence is fulness of joy; at thy right hand there are pleasures evermore. "

The Psalmist David was shown by God many paths of life. From a young Shepherd, to King of Israel there was joy in God' presence. David did express sorrow in his poems but they did not out number his praises. He fully recognized God as his Lord, his guide and to be worshipped daily.

We continue to have psalmists, Musicians, writers, readers of David's 150 Psalms. In today's scripture text we notice the expression of joy and the pleasures of being shown the path of life.

There is another poet whose 'vision' inspires me to often include in my poetry the joy and pleasures found within living with nature! Robert Frost wrote inspiring words in: "The Road Not Taken ".

Thanks Be To God for my parents who introduced me to the poet Robert Frost. My parents followed many roads not taken! I was inspired as a child to take walks up a stony road for barefeet and snow drifted for boots. The road was not taken as a "super highway". We had time to have God show the beauty of His earth. Oh, the joy of meeting face to face with a deer whose pleasures of grazing peacefully as we share the same path!

Thanks Be To God for my parents who allowed teachers to include Robert Frost among the inspirational poets. My teachers led us down many roads not taken! I was inspired as a child to walk the aisles of the classroom and the hallways of Prattsburg Central School. The hallways were not supposed to represent a "super highway". We were encouraged to take time to attend Religious Study Classes weekly to have God show the beauty of His world. Oh, the joy of meeting face to face with a friend whose pleasures of walking peacefully as we share the same path!

Prayer: Thanks be to You God for the path not taken.

November 29 Thanks Be To God

Scripture Text: Isaiah 51: 3

"For the Lord shall comfort Zion: he will comfort all her waste places; and he will make her wilderness like Eden, and her desert like the garden of the Lord; joy and gladness shall be found therein, thanksgiving, and the voice of melody. "

The Prophet Isaiah proclaims the comfort of the Lord. Thanks Be To God, Creator of nature and such beautiful places!

Man of the wilderness, allow God to create an Eden within your forest. There is joy and gladness found there. Thanks Be To God as He allowed His Son, Jesus to spend time in the wilderness and come out defeating Satan! I am reminded that I have to get beyond the outskirts of the wilderness to find Eden deep within.

Man of the desert, allow God to create His garden within your canyons. There is thanksgiving and the voice of melody. Thanks Be To God as He allowed His Son, Jesus to spend time in the desert and come out feeding five thousand people! I am reminded that I have to get beyond the sand of the desert to find the Garden of the Lord between the mountains.

Prayer: Thanks be to You God, Creator of the wilderness, deserts and gardens.

November 30 Thanks Be To God

Scripture Text: Isaiah 3: 41

"Let us lift up our heart with our hands unto God in the heavens. "

The Prophet Isaiah encourages us to give thanks to God daily. Our hearts and hands praise the goodness of our God.

Our heart moves to the beat while the blood circulates through our body. My sister Sue learned this through nursing school.

Our hands move to perform while the rest of the body comes into motion. My sister Sue is talented in crafts and has shared her works in the form of gifts for family, friends and hospital co-workers.

December 1 The Road Taken

Scripture Text: Genesis 1: 26

"And God said, Let us make man in our own image, after our likeness: and let them have dominion over the fish of the sea, and over the fowl of the air, and over the cattle, and over all the earth, and over every creeping thing that creepeth upon the earth. "

The Prophet Moses wrote in his first book the creation of heaven and earth. He writes of how God begins life on earth by creating man. The Road Taken for man would be as God said:

"Let us make man in our own image" God plans the road for man with another....The Spirit of God. Together they plan the road for the beginning of earth. Now they plan the road to take after their likeness. The Road Taken would be the first for man! God of Wisdom; Creator of heaven, earth, and man, take us too!

"Let them have dominion over all the earth" God paves the road for man with another...The Spirit of God. Together they pave the road for the first humans. Still, they pave the road after their likeness. The Road Taken would be the first for man and woman! God of Wisdom: Creator of Adam and Eve, pave the road for us!

The Road Taken by God and His Spirit is for us to travel. God and His Spirit planned and paved the road to Christmas! Let us take it today!

Prayer: Dear God and Spirit of God, I remember that You are still creating.

December 2 The Road Taken

Scripture Text: Genesis 3: 1

"Now the serpent was more subtil than any beast of the field which the Lord God had made. And he said unto the woman, Yea, hath God said, Ye shall not eat of every tree of the garden?"

The Prophet Moses continues his account of God and the Spirit's creation. He writes of how God allows man and creature to interact. Even though man has dominion over every creeping thing there are temptations along the way. The road of temptations for man is as God said:

"Eat not of the tree of good and evil...for thou shall surely die. "(Genesis 2: 17). God plans the road for man and allows the serpent to follow too. Together man and the serpent challenge each other. Now they will travel the road planned by God or the Devil. God of Wisdom, Creator of man, take us on Your smooth road!

"Hast thou eaten of the tree, whereof I commanded thee that thou shouldest not eat?" (Genesis 3: 11) God paves the road for man and the serpent to travel together. Together man and the serpent challenge involves good and evil. Still they will travel the road paved of stones or of gold. God of Wisdom, Creator of generations, pave the smooth road for us!

The Road Taken by God, Spirit and Man that defeats the Devil is for us to travel. God, His Spirit, and His Humans planned and paved the road to Christmas. Let us take it today!

Prayer: Dear God and Holy Spirit, You are still in control of Your creation.

December 3 The Road Taken

Scripture Text: II Samuel 2:11

"And the time that David was king in Hebron over the house of Judah, was seven years and six months."

II Samuel is also called the second book of the kings. The account of the beginning of David's reign is recorded . God and His Spirit planned and paved the road to Christmas to include kings such as David:

"The God of Israel said, the Rock of Israel spake to me, He that ruler over man must be just, ruling in the fear of God. "

II Samuel 23: 3 God and His Spirit plan the road to Christmas with King David. Together they plan the beginning of a kingdom here on earth. God and His Spirit had already taken Moses, Noah, Joshua, Judges, and Ruth. They took the road after the likeness of God and His Spirit. God of Wisdom, Creator of heaven, earth, and leaders, take us too!

"But his delight is in the law of the Lord, and in his law doeth he meditate day and night."

Psalms 1: 2 God and His Spirit pave the road to Christmas with King David. Together they pave the way for kings here on earth. God and His Spirit had already taken princes, priests and Levites. They took the road after the likeness of God and His Spirit. God of Wisdom, Creator of David, pave the road for us!

Prayer: Dear God and Spirit of God, You still reign!

December 4 The Road Taken

Scripture Text: Ezra 1: 2

"Thus saith Cyrus, king of Persia, The Lord of heaven hath given me all the kingdoms of the earth; he hath charged me to build him an house at Jerusalem, which is in Judah."

The Prophet Ezra records the words of Cyrus, king of Persia; the plan of God, His Spirit, and King David for the road to Christmas:

"The Lord hath given me all the kingdoms of earth" Ezra records the tribes, leaders, and Levites that help to build an house at Jerusalem. The road to Christmas would include plans for houses, temples for God and His Spirit's people (blueprints!). God of Wisdom, Creator of kingdoms and temples on Your path, take us!

"And thou, Ezra, after the wisdom of thy God, that is in thine hand, set magistrates and judges, which May judge all the people that are beyond the river, all such as know the laws of thy God, and teach them that know them not."

Ezra 7:25 Ezra gives account of his appointment as chief ruler by King Artaxerxes. He qualified because of being a ready scribe of the law of Moses (7: 6) The road to Christmas would include pavement for God, His Spirit, and chief rulers (contractors!). God of Wisdom, Creator of rulers and kingdoms on Your path, take us!

The Road Taken by God and His Spirit is for us to travel.

God and His Spirit planned and paved the road to Christmas. Let us take it today!

Prayer: Dear God and Spirit of God, You are still creating in Your likeness.

December 5 The Road Taken

Scripture Text: Proverbs 1: 1, 2

"The proverbs of Solomon the son of David, the king of Israel; to show wisdom and instruction; to perceive the words of understanding..."

King Solomon wrote in Proverbs and The Song of Solomon of how God and His Spirit plans and paves the road to Christmas for wise rulers as He said:

"Trust in the Lord with all thine heart; and lean not unto thine own understanding. And in all thy ways acknowledge him, and he shall direct thy paths." (Proverbs 3: 5, 6) God, His Spirit, rulers, and men of wisdom plan the road to Christmas. The Road Taken would be one of instruction for man. God and His Spirit of wisdom within Your earthly kingdom; take us!

"My vineyard which is mine, is before me; thou, O Solomon, must have a thousand, and those that keep the fruit thereof two hundred. "God, His Spirit, rulers, and men of wisdom pave the road to Christmas. The Road Taken would be one of wealth for man. God and His Spirit of wealth within Your earthly kingdom; take us!

The Road Taken by God and His Spirit is for us to travel. God and His Spirit planned and paved the road to Christmas. Let us take it today!

Prayer: Dear God and Spirit of God, I begin taking Your road to Christmas.

December 6 The Road Taken

Scripture Text: Ecclesiastes 1: 1 - 3

"The words of the Preacher, the son of David, king in Jerusalem. Vanity of vanities, saith the Preacher, vanity of vanities; all is vanity. What profit hath a man of all his labour which he taketh under the sun?"

The Preacher Ecclesiastes wrote that all is vanity. God and His Spirit created man to follow the laws and commands of earthly kings but more importantly to find purpose in taking the road to Christmas:

"To everything there is a season, and a time to every purpose under the heaven: "(3:1)

"I returned and saw under the sun, that the race is not to the swift, nor the battle to the strong, neither yet bread to the wine, nor riches to men of understanding, nor yet favour to men of skill but time and chance happeneth to them all." (9: 11)

"The preacher sought to find out acceptable words, and that which was written was upright, even words of truth. (12:10)

The Road Taken by God and His Spirit is for us to travel. God and His Spirit planned and paved the road to Christmas. Let us take it today!

Prayer: Dear God and Spirit of God, I begin taking on Your race.

December 7 The Road Taken

Scripture Text: Isaiah 1: 10

"Hear the word of the Lord, ye rulers of Sodom, give ear unto the law of our God, ye people of Gomorrah. "

The Prophet Isaiah writes about the creation of law by God. He writes of how rulers of all nations (even sinful ones) should be reminded that The Road Taken for man would be as God said:

"Come now, and let us reason together, saith the Lord, though your sins be as scarlet, they shall be as white as snow, though they be as red like crimsom, they shall be as wool. "(1: 18)

"Oh house of Jacob, come ye, and let us walk in the light of the Lord." (2: 5)

"And I heard the voice of the Lord, saying, Whom shall I send, and who will go for us? Thus said I, Here am I; send me." (6:8)

"For unto us a child is born, unto us a son is given: and the government shall be upon his shoulders, and his name shall be called Wonderful, Counsellor, The Mighty God, The Ever- lasting Father, The Prince of Peace." (9: 6)

The Road Taken by God and His Spirit is for us to travel daily.

Prayer: Dear God and Spirit of God, I travel Your planned and paved road.

December 8 The Road Taken

Scripture Text: Jeremiah 1:7

"But the Lord said unto me, Say not, I am a child: for thou shall go to all that I send thee, and whatsoever I command thee thou shalt speak."

The Prophet Jeremiah wrote in his first and second books (the latter having the title; Lamentations) of how God and His Spirit continue to create man. The road to Christmas taken by man would be as God said:

"Thus saith the Lord, What iniquity have your fathers found in me, that they are gone far from me, and have walked after vanity, and are become vain? "(2: 5)

"And the Lord said unto me, The backsliding Israel hath justified herself more than treacherous Judah. "(3: 11)

"But this thing commanded I them saying, obey my voice, and I will be your God, and ye shall be my people, and walk ye in all the ways that I have commanded you, that it May be well unto you." (7:23)

"Oh, house of Israel, cannot I do with you, as the potter? saith the Lord. Behold, as the clay is in the potter's hand, so are ye in mine hand, O house of Israel." (18: 6)

"How doth the city sit solitary, that was full of people! how she is become as a widow! she that was great among the nations, and princess among the provinces, how is she become tributary! "(Lamentations 1: 1)

"It is of the Lord's mercies that we are not consumed, because his compassions fail not. "(Lamentation 3: 22)

The Road Taken by God and His Spirit is for us to travel. God and His Spirit planned and paved the road to Christmas. Let us take it today!

Prayer: Dear God and Spirit of God, I begin following Your passion.

December 9 The Road Taken

Scripture Text: Ezekiel 1: 1

"Now it came to pass in the thirtieth year, in the fourth month, in the fifth day of the month, as I was among the captivated by the river of Chebar, that the heavens were , and I saw visions of God."

The Prophet Ezekiel wrote in his book the vivid visions of God and how The Road Taken for man would be as God said:

"Then said he unto me, Son of man, hast thou seen what the ancients of the house of Israel do in the dark, every man in the chambers of his imagery? for they say, the Lord seeth us not; the Lord has forsaken the earth. "(8: 12)

"Therefore thus saith the Lord God; As the vine tree among the trees of the forest, which I have given to the fire for fuel, so will I give the inhabitants of Jerusalem." (15:6)

"And I will make them and the places round about my hill a blessing: and I will cause the shower to come down in his season; there shall be showers of blessing. "

The Road Taken by God and His Spirit is for us to travel. God and His Spirit planned and paved the road to Christmas! Let us take it today!

Prayer: Dear God and Spirit of God, I begin taking Your showers of blessings!

December 10 The Road Taken

Scripture Text: Daniel 2:19

"Then was the secret revealed unto Daniel in a night vision. Then Daniel blessed the God of heaven. "

Daniel interpreted the dreams of powerful kings. He would include what God said:

"As for these four children, God gave them knowledge and skill in all learnng and wisdom: and Daniel had understanding in all visions and dreams."

(1: 17)

"Then Nebuchadnezzar spake, and said, blessed be the God of Shadrach, Meschach, and Abednego, who has sent his angel, and delivered his servants that trusted in him, and have changed the king's word, and yielded their bodies, that they might no serve nor worship any god, except their own God. "(3: 28)

"Then was the king exceeding glad for him, and commanded that they should take Daniel out of the den. So Daniel was taken up out of the den, and no manner of hurt was found upon him, because he believed in God. (6: 23)

"But thou, O Daniel, shut up the words, and seal the book, even to the time of the end: many shall run to and fro, and knowledge shall be increased." (12: 4)

The Road Taken by God and His Spirit is for us to travel. God and His Spirit planned and paved the road to Christmas. Let us take it today!

Prayer: Dear God and Spirit of God. I begin learning from Your plans.

December 11 The Road Taken

Scripture Text: Hosea 4: 1

"Hear the word of the Lord, ye children of Israel: for the Lord hath a controversy with the inhabitants of the land, because there is no truth, nor mercy, nor knowledge of God in the land. "

The Prophet Hosea writes about God and His Spirit's road to Christmas not being followed. God and His Spirit speak in truth and mercy:

"For I desired mercy, and not sacrifice, and the knowledge of God, more than burnt offerings. "(6: 6)

"What will ye do in the solemn day, and in the day of the feast of the Lord? "(9:5)

"Therefore turn thou to thy God, keep mercy and judgment, and wait on thy God continually. (12: 6)

"I will be as the dew unto Israel : he shall grow as the lily, and cast forth his roots as Lebanon. His branches shall spread, and his beauty as the olive tree, and his smell as Lebanon. They that dwell under his shadow; they shall return, they shall revive as the corn, and grow as the vine: the scent thereof shall be as the wine of Lebanon. "(14: 5- 7)

The Road Taken by God and His Spirit is for us to travel. God and His Spirit planned and paved the road to Christmas. Let us take it!

Prayer: Dear God and Spirit of God, I begin walking Your paved road.

December 12 The Road Taken

Scripture Text: Joel 1: 6

"For a nation is come upon my land, stong, and without number, whose teeth are the teeth of a lion, and he hath the cheek teeth of a great lion."

The Prophet Joel writes of the emergence of a great nation. He writes of how God and His Spirit plan and pave the road of Christmas. The road would be as God said:

"Fear not, O land; be glad and rejoice: for the Lord will do great things. "(2: 21)

"And it shall come to pass, that whosoever shall call upon the name of the Lord shall be delivered; for in mount Zion and in Jerusalem shall be deliverance, as the Lord hath said, and in the remnant whom the Lord shall call." (2:32)

"The Lord also shall roar out of Zion, and utter his voice from Jerusalem; and the heavens and the earth shall shake, but the Lord will be the hope of his people, and the strength of the children of Israel. "(3: 16)

The Road Taken by God and His Spirit is for us to travel. God and His Spirit planned and paved the road to Christmas! Let us take it today!

Prayer: Dear God and Spirit of God, I begin following Your great plan.

December 13 The Road Taken

Scripture Text: Amos 2: 6

"Thus saith the Lord; for three transgressions of Israel, and for four, I will not turn away the punishment thereof; because they sold the righteous for silver and the poor for a pair of shoes."

The Prophet Amos writes about the transgression that hinder God and His Spirit's planning and paving the road to Christmas. The Road

Taken for man would be as God said:

"For thus saith the Lord God; unto the house of Israel, Seek ye me and ye shall live. "(5: 4)

"And the Lord said unto me, Amos what seeth thou? And I said, a plumbline. Then saith the Lord, Behold, I will set a plumbline in the midst of my people Israel; I will not again pass by them any more. (7: 8)

"In that day I will raise up the tabernacle of David that is fallen, and close up the breaches thereof, and I will raise up his ruins, and I will build it as in the days of old. "(9: 11)

The Road Taken by God and His Spirit is for us to travel. God and His Spirit planned and paved the road to Christmas! Let us take it today!

Prayer: Dear God and Spirit of God, I watch Your plumbline.

December 14 The Road Taken

Scripture Text: Obadiah (verse 1)

"The vision of Obadiah. Thus saith the Lord God concerning Edom: We have heard a rumour from the Lord, and an ambassador is sent, among the heathen, Arise ye, and let us rise up against her in battle. "

The Prophet Obadiah writes down his vision and what God told him. The planning and the paving by God and His Spirit of The Road Taken would be as God said:

"But upon mount Zion shall be deliverance, and there shall be holiness, and the house of Jacob shall possess their possessions. "(verse 17)

"And saviours shall come up on mount Zion to judge the mount of Esau; and the kingdom shall be the Lord's. "(verse 21)

The Road Taken by God and His Spirit is for us to travel. God and His Spirit planned and paved the road to Christmas! Let us take it today!

Prayer: Dear God and Spirit of God, I begin accepting Your deliverances.

December 15 The Road Taken

Scripture Text: Jonah 1: 2

"Arise, go to Nineveh, that great city, and cry against it; for their wickedness is come up before me. "

The Prophet Jonah writes about his encounter with one of God's sea creatures when following the command to go to Nineveh. The road to Christmas would be as God said:

"And the word of the Lord came upon Jonah the second time, saying; arise go unto Ninevah, that great city, and preach unto it the preaching that I bid thee. "(2: 1, 2)

"Then said the Lord, Doest thou well to be angry? "(4: 4) "And God said to Jonah, Doest thou well to be angry for the gourd? And he said, I do well to be angry, even unto death. "(4:9)

The Road Taken by God and His Spirit is for us to travel. God and His Spirit planned and paved the road to Christmas. Let us take it!

Prayer: Dear God and Spirit of God, I begin encountering Your plan.

December 16 The Road Taken

Scripture Text: Micah 1: 2

"Hear, all ye people, Hearken, O earth, and all that therein is: and let the Lord God be witness against you, the Lord from his holy temple."

The Prophet Micah urges us to listen to the commands of the Lord God created in the beginning of creation! The Road Taken would be planned and paved as God said:

"I will surely assemble, O Jacob, all of thee; I will surely gather the remnant of Israel, I will put them together as the sheep of Bozrah, as the flock in the midst of their fold; they shall make great noise by the reason of the multitude of men. "(2: 12)

"Now why doest thou cry out aloud? is there no king in thee? is thy counsellor perished? for pangs have taken thee as a woman in travail." (4:9)

"He hath shewed thee, O man, what is good; and what doth the Lord requireth of thee, but to do justly, and to love mercy, and to walk humbly with thy God? "(6: 8)

The Road Taken by God and His Spirit is for us to travel. God and His Spirit planned and paved the road to Christmas. Let us take it too!

Prayer: Dear God and Spirit of God, I begin meeting Your requirements.

December 17 The Road Taken

Scripture Text: Habakkuk 1: 2

"O Lord, How long shall I cry, and thou wilt not hear! Even cry out unto thee of violence, and thou wilt not save! "

The Prophet Habakkuk questions the Lord's salvation of His creation of heaven and earth. The Road Taken is as God said:

"And the Lord answered me, Write the vision, and make it plain upon tables, that he May run that readeth it. (2: 2)

"For the earth shall be filled with the knowlege of the glory of the glory of the Lord, as the waters cover the sea. "(2: 14)

"Yet I will rejoice in the Lord, I will joy in the God of my salvation." (3: 18)

The Road Taken by God and His Spirit is for us to travel. God and His Spirit planned and paved the road to Christmas! Let us take it today!

Prayer: Dear God and Spirit of God, I begin taking Your plain road.

December 18 The Road Taken

Scripture Text: Zephaniah 1: 7

"Hold thy peace at the presence of the Lord God: for the day of the Lord is at hand; for the Lord hath prepared a sacrifice, he hath bid his guests. "

The Prophet Zephaniah writes about the Lord preparing a sacrifice. The road prepared by the Lord is as God said:

"Seek ye the Lord, all ye meek of the earth, which have wrought his judgment; seek righteousness, seek meekness: it May be ye shall be hid in the day of the Lord's anger." (2: 3)

"The Lord thy God in the midst of thee is mighty; he will save, he will rejoice over thee with joy; he will rest in his love. he will joy over thee with singing. "(3: 17)

"Behold at that time I will undo all that afflict thee: and I will save her that halteth, and gather her that was driven out; and I will get them praise and fame in every land where they have been put to shame. "(3: 19)

The Road Taken by God and His Spirit is for us to travel. God and His Spirit planned and paved the road to Christmas! Let us take it today!

Prayer: Dear God and Spirit of God, I seek Your righteousness.

December 19 The Road Taken

Scripture Text: Haggai 1: 7, 8

"Thus saith the Lord of hosts, Consider your ways. Go up to the mountain, and bring wood, and build the house; and I will take pleasure in it, and I will be glorified. Saith the Lord ."

The Prophet Haggai urged the people to consider their ways. He writes of how the people are to take the road provided by God and listen to what God says:

"For thus saith the Lord of hosts; Yet once, it is a little while, and

I will shake the heavens, and the earth, and the sea, and the dry land; and I will shake all nations, and the desire of all nations shall come: and I will fill this house with glory; saith the Lord." (2: 6, 7)

"Consider now from this day and upward, from the four and twentieth day of the ninth month, even from the day tht the foundation of the Lord's temple was laid, consider it. (2: 18)

"And I will overthrow the throne of kingdoms, and I will destroy the strength of the kingdoms of the heathen; and I will overthrow the chariots, and those that ride in them; and the horses, and their riders shall come down, every one by the sword of his brother." (2: 22)

The Road Taken by God and His Spirit is for us to travel. God and HIs spirit planned and paved the road to Christmas! Let us take it today!

Prayer: Dear God and Spirit of God, I daily consider Your ways.

December 20 The Road Taken

Scripture Text: Zechariah 1: 3

"Therefore say thou unto them, Thus saith the Lord of Hosts; Turn ye unto me saith the Lord of hosts, and I will turn unto you , saith the Lord of Hosts."

The Prophet Zechariah calls upon the Lord of Hosts and tells about the power of God and what He has to say:

"For thus saith the Lord of hosts; after the glory he has sent me unto the nations which spoiled you: for he that toucheth you, toucheth the apple of his eye." (2: 8)

"Sing and rejoice, O daughter of Zion: for lo, I come , and I will dwell in the midst of thee, saith the Lord. "(2: 10)

"....Thus speaketh the Lord of hosts, saying, Behold the man whose name is the BRANCH; and he shall grow up out of his place, and he shall build the temple of the Lord. (6 : 12)

"Rejoice greatly, O daughter of Zion; shout, O daughter of Jerusalem: behold thy King cometh unto thee, he is just and having salvation; lowly, and riding upon an ass, and a colt the foal of an ass. "(9: 9)

The Road Taken by God and His Spirit is for us to travel. God and His Spirit planned and paved the road to Christmas! Let us take it today!

Prayer: Dear God and Spirit of God, I turn to You...Hosts.

December 21 The Road Taken

Scripture Text: Malachi 1: 2, 3

"I have loved you, saith the Lord, Yet ye say, Wherein hast thou loved us? Was not Esau Jacob's brother? saith the Lord; yet I loved Jacob, and I hated Esau , and laid his mountains and his heritage waste for the dragons of the wilderness. "

The Prophet Malachi writes down his burden concerning the love and hate of the Lord from the beginning of creation . The Road Taken by man would be as God said:

"For the priest's lips should keep knowledge, and they should seek the the law at his mouth; for he is the messenger of the Lord of hosts." (2: 2)

"Will a man rob God? Yet ye have robbed me. But ye say, wherein have we robbed thee? In tithes and offerings." (3: 8)

"But unto you that fear my name shall the Sun of righteousness arise with healing in his wings; and ye shall go forth, and grow up as calves of the stall." (4: 2)

"And he shall turn the heart of the fathers to the children, and the heart of the children to their fathers, lest I come and smite the earth with a curse. "

The Road Taken by God and His Spirit is for us to travel. God and His Spirit planned and paved the road to Christmas! Let us take it today!

Prayer: Dear God and Spirit of God, I allow You to carry my burdens.

December 22 The Road Taken

Scripture Text: Luke 1: 5 & 36 & 48

"There was in the days of Herod, the king of Judeas, a certain priest named Zacharias, of the course of Abia; and his wife was of the daughters of Aaron, and her name was Elisabeth. And, behold, thy cousin Elisabeth, she hath also conceived a son in her old age. For he hath regarded the low estate of his handmaiden: for, behold, from henceforth all generations shall call me blessed."

Saint Luke recorded in his gospel God's road to Christmas. God's road would include the Virgin Mary's family. Mary would converse with God about her cousin Elisabeth:

Elisabeth and Mary were cousins and of the daughters of Aaron. God planned and prepared the road to take in the days of Herod.

Elisabeth and Mary were to convieve through God's plan and preparation within Judea.

Mary conversed with God about her low estate; handmaiden. She knew she had to travel with God and knew she would have all generations call her "blessed"

The Road Taken by God, His Spirit and Mary's family is for us to travel. God and His Spirit plan and pave the road to Christmas! Let us take it today!

Prayer: Dear God and Holy Spirit. You are still creating families.

December 23 The Road Taken

Scripture Text: Matthew 1: 17 : Luke 1: 27

"So all the generations from Abraham to David are fourteen generations; and from David until the carrying away into Babylon are fourteen generations; and from the carrying away into Babylon unto Christ are fourteen generations."

"To a virgin espoused to a man whose name was Joseph, of the house of David, and the virgin's name was Mary."

Matthew and Luke include in their gospels (good news) the lineage of Joseph. We read how God continues to allow His dominant creation; man to take His road to Christmas. Joseph would converse with God about his family:

The generation of David was preceded by fourteen generations. Joseph's family followed God's plan for salvation. We must not forget the one hundred and fifty psalms written and passed down by David.

Then, from King David to the carrying away into Babylon was another fourteen generations. We must not forget the Children of Israel recorded in the books of the Old Testament. Their God had a plan for them to all take the road to Christmas.

Finally, from the carrying away into Babylon unto Christ was another fourteen generations. We must not forget the twenty books written as part of the Old Testament and by kings and prophets. These twenty books included Proverbs, Isaiah, Micah, and Malachi. God's plan for the road to Christmas would be passed down to Joseph's family.

Joseph's family must have conversed with God about His paving the road to Christmas; especially when they received the news that a virgin was epoused to their son, nephew, grandson, great grandson and greats! Now the paved road to Christmas was becoming 'close to home'; right in the family's backyard! God's paving the road for the house of David!

Prayer: Dear God and Spirit of God, You are still creating more generations.

December 24 The Road Taken

Scripture Text: Luke 1: 35; Matthew 1:24

"And the angel answered and said unto her, The Holy Ghost shall come upon thee, and the power of the Highest shall overshadow thee; therefore that holy thing which shall be born of thee shall be called the Son of God. "" Then Joseph being raised from sleep did as the angel of the lord had bidden him, and took unto him his wife. "

Matthew and Luke continue as the two gospel writers to record God's plan for Mary and Joseph to travel the road to Christmas. There would be plenty of conversing with God!

Luke records Mary asking God's angel: "How shall this be, seeing I know not a man? "The angel converses with Mary and reminds her of the power of God and her son would be of God; holy and overshadow her!

Matthew records Joseph responding to one of God's angels through a dream. He asked of the angel: "...being a just man, and not willing to make her a publick example, was minded to put her away privily." The angel converses with Joseph and reminds him of the need to fulfill the dream full of God's power and that his son would be of God, holy and born of a virgin.

The God and His Spirit's road to Christmas has been paved for Mary and Joseph. Let us continue traveling this same planned and paved road.

Prayer: Dear God and Spirit of God, I take Your road to Christmas today.

December 25 The Road Taken

Scripture Text: Matthew 1: 20, Mark 1: 7, Luke 1: 30, John 1: 23

"And while he thought on these things, behold, the angel of the Lord appeared unto him in a dream, saying Joseph, thou son of David, fear not to take unto thee Mary thy wife; for that which is conceived in her is of the Holy Ghost. "

"And preached saying, There cometh one mightier than I after me, the lachet of whose shoes I am not worthy to stoop down and unloose." "And the angel said unto her, Fear not, Mary: for thou hast found favour with God. "" He said, I am the voice of one crying in the wilderness , Make straight the way of the Lord, as said the prophet Esaias."

Now there are four gospel writers announcing Christmas ! God and His Spirit planned and paved the road to the birth of Jesus! Today we recognize the appearance of the Angel Gabriel (Luke 1: 19) who shared the good news; good tidings, Christmas Day, and the New Testament!

The Road Taken by God, His Spirit, Mary and Joseph and families, and the Angel Gabriel continues to be planned and paved for us to travel anytime; with our mighty Savious; without fear, and straight down without hesitation!

Prayer: Dear God and Spirit of God, Your angels continue announcing Christmas!

December 26 The Road Taken

Scripture Text: Luke 2: 1- 4

"And it came to pass in those days, that there went out a decree from Caesar Augustus, that all the world should be taxed. (And this taxing was first made when Cyrenius was governor of Syria.) And all went to be taxed, every into his own city. And Joseph also went up from Galilee, out of the city of Nazareth, into Judea, unto the city of David, which is called Bethlehem (because he was of the house and lineage of David."

Saint Luke includes in God's planning and paving of the road to Christmas the role of the kings, rulers, and political influence.

Caesar Augustus sent out a decree that all the world should be taxed. Amidst God's plan are the necessary man made laws. The Road Taken would be maintained by the payment of taxes!

Taxing was first made when Cyrenius was governor of Syria. The past generations were familiar with the influence of taxation. The Road Taken would be maintained by the rulers of nations.

Joseph went into his own city of David; Bethlehem. This is part of the tradition of the house and lineage of David. The road with Christ would be maintained by generations with inheritance!

Prayer: Dear God and Spirit of God, You maintain the road to Christmas.

December 27 The Road Taken

Scripture Text: Luke 2: 7

"And she brought forth her firstborn son, and wrapped him in swaddling clothes, and laid him in a manger,because there was no room for them in the inn."

Saint Luke records how Mary and Joseph were in Bethlehem. Both the innkeeper (who had no room) and the tender of the cattle (who had room in a manger) witnessed Mary, Joseph and their firstborn son.

Baby Jesus was wrapped in swaddling clothes! (Luke 2: 7) The innkeeper might not have even looked up when Mary, Joseph and Baby Jesus asked for a room. We know that God and His Spirit were planning and paving the road for Christ to be followed! The tender of the cattle might not have even looked up when Mary, Joseph and Baby Jesus settled down in his manger. We know that God and His Spirit had planned and paved the road for Christ to include rest stops!

Baby Jesus and His parents would be surrounded by gifts brought by the wisemen (kings)!. (Matthew 2: 11) and shepherds who just had to witness this event! (Luke 2: 15, 16) The innkeeper probably looked up when he saw them all coming through Bethlehem; He May have scurried to find enough rooms! We know that God and His Spirit already planned the road for Christ to be followed to the manger! The care-tender of the cattle probably looked up when he saw them all coming through Bethlehem; going right by the inn; towards his stable! He May have scurried to find enough room in the manger! We know that God and His Spirit already planned the road for Christ to be followed to the manger!

Prayer: Dear God and Spirit of God, Your gifts of Christmas are precious!

December 28 The Road Taken

Scripture Text: John 1: 6 - 8

"There was a man sent from God, whose name was John. The same came for a witness, to bear witness of the Light, that all men through him might believe. He was not that Light, but was sent to bear witness of that Light. "

John was sent to prepare the way for Levites to follow Christ on the road planned and paved by God and His Spirit. The Levites from Jerusalem would ask of John: "Who art thou? "

Saint Luke (3: 4) records John The Baptist's response to the Levites' question (Luke being one of those Levites!) how he would travel the road with Christ and who he was according to what God said: "As it is written in the book of the words of Esaias the prophet, saying, The voice of one crying in the wilderness, Prepare ye the way of the Lord, make his paths straight. "

John was sent to prepare the way for Pharisees to follow Christon the road planned and paved by God and His Spirit. The Pharisees which were sent asked John: "Why baptisest thou then, if thou be not the Christ, nor Elias, neither that prophet? "

Mark (1:4) records John the Babtist's response to the Pharisees and the Disciples (Mark being one of the Twelve Disciples) how he would prepare the road with Christ and how he was to do this according to what God said: "John did baptize in the wilderness, and preach the baptism of repentance for the remission of sins."

Prayer: Dear God and Spirit of God, Your way is the best way to follow.

December 29 The Road Taken

Scripture Text: Matthew 2: 3

"When Herod the king had heard these things, he was troubled, and all of Jerusalem with him. "

What did Matthew record about King Herod ? "Now when Jesus was born in Bethlehem of Judea in the days of Herod the king, behold there came wise men from the east to Jerusalem, Saying, Where is he that is born King of the Jews? For we have seen his star in the east, and are come to worship him. (Matthew 2: 1, 2)

What did Mark record about King Herod? "As it is written in the prophets, Behold, I send my messenger before thy face, which shall prepare thy way before thee. The voice of one crying in the wilderness, and preach the baptism of repentance for the remission of sin." (Mark 1: 2, 3) King Herod must have read of the prophets and became troubled by news that would affect the decrees of his kingdom.

What did Luke record about King Herod ? "And the shepherd returned, glorifying and praising God for all the things that they had heard and seen, as it was told unto them. And when eight days were accomplished for the circumscising of the child, his name was called Jesus, which was so named of the angel before he was conceived in the womb." (Luke 2: 20, 21) King Herod must have been familiar with the laws of the Jews and became troubled by news that Jesus was not among the newborn males that were killed.

What did John record about Herod ? "There was a man sent from God, whose name was John. The same came for a witness, to bear witness of the Light, that all men through him might believe. He was not that Light, but was sent to bear witness of that Light. "(John 1: 6-8) King Herod must have been familiar with the prophecies of a new King, The Light, and King of the Jews and became trouble that Jesus could take right over the earthly kingdoms.

Prayer: Dear God and Spirit of God, and Your Son; the King of Kings.

December 30 The Road Taken

Scripture Text: Matthew 2: 19

"But when Herod was dead, behold an angel of the Lord appeared in a dream to Joseph in Egypt."

Matthew recorded in his good news of how Joseph (Jesus' father) had a dream. What was Joseph directed to do by God, His Spirit, and an angel of the Lord?

Upon King Herod's death there were directions given to Joseph to take Mary and Baby Jesus and go to Israel. Now it appeared that the threat was gone for a return of family. (2:20)

What caused Joseph to change where God, His Spirit and an angel of the Lord directed him? There yet remained a threat for baby Jesus, Mary and Joseph...Herod's son reigned!(2: 21)

What was fulfilled by God, His Spirit, and an angel for Mary, Joseph and Baby Jesus? Without delay the prophecy was fulfilled; Nazareth would be the family site; home. (2: 22)

Prayer: God, and Spirit of God,

begin taking Your planned and paved road with Christ today remembering that You are still creating in Your own image; likeness.

December 31 The Road Taken

Scripture Text: Matthew 1: 22, 23

Now all this was done, that it might be fulfilled which was spoken of the Lord by the prophet , saying, Behold, a virgin shall be with child, and shall bring forth a son, and they shall call his name Emmanuel, which being interpreted is, God with us."

Matthew records the name given to the infant Jesus; Emmanuel. God with us , His Spirit with us, and now Jesus with us; the Trinity with us:

The Trinity has been with us through Resolutions, the Love Chapter and foundations. There have been promises made, adoration shown and steps taken towards fulfillment of the promises started by the Trinity.

The Trinity has been taking with us Music, Bouquets and Precious Stones. There has been plenty of songs written, arrangements made, and gems collected first by the Trinity.

The Trinity has been caring for Wise Creatures, using Wise Words, and teaching the ABC's of Wisdom. There have been human companions, passed down speeches, sermons and the memorizing of the alphabet and scripture verses.

The Trinity has been showing Wit and Wisdom, receiving thanks from the family, and preparing the road planned by them. There have been generations, many thanksgivings, and the searching of scriptures in order to follow the prepared road.

Prayer: Dear Trinity Team, thank You for the daily pearls of wisdom to ponder!

Would you like to see your manuscript become a book?

If you are interested in becoming a PublishAmerica author, please submit your manuscript for possible publication to us at:

acquisitions@publishamerica.com

You may also mail in your manuscript to:

**PublishAmerica
PO Box 151
Frederick, MD 21705**

www.publishamerica.com

CPSIA information can be obtained at www.ICGtesting.com
Printed in the USA
BVOW042143010512

289193BV00001B/83/P